A HISTORY OF GORTON AND O[

by ERNEST FRANCE

First Published 1989

351 Parrs Wood Road
Didsbury
Manchester
M20 6JF

Printed and bound by Manchester Free Press. Tel: 061-864 4540.

ACKNOWLEDGEMENTS

I would like to thank all who in various ways have helped in the preparation of this history of Gorton and Openshaw:

Mr. D. Taylor of the Local History Library and Miss J. Ayton of the Archives Department of the Manchester Central Library and their colleagues.

The Editor of the Ashton Reporter.

Mr. W. France, Mr. J.H. France, Mr. S. Nelson, Mr. J. Cunliffe, Mr. S.J. Cunliffe.

Mr, J.P. Boydell of the Gorton Philharmonic Society and Mr. W.D. Hanson of the Gorton Male Voice Choir.

Mr. B.E. Bagshaw of Crossley Engines and Mr. E. Russell, formerly of the Vaughan Crane Company.

Mr. F.E. Stapleton, Mr. G. Barnes, and Mrs. J.M. Barnes, head teachers of St. James C.E. Primary School, Openshaw C.E. Primary School and Aspinal Primary School respectively.

Mr. N. Burns, Mr. A.P. King, Mrs. Lynn Rhodes.

The Rev. G.C. Beeson, minister of St. James' Church, Gorton; the Rev. R. Parker, secretary of the Lancashire Congregational Union; Mr. E.A. Rose, secretary of the Methodist Historical Society; Mr. C.J. Damp, secretary of the Hope Congregational Church.

Mrs. J. Earl, Mrs. K. Charlton.

CHAPTER I

A CHRONICLE OF GORTON AND OPENSHAW

E.M.R. East Manchester Reporter
G.H.R. Gorton Historical Recorder, written by John Higson
A.W.R. Ashton Weekly Reporter
A.S.R. Ashton and Stalybridge Reporter
M.C.N. Manchester City News
G.O.R. Gorton and Openshaw Reporter
S.A. Stockport Advertiser
A.R. Ashton Reporter
G.O.B.R. Gorton, Openshaw and Bradford Reporter
M.E.N. Manchester Evening News

43 A.D.
The Roman emperor, Claudius, began the conquest of Britain.

79 A.D
The Romans built a fort at the confluence of the Irwell and the Medlock. The fort was called Mamucium.

3rd Century A.D.
Anglo-Saxons began raids on Britain.

410 A.D.
Last of the Romans left Britain. After this date Anglo-Saxons began to settle in Britain. To meet threat from the Anglo-Saxons of Mercia the people of south-east Lancashire built the Nico Ditch.

7th Century A.D.
The settlement of south Lancashire by the Anglo-Saxons began.

925 A.D.
Anglo-Saxon Chronicle records that Edward the Elder took possession of Mameceaster. Mameceaster was the Anglo-Saxon name for the Roman fort. It was used later to mean the town of Manchester.

1066
King Harold was defeated by Duke William of Normandy at the Battle of Hastings. The Norman Conquest began.

1087
Domesday Book was compiled. There is a reference to Manchester:

"The Church of St. Mary and the Church of St. Michael hold in Mameceaster one ploughland, free from all customs but the geld (Danegeld)."

1237
The earliest reference to Gorton and Openshaw, spelled "Openshae", appears in a list, dated 1237 to 1238, of townships which had to pay a tax known as the "30th".

1320
For the first time in the history of Gorton the names of Gorton people were recorded. This was in a survey of the manor of Manchester made in 1322. They are : Henry the Reve, Geoffrey of the Abbey, Thomas of the Olres (Alders), Hugh of the Abbey, Emma the Widow, Hugh son of Richard. There is a reference in the survey to a flour mill in Gorton and a peat moss in Openshaw. The population of Gorton at this time was probably about 60, that of Openshaw about 16.

1531
Gorton chapel built about this time.

1592
The Bishop of Chester reported that the curate of Gorton Chapel kept a school. This does not prove that there was a separate school building. The children may have been taught in the church.

1636
Samuel Gorton, a London clothier, born in Gorton, sailed for Massachusetts because of his fear of religious persecution and there founded a religious sect, known as the Gortonites. A feature of the Gortonites was a real contempt for the regular clergy and for all outward forms of religion. For a year or two his extreme views led him into trouble and he was publicly whipped for insulting the clergy and the magistrates. *(G.O.R. 23.6.1950).*

1641
The men of Gorton and Openshaw show their support for Parliament by "taking the Protestation" i.e. allowing their names to be entered on a list known as a "Protestation". The estimated population of Gorton, based on the list, is 320 ; that of Openshaw, 117.

1642, July 15th
On July 15th, 1642, Lord Strange, the son of Lord Derby and a supporter of King Charles, came into Manchester to attend a banquet. Whilst the banquet was in progress, a number of Manchester citizens, supporters of Parliament, blocked up the two ends of the street. An attempt was made to disperse them and in the fighting one of the gentlemen of Lord Strange's party was struck on the head, whereupon his assailant, Richard Percival, a linen weaver of Kirkmanshulme, was killed on the spot. He is said to be the first casualty of the Civil War.

1642, September
Manchester was besieged by Lord Strange, a Royalist general. The siege was lifted after a week.

25.2.1644 End of Siege of Wythenshaw Hall

Wythenshaw Hall, home of the royalist Robert Tatton and his family, had been under siege by Parliamentary forces led by Colonel Duckinfield of Duckinfield House. On Sunday, 25th February, the Hall, shattered by cannon brought up from Manchester, finally surrendered.

1653 G.H.R.

Humphrey Chetham died aged 74. He lived at Clayton Hall and attended Gorton Chapel. He came on horseback down the fields attached to the Hall farm and thence up the old "Green Lane". He left £200 to buy "Godly English books, such as Calvin's, Preston's and Perkin's works, comments or annotations upon the Bible, or some parts thereof" or such books as would be thought fit by his executors and place them in the churches of Manchester and Bolton-le-Moors and in the chapels of Turton, Walmesley and Gorton. They had to be securely chained to a desk. The Gorton Library was kept in an oblong oaken chest. It consisted of fifty five books with a chain attached. *(The Gorton Chapel books have now been removed to Chetham's Library, Long Millgate).*

1680 G.H.R

About this period brick buildings began to supersede the "ancient raddle and daub".

("Raddle and daub" or "Wattle and daub" as it is usually called was the ancient method of making walls. Wooden laths were interwoven and interstices were filled with "daub", a kind of plaster made mainly from clay.)

May 10th, 1694 History of Newton Chapelry

On May 10th, 1694, Mary, widow of Dr. Birch, was "buried in the somerhouse in the garden in Grindloe" *(Manchester Collegiate Register)*, and about 1874 at Grindlow House a large coffin was found in the garden by the summer-house, with traces of an inscription containing the name Mary.

(The Gorton Historical Recorder says that both Dr. Birch and his wife were buried at Longsight Hall; Longsight Hall and Grindlow House were evidently one and the same.)

1703

The Dissenting Chapel, the forerunner of Brookfield Church, was built behind Far Lane in an angle formed by the Gore Brook.

1711 G.H.R.

At this time bleaching of linen yarn was carried on to a pretty large extent, a great portion of the land in the township being at times covered with yarn, the large crofters employing parish apprentices etc.

("parish apprentices" were probably young inmates of the poor-house)

1715 G.H.R.

John Gorton, a miller's servant man lived in Preston. Being in Preston Brook in 1715, he saw a man secrete something in a turf stack, which afterwards proved to be an immense sum of money. He took the money and came to Gorton, where he purchased at various times the Gorton Hall estate, the Chapel Farm, Towncroft Farm, Green Style Farm and what is now called the Bridge House Farm.

(It could be that the story of John Gorton's find was invented to explain his acquisition of wealth.)

1717

The Bishop of Chester reported that there was a school in Gorton, built by contributions. It stood in the yard of Gorton Chapel.

1718 G.H.R.

George Aspinall of Reddish, blacksmith, buried at Gorton Chapel. The hamlet jointly situate in Gorton, Reddish and Denton, was named after him.

1724

The Manchester and Buxton Turnpike Trust was established in 1724. It was responsible for improving and maintaining Stockport Road in good repair.

1731

The Manchester and Saltersbrook Turnpike Trust was established in 1731. It was responsible for improving and maintaining Ashton Old Road in good repair.

1737 G.H.R

Maiden's Bridge was erected across the Gore Brook near Far Lane. Previously, stepping stones, known as "hipping stones", were used.

1743 G.H.R.

Stocks erected on vacant land opposite George and Dragon, now Chapel House.

1745

On the 29th November Prince Charles, the Young Pretender, and his army arrived in Manchester. The Prince lodged at the house of Mr Dickenson in Market Street. On the morning of Sunday, December 1st, Charles and his army set out along Stockport Road on their march south. The horse soldiers, the pack-horses and the waggons turned right at Slade Lane, continued along Burnage Lane, crossed the Mersey at Didsbury and from there marched on to Macclesfield via Cheadle, Wilmslow and Alderley Edge. Prince Charles with the infantry continued along Stockport Road and forded the Mersey at Tiviot Dale, the bridge being down. They then marched through Stockport and along what is now Wellington Road South, eventually rendezvousing with the horse soldiers, pack-horses and waggons in Macclesfield. During the Pretender's brief stay in Manchester a company of his soldiers bivouacked in a field near to where Gorton House now stands.

1752 G.H.R.

Year begins on January 1st instead of March 25th. The day following September 2nd was called and reckoned as September 14th. The old calendar was the Julian and the new one, the Gregorian.

(The change in calendar brought England into line with the continent.)

1755

A new Gorton Chapel, dedicated to St. Thomas, was built.

1770 G.H.R.

George Birch of Gorton formed a new length of road, since named Gorton Lane, from Ardwick Toll-bar, Ashton Old Road, to Gorton Brook. He was the owner of all the land through which it passed as well as Gorton Brook.

1771-2 G.H.R.
Practice of cultivating potatoes as a regular field crop began to acquire supporters. Grain crops had failed. Famine led to the discovery of value of potatoes, which had been hitherto confined to garden cultivation and only regarded as a luxury. They were fed also to live-stock.

1772 G.H.R.
A sum of £152 11s 6d was voluntarily subscribed by the landowners and inhabitants of Gorton towards repairing the highways.

1775 March 24th The Gorton Death Book
(transcribed by John Higson)
Three children poisoned with Yew by their mother in Longsight with intent to kill the worms.

1776 G.H.R.
Amicable Society or sick club begun in Openshaw. Removed to George and Dragon, Gorton, in 1788. 121 members. Friendly Society or elder sick club begun at Horse and Farrier. 161 members. *(George and Dragon and Horse and Farrier later renamed Chapel House and Black Horse respectively.)*

1778 G.H.R.
Gorton makes little progress in population. It yet consists of single and scattered farm-houses. A few small groups built near the chapel, Abbey Hey, Winning Hill, Ashton Fold and Longsight.
(Winning Hill is now known as Ryder Brow. Ashton Fold was the name given to a group of cottages behind the site of Wellington Street Baptists.)

1780 G.H.R.
Rush cart went out on the Friday before the 1st Sunday in September, visiting Mr Grimshaw's High Bank and also the locality of Gorton Brook. On that night or Saturday morning, rushes were "teemed" down near the Chapel Gate, then strewn on the bottom of pews, and in the aisle. On this day also, the band, accompanied by the "pikemen" carrying staves surmounted with brass eagles, perambulated the village, stopping nowhere, neither soliciting any contributions.

1782-3 G.H.R.
Expended on Poor-house, High Bank, £1 12s 9 ½d. Paid Samuel Stansfield, mil:man (militia man) £4 4s.

Three cottages erected near Kirk Lane by Mr Joseph Taylor of Openshaw, one of the chapel-wardens. They were named Briton's Row, from a favourite assertion of his, when he used to say with much gusto, "I am a Briton".

A row of houses erected at the foot of Ryder Brow; they are now known as "Bottom o' th' Brow" and bear the initials "ESA 1782".

1783
The day school in the Gorton Chapel yard was closed down. It was replaced by a new school at the corner of Cross Lane and Wellington Street, known in later years as Gorton Old Endowed.

1786
The first factory in Fairfield was built in this year. It was described as being a low building. The motive power was provided by a horse, driven by a boy, which turned a large wheel, which in turn worked a "cotton Billy". Presumably this was a spinning machine.

The factory hours were from 6 a.m. to 8 p.m. Children as young as six were employed. They received 2s 6d per week. *(See an "Account of the rise and progress of the cotton trade in Droylsden and Fairfield" by James Bowker of Fairfield, included in John Higson's newspaper cuttings.)*

1796
Stockport Canal is opened.

1797 March 25th Gorton Death Book
George Bertenshaw cut his wife's throat and his own in Sinderland Hall, Eight Aker field, Little Moss (Droylsden), as they were coming home from Manchester, with a knife that he had bought that day for that purpose. May thay Lord receive her and they were buried together 29 Day after dark at Ashton under Lyne.
(It is not known who compiled the Gorton Death Book. The transcription is in the Archives Department of the Manchester Central Library.)

1804 G.H.R.
On the Friday preceding the first Sunday in September, the annual rush-bearing ceremony was held. It was accepted as a prelude to a week's gaiety. Persons came to the village of Gorton from miles around. On that auspicious morning James Hibbert of Foxfold and his assistants might be observed preparing rushes and, while they were erecting a pyramid and decking it out with silver plate and garlands, the Morice dancers were as eagerly decking themselves out with holiday attire.

A number of horses were selected to convey the rush-cart and the Gorton Band accompanied the procession. The dancers and young couples tripped it on the light fantastic toe to the tune of the Morice dance.

The great event of the week, however, was in Foxfold, where, according to the record, there was generally a bear bait. This commenced at 6.00 a.m. and was renewed at intervals of four hours until nightfall.

Bear and badger baiting were held on vacant land adjoining the Black Horse, Bottom o' th' Brow, and bull baits at the George and Dragon.
(Foxfold was a group of cottages to the west of Tan Yard Brow. One of the cottages was converted into a beer-house and took the name of the 'Lord Nelson'. Bottom o' th' Brow is a continuation of Far Lane. 'George and Dragon' was the old name of the Chapel House. It stood on Wellington Street near the Church.

Bull baiting was a popular sport. In 1829 there were five bull baits in or near Gorton viz. the Plough Inn, the Chapel House, the Lamb Tavern, the Bull's Head near Aspinall Smithy and "Marchington's" in Abbey Hey. "Marchington's" was a field, owned by James Marchington, a brewer.
Bull dogs were held in high esteem and a prize, usually a brass collar was awarded to the owner of the dog that best pinned the

bull i.e. caught and maintained its hold of the gristle near the nose of the animal.)

1805 G.H.R.
October 21st.
Lord Nelson was killed in the battle of Trafalgar.
December 5th.
General thanksgiving for the victory was observed.
December 10th.
A holiday was given at Gorton Old Endowed School. Most of the Gorton females purchased dress pieces of Nelson mourning print, scarlet and black stripes.

1807-8 G.H.R
During this period, wages for weaving nearly all sorts of cotton goods were reduced, in consequence of which turn-outs (strikes) and riots took place in various parts of the county.

1810 G.H.R.
Maiden's Bridge widened.

1811 G.H.R.
Population of Gorton - males 557, females 626. Total 1,183. There were 225 families, of whom 21 were chiefly employed in agriculture, 201 in trade and manufacture and 3 otherwise employed.
221 inhabited and 6 empty houses.

The hatting trade was very brisk. Many handloom weavers are out of employment.

1812 G.H.R.
Rising of the Luddites. A party of them came to John Ashton's shop, Chapel Houses, and retailed flour at their own prices. Numerous hatters from Denton were apprehended at Reddish Mill. They were afterwards transported to Australia and commenced the hatting business and being able to make and finish them they were very successful.
(The Luddites were followers of a mythical "King Ludd". The movement began in Nottinghamshire as a protest against the use of "wide" stocking frames, which, so it was claimed, were causing unemployment amongst stocking-workers. The success of the Nottinghamshire Luddites inspired imitation by Lancashire and Cheshire handloom weavers, who believed that the power-loom was throwing them out of work. Factories which housed the power-looms were broken into and the machines smashed. The real cause of unemployment was, however, not the power-loom but the Napoleonic War, which had closed the European market to British goods.)

1818
The Manchester, Hyde and Mottram Turnpike Trust was established. It built Hyde Road, which was an entirely new road.

1825 G.H.R.
Gorton Mill commenced working. There was a procession round the village and a supper at the Plough Inn.

1826 G.H.R.
Gorton reservoirs completed.

James Barlow of Levenshulme, yeoman, died March 15th, aged 90 years. He was a Calvinist and the last survivor of the old trustees of the Dissenting Chapel. His coffin was prepared by his own directions some years before. He chose a suitable oak on his Levenshulme estate, caused it to be cut down and formed it into a coffin, which he kept ready for use. He was interred in a tomb in his garden on Winning Hill, Gorton, where his wife had been entombed in 1816. *(See G.O.R. 14.5.1965)*

1829 G.H.R.
Ancient half-timbered farm-house, known as Town Croft, taken down and replaced by Gorton Villa by Mr William Harrison Lees.
(Mr Lees was one of the owners of Gorton Mill.)

All paupers working for the township to have only 1s 6d per day. 17 paupers including a woman with her five young children deserted by her husband - received 8s weekly.

Large house next to Gorton Chapel to be used for the town's business.

1830 G.H.R.
Mr John Grimshaw ordered to pay £100 to the overseers. This was the purchase money of "Chatsworth Hall", Gorton's alms-house, which had been sold to the commissioners of the Manchester and Stockport Turnpike. *(As the alms-house was on High Bank, the road being widened must have been Hyde Road and the turnpike trust in question, the Manchester, Hyde and Mottram Turnpike Trust.)*

Coffin found in a heap of soil near Debdale Lane. It had contained the corpse of Mrs Booth and had been brought from Denton Chapel Yard by the resurrectionists *(body snatchers - they sold the bodies to hospitals for dissection).*

1831 G.H.R.
Population of Gorton : 1294 males 1329 females
496 families : 57 being independent means, 35 engaged in agriculture and 404 in trade and manufacture.

New poor-house, consisting of lock-up, poor-house and town's offices, was erected in Wellington Street near the centre of the village at a cost of £1,079 12s 6d.

1832 G.H.R.
Ralph Stanley ordered to purchase iron bedstocks for the workhouse. October 14th.

Particular instructions to be given all the constables to prevent all vagrants and beggars asking alms in the township, who are to order them out of the township; if they do not cease, they are to be taken before the magistrates, and convicted. Public notice-boards to be put up at the principal entrances, cautioning all vagrants and beggars from coming into the township viz. one at or near the Plough Inn, one near Smith's houses, one near the toll-bar leading to Stockport and one in Abbey Hey Lane. April 27th.

The "Railway and Cotton Tree £20 Money Club" established at that tavern near the Old School. Subscription 10s monthly. July 16th.

1832 G.H.R.
William and Aaron Lees of Gorton Mill, Abbey Hey Lane, employed 711 workers.

female 190 under 18
228 upwards of 18
Monday to Friday 6.30 a.m. to 8 p.m.
8 - 8.30 breakfast
1 - 2 dinner

No stoppage for tea but it is allowed to be brought and eaten at intervals.

Saturday 6 a.m. to 4.30 p.m. except half an hour for breakfast and 1 hour for dinner.

Total number of hours worked in a week - 69
Average wage £1 3s 6d per fortnight.

1834 G.H.R.
Constables to give notice to the inhabitants to "keep their dogs up or they will be compelled". May 30 *(Presumably the inhabitants were being asked to keep them under control.)*

1835 G.H.R.
Select vestry agreed to pay the expense of John Hall's gun, it being broken whilst Joseph Hall and James Gresty were shooting dogs by order of the constables. September 4th. *(The select vestry was the ruling authority of the village.)*

Act of Parliament passed prohibiting the baiting of animals succeeded in repressing the usual bull, bear, badger baits in Gorton and other wakes.

1836 G.H.R.
New road formed from Abbey Hey Lane to Openshaw designated Lees street. Messrs John Lees and Sons erected eight cottages in it. John Jennison, a Stockport handloom weaver, bought a tavern, called Belle Vue, and half an acre of land from John Walker.

1837 G.H.R.
Cow Club to insure against loss of black cattle, supported by contributions and honorary subscriptions of £1. Abolished 1845.

Agreed that Susan Nicholson, now in the workhouse, be allowed half an ounce of bacco per week. This contrasts with the present bastille arrangements. January 13th.

Robert Rider, aged 48, ordered to come into the workhouse. He became useful in his new sphere, taking the juveniles out on airing in the fields on the weekday and to church on the Sabbath.

Agreed that Mary Ann, child of John Walker, must not be sent by the overseers to Van Dieman's Land with its mother. July 28th. *(Van Dieman's Land was the old name for Tasmania.)*

1838 G.H.R.
Queen Victoria crowned. Grand procession at Manchester; the only equestrian musicians were the Gorton *(Aspinall Smithy)* Old Band. June 28th.

Work on the Sheffield, Ashton-under-Lyne and Manchester Railway commenced near Green Lane.

1839 G.H.R.
Members of several Gorton families attend torchlight meeting in the vicinity of Ashton-under-Lyne. Some have polished pikes in their possession and many have their dwellings adorned by the likeness of the Rev. Joseph Rayner, the people's friend. *(These Gorton families were members of the Chartist movement, which took its name from a charter of six points. The six points were: a vote for all adult males, the secret ballot, annual parliaments, abolition of the property qualification for M.P.'s, payment of M.P.'s and equal electoral districts.)*

1840 G.H.R.
Gorton Mills stopped working. Nearly caused desertion of village. July.

Manchester and Birmingham Railway opened to the public as far as Stockport. Numerous villagers availed themselves of the privilege of free conveyance to and from that town.

Royal Oak tavern, Cross Lane, rebuilt. This old cottage was the last thatched dwelling existing in the township.

1841
First Fairfield Station opened.

1842 G.H.R.
Alarming riots in neighbourhood, arising from want of employment and dearness of food. August 10th.
Splendid fireworks exhibition at Belle Vue by Signor Pietro (Mr Richardson) of Chapel Houses. May 2nd.

Several of the Gorton clubs and societies having considerable funds in hand, it was resolved that each member should receive £1 out of the general store.

First Gorton Station opened near Green Lane crossing on Sheffield Manchester Railway.

1843 G.H.R.
2nd annual steeple chase. A sweepstake of five sovereigns each with a purse added for bona fide hunters. A course formed over Gorton Hall (or Plough Inn), Sunny Brow, Nearer Catsknoll and Whitely Farm. Won by Mr Assheton Bennett.

1844 G.H.R.
Gorton Mills recommenced working under the tenancy of Messrs John Rylands and Sons. June.

Gorton meeting (races) established. October 4 and 5. Course formed by Messrs Bennett and Co.

1845 G.H.R.
Robert Robinson died, aged 61. He was the well-known waiter at the Waggon and Horses, Gorton, and was known as "Old Bing Bang" from a tune he practised playing on a pair of fire-tongs.

1846 G.H.R.
Demonstration in Manchester, on account of the repeal of the Corn Law. Gorton Mills "stopt", but there was no external

rejoicing in the village.

1847 G.H.R.
Mr Rylands of Gorton Mills opened his new shop on the premises and in connection with the mill, professing under the appellation of the "Gorton provision stores" to retail goods out at wholesale prices to the operatives in his employ.

Masters' memorial against the Ten Hours Bill signed by John Rylands of Gorton.

Gorton Mills provision stores fined for deficient weight.

Commenced erecting a girder bridge over railway, intended for the new diversion of Green Lane, leading to Openshaw. Caused by erection of depot *(Gorton Tank).*

Hatting trade depressed, the hatters *(body makers)* not earning on average 1s 6d per week.

1848 G.H.R.
A post office established at Mr Ralph Holt's, provision dealer, Longsight.

Permanent railway station built on Cornwall Street.

Mr John Buckley erected a commodious public-house, "The Cornwall Inn", near the Gorton Station. *(The Cornwall Inn is now the Railway Inn).*

1849 G.H.R.
A packet commenced plying on the canal between Gorton station or rather Openshaw bridge and Lancashire Hill, Stockport. Fare 4d. April 2nd.
Discontinued on the opening of the branch line from Guide Bridge to Stockport. September 8th.

Cholera epidemic. John Smith of John Street, newsvendor etc. taken ill on 11 September, died on 13th. Wife attacked on 14th, died on 16th. Son attacked but recovered, son's wife attacked on 19th, died on 20th. Widower has seven children.

Felt hat trade depressed. Decline may in part be traced to the now general wear of silk hats for men and caps for boys. A few years ago it was common for the youth of both sexes to wear unfinished felt hats: whilst those for boys were left their natural colours, those intended for girls were generally dyed blue.

At a meeting of the factory operatives at the Church Inn, Droylsden, votes of thanks were passed to Messrs John Rylands & Sons, Gorton, and Messrs Orrell of Openshaw for not running their engines more than 10 hours per day.

(In 1848 the Ten Hours Act, limiting the working day of women and young persons to ten hours, had become operative. However, some employers had found a loophole in the Act and were keeping their factories open for longer periods by compelling the women and young persons to work shifts. The hopes of the men that the Act would automatically reduce their working day were thus frustrated. John Rylands and Messrs Orrel were honourable exceptions.)

1850 G.H.R.
May, daughter of James Barnes of Wellington Street, aged thirteen, killed at Gorton Mills. Her neckerchief caught on a line shaft, which turned the mechanics shop and was not boxed off. She was hurled round before the engines could be stopped and died of internal injuries.

8.5.1858 A.W.R.
On Tuesday afternoon the first brick was laid of a new cotton mill about to be erected by Mr John Buckley, in a field bounded by Prestwick brook, a few hundred yards east of Gorton Church. The mill is to be four storeys high and eight windows long, the internal measurements being 81 feet long and 84 feet wide.

11.9.1858 A.W.R.
Gorton Wakes This festival has been better patronised than for some years past. There were two or three 'acting shows', waxwork exhibitions, several toy bazaars and a very considerable number of stalls for the sale of gingerbread, fruit, sweetmeats etc. The several public houses and beershops had their attractions and diversities of 'old English sports' but the throng of sight-seekers and the principal paraphernalia were congregated round the Plough Inn, the real centre of the village.

18.12.1858 A.W.R.
On Monday morning week Joseph Esford, a lad of nine years of age, climbed up one of the carts or barrels in Openshaw, which supply that township and Droylsden with water. He fell off and the wheel passed over his head.

The Donkey that would not go
One day last week a Droylsden itinerating green-grocer was met traversing the highway and shafting a cart, whilst his donkey complacently walked by his side. On being interrogated as to the cause of this singular spectacle, the kind-hearted master good-humouredly replied that the lazy animal would not work and he was trying to shame it into a sense of duty. *(Droylsden was known as the 'silly country'. This is but one example of the humourous tales that were told about its inhabitants. Another tale was that they put a pig on a wall so that it could see the procession.)*

10.9.1859 A.S.R.
Gorton and Openshaw Wakes
The highway from the New Inn (Half Way House) to Pin Mill Brow presented a most gay and lively appearance. The various workshops in the localities ceased to work on the Monday and Tuesday. On Monday the various licensed houses were the first to be decked with flags, banners etc. containing various devices.

12.5.1860 A.S.R.
Mr Walters M.P. defied any person to lay his hands on any single grievance now affecting the working classes as a class. What the working classes really wanted was less work, more pay and a glass of beer on Sundays.

18.10.1862 A.W.R.
The Openshaw Relief Committee gave help to 67 families comprising 264 individuals. The cost was £10 16s. Mr Jack Ashbury gave £100 to the Committee. The Committee also received £10 per fortnight from employees of the Gorton depot

of the Sheffield and Lincolnshire Railway Company (Gorton Tank).

29.11.1862 A.W.R.
The City of London Relief Committee at their weekly meeting voted the sum of £38,825 in all towards the prevailing distress. Gorton received £200 and Droylsden, £350.

20.12.1862 A.W.R.
In Droylsden, relief took the following forms:
(1) Bread and soup given out at the King Street Schoolroom.
(2) Distribution of food such as ham and bacon.
(3) Distribution of coal, clothing and clothing tickets.
(4) School money paid on behalf of poor children.
(The poverty, which these various committees sought to relieve, was due mainly to the American Civil War. This began on 12.4.1861 with an attack by southern troops on Fort Sumter. The blockade of southern ports by the north deprived Lancashire mills of raw cotton, with the result that large numbers of mill-workers where thrown out of work. The war ended on May 26th, 1865.)

March 1863
The Ashton and Stalybridge Reporter reports riots at Stalybridge, Ashton, Dukinfield, Mossley and Hyde, due to unemployment in cotton manufacturing.

11.4.1863 A.S.R editorial comment
The poor of Lancashire have had a surfeit of good advice lately. But unhappily for their clever and eminent advisers, the various panaceas they purpose are on a par with the advice of a benevolent physician, who suggested to a poor consumptive patient the propriety of a voyage to Madeira. When poor folks are told that a sheet of paper makes a good blanket or that a herring may be cooked so as to afford a meal for eleven persons, they may be pardoned for incredulity.

18.11.1863
Gorton Local Board of Health established. Openshaw Local Board of Health established about the same time.

5.3.1864
Manchester Gas Committee agree to enter into a contract with Gorton Local Board to supply gas to public lamps in Cross Street and Gore Street, Hyde Road. To be lit and extinguished at same hours as Openshaw.

28.5.1864 M.C.N.
We are pleased to find that, among the thousands of children who have enjoyed the festivities of the past week, the boys and girls of this establishment *(The Chorlton Union Workhouse)* have not been forgotten. Early on Saturday morning three lurries, a van and another conveyance were seen wending their way to Alderly Edge, freighted with their living loads and provisions for the day. In the foremost was the Juvenile House Band, playing lively airs, and sporting Union Jacks, fluttering in the breeze. Arrived at Alderly, a substantial foundation of bread and meat with milk commenced the day's proceedings; afterwards oranges, nuts and sweets were freely distributed. For tea the governors had provided for each child a cake of ample dimensions with another supply of milk. The usual sports were entered into with great zest by the juvenile party. Races were run in sacks and out of sacks and many a boy can boast of his own exploits to his friends at home by exhibiting the fairly earned addition to his limited exchequer; while the girls, with well-filled pocket handkerchiefs, have ample proof of the guardians' liberality and the practical tendency of the lessons on care and economy, which are being instilled into the little hearts of those future members of Old England.

17.12.1864 M.C.N.
The Gorton Ratepayers Association object to the building of the new town hall as 'other improvements for the benefit of the inhabitants at present are more necessary, viz. a plentiful supply of good light, better roads and better drainage'.

31.12.1864 M.C.N.
Yesterday Messrs Beyer Peacock and Co., Machinists, Gorton foundry, gave their 10th annual dinner to the workpeople in their employ at the Belle Vue Gardens. At half-past ten, upwards of 1500 workpeople assembled in the foundry yard at Gorton, where in addition to receiving a ticket for a really first-class dinner, each man was presented with a shilling and two 'cheques', with which to enjoy himself during the afternoon according to his fancy.

Mr Beyer said that the principle which he adopted was to treat his hands as fellowmen *(applause)*. He had always found that the more wages he paid a man, the cheaper was that man's services, for then the labourer felt it to be his interest to serve his employer.

17.6.1865 M.C.N.
The Whitweek supplies at Belle Vue were: 100 hams cut into sandwiches, 20,000 penny buns, 1,500 4lb loaves, 500 currant buns, 40,000 Eccles cakes, 40,000 buttered biscuits, 25 large calves made into veal pies. Nearly 100,000 persons were admitted.

25.11.1865 M.C.N.
The Openshaw Ratepayers Association complained that the contents of ashpits had been left on the surface of South Street and suggested that the Local Board should undertake the work of emptying ashpits. There was also a complaint about the state of Wellington Street: workers on their way to Beyer Peacock's were up to their knees in mud. One member observed that the streets of Gorton were as bad as those of Openshaw and that there was no advantage in moving.

17.9.1867
A prison van carrying two Fenian leaders, Kelly and Deasy, was ambushed on its way to Belle Vue gaol under the railway arch on Hyde Road near Grey Street. In an attempt to force Police-sergeant Brett, who was accompanying the prisoners, to hand the keys through the ventilator, shots were fired through the door. One of them killed Police-sergeant Brett. Kelly and Deasy escaped and were never caught. Three Fenians, Allen, O'Brien and Larkin were arrested and after a trial were hanged at the New Bailey Prison in Salford. They are known as the "Manchester Martyrs".
(The aim of the Fenian Society was to gain Home Rule for Ireland.)

8.1.1870 G.O.R.
Ryland's Mill working 6 a.m. to 6 p.m.

22.1.1870 G.O.R.
A sparrow shooting contest came off at Mr John Williamson's Old House at Home, Abbey Hey.

In a letter on West Gorton a correspondent wrote, 'The first noticeable peculiarity which will strike the visitor is mud, the presence of which can easily be accounted for by the fact that West Gorton possesses one-and-a-half properly laid out streets."

5.3.1870 G.O.R.
Hunting Season. The harriers met on Wednesday at Mr W. Jennison's Waggon and Horses Inn, Hyde Road. There was a good 'turn-out'. Several horsemen were present including Messrs Harrison of Ashton, Ellison of Glossop and Jennison of Gorton. The dogs were followed by a large number of the neighbouring sportsmen, who heartily enjoyed the sport. Although the day was not favourable, nor the game so plentiful, yet none regretted following the cry of the dogs.

23.7.1870 G.O.R.
"Turn-out" *(strike)* at Ryland's mill for an advance of wages. The self-actor minders *(spinners)* wanted an advance of 5%. The large mill was closed by the master. This conduct on the part of the master had thrown quite a gloom over the whole neighbourhood.

30.7.1870 G.O.R.
Ryland's spinners went back and agreed to be paid by the Stockport list.

27.8.1870 G.O.R.
Employment adversely affected by the Franco-Prussian War. Some cotton mills closed. 150 men at the Gorton Locomotive Depot of the Manchester, Sheffield and Lincoln Railway discharged.

A complaint was made against Mr Clough that night soil had been thrown out of an ashpit in John Street and not removed. *(Peter Clough, a private contractor, was paid £500 per annum for emptying ashpits and privies).*

18.3.1871 G.O.R.
Smallpox reported in Openshaw. A family named Robinson, who live at a mangle house, has been affected. *(A mangle-house was a house with a mangle or wringing machine which was let out to women in the neighbourhood).*

9.9.1871 G.O.R.
Pump dressing in Walter Street near the Bull's Head.

8.6.1872 G.O.R.
Master and Apprentice James Henry Barlow was summoned at the County Police Court by his master, Reuben Gibson, that he being an apprentice did unlawfully leave his work without notice on the 22nd of May and did not return until the following Monday.

20.7.1872 G.O.R.
Severe floods experienced in Gorton. The garden of the Waggon and Horses was under water. Gorton railway station was flooded and trains were unable to run. Gorton reservoir overflowed. The floods were wide-spread and affected Manchester, Marple, Bury, Newton Heath and Moston, but Openshaw suffered little.

26.9.1872
Messrs Beyer Peacock and Co., Robert Booth and Co., G L Scott and others complained to the Gorton Local Board that the new road over the railway in Gorton Lane was in bad condition and that the horses, which were to assist heavy loads over, had been taken away.

26.9.1873 S.A.
Pigeon and sparrow shooting at Abbey Hey Gardens.

14.11.1873 S.A.
The members of 1,049 Diamond Lodge, of the Grand Protestant Association of Loyalist Orangemen of England, Stockport District, celebrated the never-to-be-forgotten Gunpowder Conspiracy and also the landing of King William III. The celebration took place at the Pack Horse Inn, Openshaw.

12.12.1873 S.A.
A number of the residents of Abbey Hey sat down to a supper on Friday evening last at Mr John Williamson's Old House at Home. After a hearty meal had been partaken of, the company enjoyed themselves with the usual toasts and singing, one of them remarking that he hoped they would be remembered as a civilised body now, though they used to bear the title of uncivilised.

9.1.1874 S.A.
Three children killed on railway. An accident of a shocking character occurred on New Year's Day on the Manchester, Sheffield and Lincoln railway, whereby three children, named Elizabeth M'Williams, aged 7; Ann M'Williams, aged 9; and Susannah Noran, aged 10, residing in Little Street, Gorton, lost their lives. There is a tip near the railway, used by the Ashbury Carriage Co., and the children, who had been gathering cinders under the waggons, had wandered onto the main line, just as the ten o'clock express from Oldham came up. Before the driver could stop, the engine knocked the poor children down. Another witness stated that strong fences had been erected, but had proved ineffectual.

The scholars of the Brookfield Church Sunday Schools, Hyde Road, Gorton, to the number of 300, sat down to their annual Christmas free tea party, on Saturday last. After tea, a magic lantern was exhibited and called forth rounds of applause from the crowded gathering.

20.3.1874 S.A.
At the Manchester County Police Court on Monday before Sir John Iles Mantell, a boy named John Starkie was charged with gambling. On Saturday, a constable saw the prisoner and a number of other boys playing pitch and toss in Hyde Lane, Gorton. He ran after them and succeeded in apprehending Starkie. The prisoner was fined 2s 6d, or in default of payment, seven days imprisonment.

3.5.1874 S.A.
Thomas Church summoned for a breach of his indentures as an apprentice to Messrs Webb and Co., tin-plate workers, Bank View Street, Gorton. Defendant was bound over in two sureties of £5 each to return to his employment.

30.5.1874 A.R.

Brief guides for trippers - Blackpool The new promenade is now open and there are two magnificent piers. Uncle Tom's Cabin is of old reputation, a spot where winsome gipsies told the blushing damsel the complexion, stature, name etc. of her future husband. Blackpool has at times one of the roughest coasts and unless the weather is very calm it is dangerous to either boat or bathe.

(Other resorts mentioned were Southport, Liverpool, Lytham, Fleetwood, Lancaster, Morecambe, Alderley Edge, Haddon Hall and Miller's Dale).

13.3.1875 A.R.

The walking feat of Professor Poplin

Professor Poplin walked 30 miles in 6 hours in a pair of clogs that weighed 3 lbs.

Along with the above-mentioned feat he undertook to perform seven more feats in 30 minutes, namely

1st walk half a mile frontward

2nd run half a mile

3rd run half a mile and carry 20 lbs weight on his back

4th run a coach wheel half a mile

5th pick up 20 stones one yard apart

7th pick up 15 bricks with his mouth

and other extraordinary feats.

He started from the Junction Hotel at the corner of Clowes Street, West Gorton, along Hyde Road to the canal bridge at the corner of Reddish Lane and back - the journey to be walked till the distance had been completed.

20.3.1875 A.R.

The main sewer from Clayton to Gorton Brook enters Openshaw near Clayton Lane. A number of chemical works in Clayton discharge their refuse into this sewer. Brass door knobs and candlesticks in the area are tarnished and blackened.

11.12.1875 A.R.

A lioness at large at Belle Vue

Last week a lioness escaped from its cage. When the underkeeper, Mr Walter Scott, tried to bar her way, the lioness chased him. Mr Scott ran to the cooking house, but fell before he could gain its sanctuary. The lioness would certainly have killed him, had not fate in the shape of a cat intervened. Its sudden movement distracted the lioness sufficiently long for Mr Scott to regain his feet and make his escape.

The commotion brought Mr Thomas Davy, the head animal keeper, on the scene. He took one of the lioness's cubs from the cage and, holding it in his hands, showed it to the mother. Then he turned about and walked slowly back to the cage, followed by the lioness. By this means she was safely caged in her den.

9.9.1876 A.R.

Well-dressing at Aspinall in Reddish Lane.

30.9.1876 A.R.

Smallpox at No. 16 Clyde Street and No. 79 Ducie Street, Gorton.

17.3.1877 G.O.B.R.

Bay-window houses, fronting Clayton Lane, Openshaw, to let at 4s per week. *(Advert).*

25.8.1877 G.O.B.R.

Bulgarian atrocities out-done in Openshaw and Bradford.

A number of youths of both sexes, perhaps 200 to 300 in all, known by the term 'scuttlers', have selected an open space of ground opposite to my dwelling as the centre of their operations. Their weapons of warfare are of an old fashioned kind viz. stones, pieces of brick, stick and suchlike rude implements.

Saturday, August 11th,; Sunday the 12th; Sunday the 19th and Monday, the 20th, were four of their field days. It seems there were two opposing forces. They met on the days named and commenced skirmishing. Gradually they worked nearer to each other, then the melee commenced.

On another occasion I saw a youth kicked almost to death.

(The above letter, printed under the newspaper's own caption, was signed 'A Sufferer'. 'Scuttle' means 'fight'. The origin of the word is not known.)

1.6.1878 G.O.B.R.

Gorton Local Board begin numbering of house doors.

28.9.1878 G.O.B.R.

Handbell ringing contest at Belle Vue.

The Openshaw Clothing Company of 127 Ashton Old Road, Openshaw, advertise ready-made clothing:

Boys' suits from 5s

Youth's suits from 10s

Men's tweed suits from 25s

Men's black suits from 30s

Men's black cloth trousers *(lined)* from 7s 6d

12.10.1878 G.O.B.R.

Telegraph introduced into Openshaw.

5.1.1878 G.O.B.R.

Quoiting match at the Royal Oak quoiting ground, Ogden Lane.

23.3.1878 G.O.B.R.

Scuttlers in Openshaw. Shopkeepers had to put up shutters. *(See 25.8.1877, G.O.B.R.).*

24.7.1878 G.O.B.R.

Ryder Street, Ashton Old Road, Openshaw. Capital houses, newly beautified, rent 3s 10d - Apply 50 Ryder Street. *(Advert).*

26.7.1879

The Nuisance Inspector of Gorton reported the tenants of Nos. 15 and 17 Foxfold for keeping fowls in their cellars.

8.8.1879 S.A.

William Newby, aged 14, convicted of stealing strawberries from garden of Mr R. Weaver of Kirkmanshulme Hall. Father earned 9s a week on workhouse farm. Newby was sentenced to one month hard labour.

10.1.1880 G.O.B.R.

Proposal to build a new girder bridge over the canal at Ashton Old road. *(The proposal does not appear to have been put into effect.)*

26.6.1880 G.O.B.R.
Postal authorities propose bringing a line of telegraph posts and wires along Hyde Road from Manchester to Belle Vue station.

21.8.1880 G.O.B.R.
Manchester Fire Brigade take 40 to 45 minutes to arrive at fire in Birch Street, Gorton. Difficulty due to lack of telephone communication.

8.9.1883 G.O.B.R.
The Wakes will be remembered for the wretched weather if nothing else. There has been a continuous downpour and everywhere has been ankle-deep in mud. The large Town Croft was crowded every night and fairly attended in the afternoon. The shows, which every year seem to be deteriorating more and more, have been well patronised.

On the left was a circus, the paintings outside of which represented both men and horses accomplishing impossible feats, but which divided along with the clowns the openly expressed admiration of the juveniles, as they ascended the stage to transfer the necessary coppers from their pockets to the pockets of the proprietors of the establishments.

There was a booth with fat women and an exhibition, half pictorial half mechanical, in which people could see an accurate representation of the bombardment of Alexandria and other astonishing sights for one penny. There was a ghost illusion show and marionettes and a sparring booth. To the next booth an air of mystery and perhaps curiosity was lent by an announcement that no females were admitted and in which a living giant and living cannibals were said to be on view.

There was a theatre on the stage of which the actors strutted in all the glory of tinsel and paint. There were hobby horses, steam velocipedes, small swing boats, shooting galleries, Aunt Sally establishments, shooting at a score of bottles or cups strung in a row, coco-nut shies, portrait galleries, bazaars at which every conceivable kind of toy might be purchased and stalls where you might buy coco-nuts, ginger bread, black puddings, hot peas and roasted potatoes. Finally there was a camera obscura.
(A camera obscura is a dark chamber in which an image of outside objects is thrown upon a screen. The fair appears to have been a thoroughly enjoyable one, despite the writer's derogratory opening remarks.)

22.9.1883 G.O.B.R.
The 'cart wheel' business received a severe blow at the hands of the magistrates on Wednesday. In some dozen cases, where Mr Fennah had summoned persons for the irregular or non-attendance of their children at school, he stated that the children were constantly on Hyde Road, turning cart wheels, their parents being somewhere close at hand to receive the money from them.

In every instance an order to attend school was made. If these orders were not obeyed, the next thing will be committal of the children to an Industrial School.

7.1.1888 G.O.B.R.
The new 'margarine Act' came into operation on the 1st of January. Henceforth the vendor of 'butterine' must discard that name and see that the substitute for butter they are selling is legibly labelled 'margarine'. Butter and butterine were so very similar in appearance that people hitherto might have been excused in mistaking the one for the other.

A good Christmas dinner, consisting of roast beef with potatoes and plum pudding, was given in the Wesleyan Schoolroom, Cross Lane, last Saturday, to the poorest children in Gorton. There were three sittings and altogether 545 children partook of such a dinner as the majority of them had not seen, much less tasted, during the whole of the year.

24.3.1888 G.O.B.R.
A cock-fight in an empty house opposite the Abbey Hey Hotel was stopped by Constables Brindle and Savage.

28.4.1888 G.O.B.R.
Report on the health of Gorton for the year ending February, 1888
Epidemic of measles March-June : 65 children died.
Scarlet fever in last three months : 22 deaths.
Steps taken by the Health Committee to stop the keeping of pigeons and poultry in the back rooms of houses should be extended to the back yards. *(My father's father kept pigeons in one of the back bedrooms of the Cromwell Inn on Ashton Old Road. E.F.).*

5.5.1888 G.O.B.R.
A meeting of Irishmen living in the district was held at the house of Mr Collins, Signal Inn, Cross Street, for the purpose of forming a branch of the Irish National League of Great Britain.

12.5.1888 G.O.B.R.
Gorton Villa F.C. have acquired a new ground off Church Lane (Cambert Lane), opposite the Congregational Church. The club house and the dressing room will be at the Chapel House Hotel.

Farmers and milkmen celebrate May Day by decorating their horses with flowers, ribbons and bells.

26.5.1888 G.O.B.R.
How Gorton Sunday Schools celebrated Whitsuntide.
On Thursday there were individual processions round the village, some accompanied by brass bands. Most Sunday Schools followed with a tea party and games in a field. On Friday, all the Schools, apart from St. James's and Gore Street Mission Hall, had excursions to Chatsworth, Llandudno or Llangollen. St. James's had games in a field on the Friday instead of Thursday. Gore Street Mission Hall had a lurry trip to Dunham Park on Thursday and games in a field on Friday.

23.6.1888 G.O.B.R.
The dangers of dandelion gathering.
William Smart and Fred Hamilton were summoned by John Yarwood for trespassing. A bundle of dandelions, which the lads were alleged to have pulled up, was produced in court. One of the lads said that the place was full of bricks. Mr Yarwood: "No, sir, it has been a croft, but it is hay-grass now." A fine of 6d each and the costs was imposed.

5.1.1889 G.O.R.
Street pastimes.
William Henry Stevenson, George Halliwell, Walter Withington, John Rider and William Boon were summoned by Constable Wilson for causing an obstruction in Queen's Road, Gorton, on the afternoon of Sunday, December 23rd. They were pulling each other about and kicking a piece of timber. One of the defendants said they had a small piece of rubber and were going all the time they were kicking it. They were fined 6d each.

9.2.1889 G.O.R.
18 fowls kept in one house in Grey Street, Gorton.

1889
Little Droylsden was added to Openshaw.

22.6.1889 A.R.
"Openshaw v. Gorton" appears to have been the title of the battle waged in Newtown on Sunday. Nine lads, resident in Gorton and Openshaw, were charged on Monday with scuttling at Gorton on the previous day. The evidence revealed an extraordinary state of things. According to one of the witnesses the bother commenced soon after breakfast and was going on more or less all day. When Constable Wilson arrived on the scene, a little before seven o'clock in the evening, he found gathered on one side of Gorton Brook some lads and lasses from Openshaw and on the opposite side of the brook a similar gang of lads and lasses belonging to Gorton. They were engaged in the delightful occupation of storming each other.

Some of them, said the officer, had their belts off, but they were not sufficiently close to be able to use them. This is bad, but the state of terrorism excited by the scuttlers' conduct is worse. In explanation of the fact that the rowdyism was allowed to go on for so long a time, it was stated that the people living in the vicinity were afraid to inform the police, as they know that the result would be that their windows would be broken.
This will give to those people who happily live in districts where scuttling is unknown some idea of what it means.
(Gorton Brook was the name given to that part of the Cornbrook which flows below Gorton Lane and it must have been near there that the battle took place. "Newtown" may be a misspelling of "Newton", meaning "Newton detached", the other name for Kirkmanshulme. If so, it is still incorrect, for Gorton Brook is some distance from Kirkmanshulme.)

28.6.1890 G.O.R
Prospective development of Abbey Hey district.
The well-known grounds attached to the Abbey Hey Hotel will soon be a thing of the past. A new street *(Jackson/Jetson Street)* will cut across the Abbey Hey Grounds with a second street at right angles to it *(Kenyon Street)*. Members of the Gorton Cricket Club, who hold their ground subject to a six months notice to quit, are somewhat apprehensive that this street will be carried forward so far in the direction of this field as to necessitate their having to relinquish it.
(At this time the Vine Street railway cutting had not yet been made. The Abbey Hey portion of Vine Street was then called Hodson Street. There were a few houses on thewest side of Hodson Street near to Abbey Hey Lane. They were pulled down when the cutting was made.)

9.8.1890 G.O.R.
East Gorton is progressing rapidly. In the new street, which has just been opened out from Chapman Street to Goose Green, ten houses are being erected at one point and several others near the mill. *(The new street was High Street, now called Highmead Street.)* In Lees Street, near Gorton cricket Ground, another row of property is about to be put up.

There is a shortage of accommodation, with the result that rents have been raised.

16.8.1890 G.O.R.
"What age are you?", the taskman said,
Outside the workshop door;
The youngster blushed and soft replied,
"Please Sir, I'm twenty-four".
"Too young, too young", then said the boss,
"We've lots of lads to drive,
Go somewhere else - call later on,
Come when you're twenty-five".

Then turning to another man,
"What age have you put on?
You seem to know a thing or two".
"Yes Sir, I'm forty-one".
"Too old, too old," the taskman cries,
"For now we draw the line
At one year less, so come again
When you are thirty-nine".

(Signed) Amalg.Eng.

30.8.1890 G.O.R.
Market, opened on Wakes ground Lower Openshaw, lit by flaring naphtha lamps.

6.9.1890 G.O.R.
Openshaw Wakes held on land at rear of Openshaw Inn.

3.1.1891 G.O.R.
Dog collars engraved with names and addresses of owners are on sale at the Reporter Office upon the shortest notice at most reasonable prices.

A number of Gortonians will remember the last day of 1890. They were summoned for keeping dogs without licences. At the Gorton Petty Sessions Mr Leresche ordered them to pay certain penalties. On the following day they were supposed to take out a new licence for the year upon which we have now entered.

10.1.1891 G.O.R.
Employees of Messrs Jennison have been filling the Belle Vue ice-houses with ice taken from a pond off Kirkmanshulme Lane.

17.1.1891 G.O.R.
Paper hanging from ½d per piece. J. Collins, house decorator, Haddon Street, near Midland Hotel, Gorton. *(Advertisement).*

24.1.1891 G.O.R.
The distress in West Gorton.
An influential committee has been formed to open a soup

kitchen in West Gorton. A yard has been lent at the corner of Sussex Street and Gorton Lane. An appeal for money, meat, bread and coal has been made.

31.1.1891 G.O.B.R.
The Scotch Railway Strike.
Mr William Mather M.P. has forwarded from Russia a contribution to the fund being raised for the benefit of the railwaymen who are on strike in Scotland. This kindly act shows that once more Mr. Mather's sympathy with the working classes of the country is real and unabated.
(Mr William Mather, M.P. for Gorton, of Woodhill, Prestwich, later became an honorary member of the Amalgamated Society of Railway Servants. He was a member of the firm of Mather and Platt.)

21.2.1891 G.O.B.R
Sir Edward Watkin, chairman of the directors of the Manchester, Sheffield and Lincoln Railway Company, delivered a lecture on the Channel Tunnel on Thursday evening in the Boys School in connection with the Gorton Tank Works.
(A tunnel had already been started on both sides of the channel.)

Mr William Mather on the importance of Education.
...... There is a great desire to know whether we are doing a fair and right thing, as regards the children of the working classes, by enabling them to become free from educational influence, so far as half time attendance is concerned, at ten years of age, if they have passed the second or third standard.
A child of ten looks a very small speck of humanity. My little girl is eleven and I should be sorry to see her leave home at five or six in the morning to work.

2.5.1892
New station at Fairfield opened, 3/8 mile east of existing station.

25.2.1893 G.O.B.R.
The Abbey Hey estate is to be opened out. The well-known sporting grounds are closed and will be covered over in future with brick and mortar tenements.
800 - 900 houses are to be erected.

19.8.1893 G.O.B.R.
Gorton Villa Football Club wound up.

23.5.1894 G.O.B.R.
Diphtheria assumed an epidemic form in Gorton in the autumn of 1893.

1901
Prices at T. Seymour Mead's, Ashton Old Road, Higher Openshaw:
Sugar 2 ¼d per lb
Tea 1s 5d per lb
Butter 1s 2d per lb
Rice 2d per lb
Almonds 1s 8d per lb
Sardines 1s 3d per tin
Salmon 8d per tin

Gorton Library opened on Church Lane (Cambert Lane). The money was provided by John Buckley, the Gorton mill-owner.

7.6.1902 G.O.B.R.
Gorton rejoiced with every other place in the country at the conclusion of the war in South Africa and the signing of peace. There were bonfires and fireworks and houses were decorated with bunting and Union Jacks. Schools and works were closed.

Ashton Old Road presented a particularly lively appearance. Union Jacks, large and small, were to be seen everywhere. On Sunday, bands of lasses and lads, arm in arm, paraded the streets of the main thoroughfare singing, "Britons never shall be slaves".

5.7.1902 G.O.B.R.
Coronation Festivities in Gorton.
On Thursday week over 10,000 children were present in the procession of the schools round the township. After parading the district the scholars went back to their respective schools and were regaled.

October 1905 Gorton Parish (St. James) Magazine

DEATHS

"I am the Resurrection and the Life, saith the Lord"

Aug 5 Alice Barber, aged 14 months.
Aug 12 Harriet Hannah Houghton, aged 40 years.
Aug 13 Lily Earnshaw, aged 3 days
Aug 14 Charles Woodhall, aged 7 months
Aug 15 Annie Lowcock, aged 3 days
Aug 16 William Heywood, aged 27 years
Aug 17 Albert Stokes, aged 16 years
Aug 21 Jane Noden, aged 10 months
Aug 21 Hannah Connell, aged 56 years
Aug 23 Thomas Bailey, aged 8 months
Aug 25 Alice Robinson, aged 63 years
Aug 26 Harold Bailey, aged 2 months
Sept 1 Harold Leeson, aged 31 years
Sept 1 Sarah Willcox, aged 66 years
Sept 1 Sam Saunders, aged 66 years
Sept 4 Harry Pickles, aged 15 weeks
Sept 4 George Holt, aged 5 months
Sept 4 Edward Regan, aged 1 day
Sept 4 Edmund Marchington, aged 72 years
Sept 6 James S. Aspinall, aged 4 months
Sept 8 Ortence Bacon, aged 35 years
Sept 13 Ada Cunningham, aged 13 months
Sept 13 Robert Henry M. Taylor, aged 1 month
Sept 14 Charles Valentine Pickering Quin, aged 22 years
Sept 15 George Bradley, aged 1 month

1906
Gorton Male Voice Choir founded. Gorton and Openshaw station built with access from Lees Street, replacing the one on Cornwall Street.

29.2.1908 G.O.B.R.
A startling tragedy at Gorton. Exciting scenes in a beer house. Man killed and woman injured. Alleged attempted double murder.
In the early hours of Friday last, February 21st, a murder took place at the Prince of Wales beerhouse on Abbey Hey Lane.

John Ramsbottom, son-in-law of the licensee, shot his wife in the breast. James M'Craw, Mrs Ramsbottom's brother, intervened and was hit in the arm and stomach. He died three quarters of an hour later.

25.4.1908 G.O.B.R.
John Ramsbottom of Abbey Hey Lane found guilty of the murder of James M'Craw.

2.1.1909 G.O.B.R.
Early in the week everything was in readiness for the payment today (Friday) of old age pensions in Gorton and Manchester. In Gorton nearly 400 applications were considered and 350 odd accepted. 36 died before they could draw their pensions. Another sad feature is the grief of those who are disqualified through having received trifling allowances of poor relief during the year.
(The pensions, which varied from 1s to 5s a week, were given at seventy years of age and were subject to a means test.)

6.3.1909 G.O.B.R.
Medical Officer of Health's monthly report:
Infantile mortality in Gorton was equal to 148 children dying under one year out of each 1,000 births.
(The corresponding figure for the U.K. for 1988 was 9.1)

The Gorton Surveyor discussed with the Chief Electrical Engineer of Manchester corporation the lighting by electricity of Hyde Road and Reddish Lane.

2.6.1909
Alhambra Theatre, Higher Openshaw, opened.

10.7.1909 G.O.B.R.
Mark Shawcross, aged 39, a labourer of Gorton, was sentenced to death for the murder of Mrs Emily Ramsbottom, aged 27, of Ellesmere Street, Gorton,. The body was found by a number of young women going to their work at Messrs Turner's tarpaulin works off Pink Bank Lane. It was lying in a lane near the Sewage Works off Brook Road.
(The lane, in which the body of Mrs Ramsbottom was found, was in fact Knutsford Vale, which for many years after was known as Murder Lane. The Sewage Works was off Mount Road not Brook Road.)

21.8.1909 G.O.B.R.
Alhambra Theatre
Great attraction this week is the great Lafayette, who has attracted large crowds and particularly was this so on Saturday, for at the matinee and the two houses at night it is estimated that between eight and nine thousand people comprised the three audiences. In the afternoon he provided the whole of the entertainment, which lasted for nearly three hours. It was produced on entirely new lines and included his new illusion-drama, "Dr Kremser". Another piece was the "Lion's Bride", the story of a maiden who is rescued from the den of a lion of apparently genuine ferocity.

30.10.1909 G.O.B.R.
High Bank Recreation Ground, Abbey Hey, opened.

29.1.1910 G.O.B.R.
Some time ago the Gorton Education Committee decided that in future no married women teachers should be appointed in the elementary schools and this week the Manchester Education Committee decided to fall into line with this and other authorities. No action, however, is to be taken with regard to the married women at present engaged in the schools. Though opposition was taken to the proposal to exclude married women, it found very little support. The opinion of the members seems to be, and very properly so, that the married woman's place was at home and not in the school. Surely it is not unreasonable to suggest that a married woman cannot teach well in the school and do her duty to her family as well. How many instances are there in the country where husband and wife are teaching in day schools, and yet there are many single women, equally as capable, unable to get a situation owing to the market for teachers being overcrowded.

26.2.1910
Moving pictures shown at Alhambra Theatre.

7.5.1910 G.O.B.R.
Midnight collection of letters begun from the Gorton sub-post office and from Cross Street.

24.9.1910 G.O.B.R.
Blackpool. Mrs Kay, Victoria Villa, 14 Kent Road.
Bed, cooking, sitting room, attendance, piano, 1s each person (per day)
3 mins. Central pier.
(Mrs. Kay was advertising "apartments" - for the working class a cheap alternative to the boarding house. Holiday makers at 14 Kent Road would provide their own food, an exception being made if for convenience Mrs. Kay provided the vegetables. Apartments were common until well after the 2nd World War.)

15.8.1914 G.O.B.R.
Poor and the War.
As an interesting example of how the poor are faring just now, the wife of a labourer in Openshaw states that her income is £1 a week. They have eight children and pay 5s a week in rent. Some few evenings ago she was charged 2d for half a pound of sugar and 2d for an ounce of tea, whilst the cost of bacon is 2s 2d a pound and butchers meat 1s.

29.8.1914 G.O.B.R.
Gorton and Openshaw Workshops Relief Committee set up. A collection has been taken in worshops for the poor.

7.11.1914 G.O.B.R.
Mr John Hodge M.P. said, "There was a worse thing then war. That was to be ridden over by a nation which had shown itself to be merciless and barbarous and a believer in might against right". He was addressing a Labour meeting at Gorton Labour Hall.

Soldiers' pay 1s per day. 9d per day deducted from a married soldier's pay as a contribution to his wife's family allowance.

19.1.1918 G.O.B.R.
The food distribution problem has reached a critical stage. On Wednesday it caused a remarkable demonstration. At eleven o'clock in the morning the men and women engaged in seven or eight of the largest munition works in the Openshaw and Gorton districts ceased work for three hours and marched down

to Albert Square in protest against the queues and to demand a national system of rationing with an equal distribution of food among all classes.

9.2.1918 G.O.B.R.
A Public Food Kitchen, said to be the most promising experiment of its kind, has been opened in Barmouth Street, Openshaw. Dinners are served between 11.30 am and 2 pm. It has a capacity for 2,000. In the first week 1500 meals were served.

Soup is 1½d per pint. Meat and vegetable stew and meat pie are both 4d.
Potatoes are 1d.

16.2.1918 G.O.B.R.
The Victoria Cross has been awarded to Lance-Corporal John Thomas of Higher Openshaw for gallantry as a sniper. When on leave he stayed with relatives at 7 Gorton Road, Openshaw.

2.3.1918 G.O.B.R.
The compulsory rationing scheme comes into operation on Monday in the Manchester area, including Openshaw, Gorton, Bradford and Clayton. A start is being made with tea, butter and margarine. Meat will be compulsorily rationed on March 25th. The allowance of tea will be one ounce per head and the allowance of butter and margarine will be four ounces per head. (per week).

4.5.1918 G.O.B.R.
Private George A. Wood, aged 20, of 45 Hobart Street, High Bank, Gorton, was killed at Zeebrugge on April 23rd. His body was brought for burial with military honours at Brookfield church. Another son Robert was killed two years ago.

29.6.1918 G.O.B.R.
The day schools in Gorton are closed for this month. There is no abatement of the influenza in Gorton and there appears to be no alternative course than isolation at home. *(This was the dreaded "Spanish 'flu". In the 1918 - 1919 epidemic it killed 228,917 people in the U.K.)*

5.4.1919 G.O.B.R.
Population of Openshaw estimated at about 30,000.
Number out of work: men 3,501, women, 7,488.
Unemployment due mainly to closing of munitions works.

3.5.1919 G.O.B.R.
The Rev. C. C. Chambers of St. George's, Abbey Hey, has expressed his objection to raising money for a war memorial by means of socials, whist drives, football matches, dances. etc.

3.5.1919 G.O.B.R.
600 homes to be erected at Gorton Mount by Manchester City Council. Rents are to be between 11s and 17s 6d.

10.5.1919 G.O.B.R.
"......... the Abbey Hey people have certainly responded promptly, though not in the way the worthy Rector could have desired. In a word, they have resented the Rector's chastening and, so far from feeling repentant at their reprehensible conduct in carrying out their worldly pleasures to aid a sacred cause, have determined to organise more dances etc." *(See 3.5.1919).*

12.7.1919 G.O.B.R.
Peace and Victory Pageant.
Sunday School Procession at Openshaw. Fine display by Non-conformists.

The Baptist School carried letters to spell Peace. The Central Openshaw United Methodists represented different nationalities. Stanley Street Wesleyan Methodists and Lees Street Congregational were resplendent and delicately beatific with wreaths of florally worked emblems of Victory.

27.6.1925 G.O.B.R.
The biggest railway locomotive ever built was given a trial run to Penistone on Sunday morning. The engine, which has been built by Messrs Beyer Peacock and Co. Ltd., was stated to have emerged from its initial run very satisfactorily. It has been built for the London North Eastern Railway Co. and will make its first public appearance at the Darlington Railway Centenary in July, when every type of engine will be on view.
It is 79 feet long with small wheels for up hill work, a 22 feet boiler and a firehole "as big as a room".

14.11.1925 G.O.B.R.
Mrs Lambert of 3 Norman Street, West Gorton, was killed at Belle Vue by a blow from a tiger, while she was engaged in cleaning out the animal's cage.

6.2.1926 G.O.B.R.
Shortage of housing in Gorton reported.

3.4.1926 G.O.B.R.
Greyhound racing proposed at Belle Vue at meeting of Belle Vue (Manchester) Ltd.

26.2.1926 G.O.B.R.
Coal 2s 6d - 3s per cwt. Mills are turning in desperation to oil fuel or closing down, if they cannot adapt their plant.
(The high price of coal was due to a shortage, which was a consequence of the miners' strike. This began on May 3rd, when the miners were joined by other workers in a general strike. The general strike lasted nine days, but the coal stoppage went on for seven months.)

31.7.1926 G.O.B.R.
Greyhound racing installed at Belle Vue this week.

19.3.1926 G.O.B.R.
Charleston Banned
The Charleston dance has not reigned long at the All Saints Schools, West Gorton. Following protests by members of the Mothers Union at a recent dance, the Rector (Rev. Wm. Binch) made a personal visit of inspection and in consequence of what he saw he ordered the dance to cease forthwith.

14.1.1928 G.O.B.R.
Many careworn faces were lit up with joy and there were many heartfelt expressions of thanks from the small army of Gorton, Openshaw and Droylsden old folks between 65 and 70 years of age who drew their first weekly pension of ten shillings.

8.9.1928 G.O.B.R.
The mill of Messrs James Moorhouse and Son Ltd, cotton manufacturers and doublers, Croft Street, Gorton, was almost

completely destroyed by fire. The mill was known as Buckley's Mill and employed 200 people, including 150 women.

23.2.1929 G.O.B.R.
The Great Frost
The street gas-lamps in Gorton, Openshaw and Droylsden have failed to function. Many houses are without water, because of burst pipes. The Great Frost killed 'Lil', the famous Belle Vue hippopotamus, valued at £1,500.

6.4.1929 G.O.B.R.
The second meeting at the new motor-cycle dirt-track at Belle Vue took place last week. There was a crowd of 12,000.

8.6.1929 G.O.B.R.
Mr Joseph Compton (Labour) increased his majority at the general election.

29.6.1929 G.O.B.R.
H D Moorhouse is to equip between 30 and 40 of his cinemas with talkies.

24.5.1930 G.O.B.R.
Remarkable interest was evinced in the flight over West Gorton of the giant airship R100, which crossed over the district about 11.30 a.m. on Thursday morning.

4.7.1931 G.O.B.R.
Godfrey Ermen Field off Abbey Hey Lane formally declared open.

14.7.1931 G.O.B.R.
Public wash-houses can only be engaged for one hour per week. Queues form at 4 a.m. to book an hour. Their popularity has followed the installation of the electric washer.

12.9.1931 G.O.B.R.
The hump-backed bridge, which carries Ashton Old Road over the canal is no more. A new bridge is to be built.

24.10.1931 G.O.B.R.
Parliamentary election results:
E.A.G. Shackleton Bailey (Con.) 21,228
J. Compton (Lab.) 16,316
Christopher Flanagan (Com.) 1,000
(In 1929 Ramsay MacDonald took office for the second time and his Labour government met the worst economic crisis the world had every known. By the end of 1931 there were 2,900,000 people unemployed - a fifth of all insured workers. Cuts in government expenditure were recommended and ten members of the Labour Cabinet resigned. With Conservative support a National Government was formed and a General Election held, with the result that Labour representation in the House of Commons was reduced to 51 members. Mr Compton was one of the casualties.)

14.11.1931 G.O.B.R.
Magistrate's comments in "Knick-Knack" Club Case.
At the magistrates' court charges of obtaining money were brought against Mrs .... in connection with a "Knick-knack" club. Mrs .... had applied to Mr F.C. Riley of Cross Street to be allowed to form a "Knick-knack" club and collect the money from the members week by week on a commission of 1s 8d in the £. Mrs ...., who was in arrears with her rent, obtained from Mr Riley suits, boots and other clothing and bedding to the amount of £24 9s, some of which she pawned. She had paid to Mr Riley only £4.

Mrs Pearson (Magistrate): Is it not customary in these "Knick-knack" clubs for only one check to be issued each week and the customers supplied in rotation so that the shopkeeper is covered each week?

Witness: That is correct but many shops adopted the present system about two years ago. In Gorton it is now the rule to hand out the goods in the first week.
The defendant was bound over
(The "Knick-knack" clubs to which Mrs Pearson was referring operated in the following way. A number of women would agree to subscribe a fixed sum each week for a number of weeks. Thus twenty women might agree to subscribe two shillings a week for twenty weeks. In the first week the club organiser would collect £2, which she would exchange at the shop for a check or voucher, redeemable only at the shop in question. The check would be given to the member whose name came first out of the hat. This would be repeated each week until each member had paid in £2 and received goods to that amount. The club organiser would receive her commission either weekly or in a lump sum.)

5.12.1931 G.O.B.R.
Councillor T Regan (Gorton North) attacks "police brutality" and refers to the police as an "army of occupation". The occasion was when the police stopped a demonstration march by the unemployed through the city.

The police were defended by Alderman Walker, who said that the march would have held up employees on their way to work.

6.5.1933 G.O.B.R.
Plans approved by the Manchester City Council for 30 houses in Chapman Street, Brown Street and Harrison Street, Gorton.

10.6.1933 G.O.B.R.
The first united procession of Church of England and Free Church Sunday Schools in Gorton took place on Saturday. There were more than 5,000 scholars and it was estimated that 20,000 people lined the route.

19.6.1933 M.E.N.
Tributes to a brave young policeman were paid at the inquest today on Constable Jewes, 25, of "A" Division, Manchester City Police. Jewes and William (Battling) Burke, 46, of the Salvation Army Hostel, Francis Street, Manchester, lost their lives on Friday night in the River Irwell, where Burke had been lowered on a rope over the bridge near Manchester Cathedral to save a kitten. Burke got into difficulties and Constable Jewes went in to save him. The verdict was that both men were accidentally drowned.
John Tudor (21) of 90 Greengate, Salford, who went to the aid of Jewes and Burke and was dragged out of the water exhausted, was complimented by the coroner.
Constable Tom Jewes resided at 25 Bransford Road, Higher Openshaw.

21.6.1933 M.E.N.
Blackpool Mrs J. Wood 29 Bairstow Street. adj. Prom.
beds 3s 6d (2 pers.) board 6s bed-breakfast 3s

Blackpool North 58 Enfield Road 2s 6d bed (2)

Blackpool Ellis & Berkin, 54 Chernley Road. Cent.
elec. and wash basins: 3s 6d 2 persons: nr stn. and sea

24.6.1933 G.O.B.R.
100,000 people lined the streets between Albert Street Police Station and Victoria Station to pay tribute to Constable Jewes. He was buried at Whittle-le-Woods near Chorley.

2.2.1935 G.O.B.R.
A deputation from the Unemployed Association of Gorton United Trades and Labour Council complain to the Public Assistance Committee that the new relief scales of the Unemployment Assistance Board are unfair. The example quoted is that a man, wife and three children receive only 7s whilst a widow with two children receives 10s 6d.

23.2.1935 G.O.B.R.
The Gorton Branch of the Manchester and District Anti-War Council arranged an exhibition, which has been said to strip war of its glory more effectively than a thousand speeches. It was staged in Lees Street Congregational Sunday School.

9.3.1935 G.O.B.R.
Demonstration against the new Unemployment Act.
The main procession included a body of women who called themselves the West Gorton Battalion of Lady Astor's Ragged Army.
(The 1935 Unemployment Act brought in the "means test" See 16.11.1935 G.O.B.R.)

23.3.1935 G.O.B.R.
Letter from a correspondent:
In a short time will come one of the year's most melancholy periods. As Easter approaches, the hikers, campers and picnickers will swarm, crowd and climb in the hill country around Manchester. They will bring with them their usual collection of noise producers - both vocal and mechanical - their trained gate-openers and their own particular brand of insolence. If chaos is a sign of progress, then the farmers, who suffer this invasion in more or less inarticulate rage, should be quite satisfied at the advance of civilisation.

(signed) Wigwam

30 m.p.h. speed limit came into effect at midnight on Sunday

11.5.1935 G.O.B.R.
Openshaw Gay Jubilee Festivities Open-air parties in the street.
One impressive display was in a street off Fairfield Road. Flags and bunting were draped across the street and round the front of houses and there was a significant notice: "Rent men need not apply until Wednesday week".

In one local street flags and bunting were being brought out for decorations and were strung from one window to another. I met an elderly lady who brought out a parcel of pennants and flags and although there was a smile on her face, I could see that she was fighting hard to keep back the tears. "The decorations were bought to celebrate the return of my husband from the war. The flags were out ready and the neighbours were joining to give him a rousing reception. But he never returned. On the morning he was leaving France for home he was fatally wounded." Sadly she put the flags away and they were not used again until Jubilee Day.

There was no centrally organised service, procession or demonstration, but in spite of that, Gorton people were not behind in demonstrating their loyalty. One Union Jack flying from the flag pole was the sole decoration of Gorton Town Hall.

The streets off Cross Street and Church Lane let themselves go. Lord Street off Hyde Road was a picture. There were streamers from every window and round the doors and it was in this street that an open-air Jubilee party was held.
(The Jubilee was the Silver Jubilee of King George V.)

1.6.1935 G.O.B.R.
Gorton's Big Peace Meeting.
500 People marched through the streets of Gorton to Debdale Park for a mass meeting and demonstration. Mr Compton urged the Labour policy of collective security. By this method it would be the easiest thing in the world to smash any warmonger and they could do it without increasing the fighting force by one single aeroplane.
(By collective security Mr Compton meant that members of the League of Nations should by concerted action stop any aggressor.)

10.8.1935 G.O.B.R.
E.A.G. Shackleton Bailey, M.P., protested against the decision of the Unemployment Assistance Board to make a reduction of a shilling in the allowance given to parents in respect of every child receiving free meals except the first child.
(Mr Shackleton Bailey was the Conservative M.P. for Gorton.)

16.11.1935 G.O.B.R.
Gorton recaptured by Labour.
J. Compton 20,039
E.A.G. Shackleton Bailey 15,833
Mr Shackleton Bailey said that the Means Test had lost them the election in Gorton, and particularly in Lower and Central Openshaw. "Mr Compton was a high type of trade union official and he had fought quite a clean fight." Mr Compton said of Shackleton Bailey, "I want to pay this compliment to my opponent - he made us go all the way. If every Conservative candidate is as hard working as Mr Bailey, then the Conservatives have something to be proud of."
(When determining the amount of unemployment benefit, the authorities took into account the assets of the applicant and the income of the members of his family. This was known as a means test.)

22.1.1937 G.O.B.R.
Death of Mr J. Compton, M.P. on 18.1.1937 reported.
(He was succeeded by Mr. William Wedgwood Benn, Labour.)

5.3.1937 G.O.B.R.
Pottery Lane Bridge.
A new railway bridge has been constructed. The roadway has been lowered, widened and considerably improved and from now on the double deck buses of Manchester Corporation need have no fear of being trapped under the bridge.

14.5.1937 G.O.B.R.
Coronation Celebrations in Openshaw and Gorton.
200 children took part in a procession through the streets of Openshaw to celebrate the coronation of George VI and Queen Elizabeth. In George Street (now Greenside Street) Park they held their own coronation ceremony, a boy and a girl being chosen to play the part of the royal couple.

Street parties were the order of the day in Gorton and Openshaw. Trestle tables were erected in the streets and covered in red, white and blue and a variety of household chairs were commandeered for seating accommodation. Loads of good things were piled on the table - I never saw a stinted tea-table in the whole of the tour.

After tea, parties and concerts were held in the streets and many had open air dancing, music being provided by piano, jazz band, accordion or radio.

The enthusiasm was boundless and the workers legion. In some cases the keenness went as far as the painting of the streets into a huge Union Jack. Kerb stones were done in red, white and blue. Ellesmere Street (between Church Lane and Cross Lane) was transformed into a fairyland of lights.

20.8.1937 G.O.B.R.
Song of the Litter Lout by J. Staley.
I thrown my finished fags away
In wood or pleasant hollow
And when in scented lane I stay
The packet soon will follow
The papers from my lunch I leave
Beside the stream so merry,
And pebbles at the bottles heave
I'm good at shying very.

With shining foil from off the chocs
I decorate the heather
And play at footer till the box
No longer holds together
A trail of orange peel so bright
Marks all the track I've taken
With now and then to left and right
Banana skins forsaken.

Some cross old codgers make a fuss
And try to spoil our pleasures
They put up cheeky signs for us
And hint at sterner measures
But I don't listen to their talk
Some folks are very bitter
I want full freedom in my walk
To dump at will my litter.

17.9.1937 G.O.B.R.
A drumhead service in memory of fallen comrades, organised by the Belle Vue (Gorton) Branch of the British Legion, took place on Saturday in All Saints Church. The only two survivors of the first contingent of the Lancashire Fusiliers who landed at Gallipoli in the historic 'Ellis Landing' also walked in the parade. They are Mr A. Conlan of Seddon Avenue, Gorton, and Mr Harry Leadbetter of Clowes Street, Gorton. Only sixteen survived the landing, the others being massacred by the Turks, and now only these two men are left.

5.11.1937 G.O.R.
The Valour will make its annual pilgrimage from Manchester to London.
(The steam locomotive Valour was built at Gorton Tank in 1920 by the Great Central Railway Company. At the front were two plates bearing the dedication "Valour", in memory of the G.C.R. employees who gave their lives for their country in the First World War. During the Armistice Day journey from Manchester to London the Valour stopped at Leicester and observed the two minutes silence.

When the Valour was broken up in 1948 one of the plates was sent to the York Railway Museum and the other was fixed to the outside wall of the Gorton Tank iron foundry. see G.O.R. 31.5.1963.)

12.11.1937 G.O.R.
Mr William Dawson of Blackburn Street, Higher Openshaw, has been a knocker up for 67 years and he claims to be the oldest "knight of the pronged stick". "Billy Dawson", who is 76 years of age, commenced knocking up when he was a mere boy. Mr Dawson's mother was a knocker up before him and she has over 50 years to her credit. Mr Dawson was born in Droylsden and his father was a weaver at a local mill. Mr Dawson began work at the same mill when he was nine.

18.3.1938 G.O.R.
Gorton's famous lollipop shop in Far Lane will soon have disappeared completely. The work of demolition is proceeding rapidly and already the building has been reduced to a mass of broken bricks, rubble and stone.

The building with its black and white markings has been admired by thousands including many visitors from abroad. The house had an old-fashioned fire-grate with a spit and small diamond-shaped windows.

22.7.1938 G.O.R.
Quantity of food that can be purchased with an unemployed man's food allowance.
7lbs of bread
3lbs of vegetables
3¼oz of fish
¾lbs meat
¾ pint of milk
1½oz of cheese
½ of an egg
½oz of butter

Gorton Tram Stops and Democracy Letter signed P.J.
When I ever hear people talking about the freedom and blessings of democracy, I always get a 'pain in the neck'. I would like to draw these people's attention to the tram and bus stops of Gorton.

Any time before nine o'clock in the morning some of the most disgusting spectacles possible can be seen at any tram stop. Crowds of men, women and young girls can be seen struggling to board the trams. It is nothing unusual for people to have their clothing torn or to have some minor injury.

20.9.1938 G.O.R.
Audenshaw's Old Hatting Master
I believe the only survivor of the golden age of the industry is Mr Adam Ashworth of Hay Street, whose works are now the last of the 18 factories at one time operating in Audenshaw.

7.10.1938 G.O.R.
"Germany Has Blackmailed Us." Mr Shackleton Bailey's Straight Talk at Gorton

Mr Shackleton Bailey said that the only alternative to the Munich Settlement was war. "Let Germany go east and waste her energy on the Russian bear. Hitler has repudiated many treaties in the past and when a man has broken pledges one by one, can you attach any importance to a general statement that he makes?"

7.4.1939 G.O.R.
George VI on a tour of Lancashire visited Melland Playing Fields.

Practice blackout last Saturday - 12.30 a.m. to 3 a.m.

12.5.1939 G.O.R.
Mr William Wedgwood Benn, M.P. for Gorton addressed a meeting in Bradford's Philips Park. He attacked the Government bill to introduce conscription.

8.9.1939 G.O.R.
Evacuation of children began on Friday, September 1st. Higher Openshaw children were evacuated to Glossop, Hadfield and district. Lower Openshaw children went to Blackpool and Gorton children to Hazel Grove and Poynton.

15.9.1939 G.O.R.
Some mothers and children returned within a week.

17.11.1939 G.O.R.
Bus-loads of children, including many from Gorton and Openshaw, arrive in Manchester on Fridays and Saturdays to spend the week-end with their parents. There are many complaints of accidents in the blackout.

1.12.1939 G.O.R.
John Jagger, M.P. for Clayton, forecast that the war would end within 6 to 8 months because of the strain on Germany.

Rationing of bacon, ham, butter and sugar will begin on 8.1.1940.

5.4.1940 G.O.R.
Manchester City Council rejected the recommendation of the Watch Committee to permit the opening of cinemas on Sunday, but agreed to games in parks on Sundays.

Alderman George Hall said, "I have never asked for Sunday games for myself and you don't need to. I and all of you here, who can afford to, can play games any Sunday we like."

17.5.1940 G.O.R.
A feature of the Whitsuntide procession of the Openshaw churches was the number of gas masks carried by the children.

12.7.1940 G.O.R.
There has been a good response in Gorton and Openshaw to the appeal by Lord Beaverbrook, the Minister of Aircraft Production, for old aluminium to be converted into aircraft.
Mr W. Wedgwood Benn, M.P. for Gorton, has rejoined the R.A.F. He is 63 years of age. He joined the Army Flying Corps in the 1st World War at the age of 37. He holds the D.S.O. and the D.F.M.

4.10.1940 G.O.R.
Rowdyism complained of in report to Manchester City Council
The standard 48 person communal shelter is not equipped with seating, lighting or sanitary facilities, although these are provided in public shelters. These factors have caused persons in certain areas to proceed to the public shelters each evening, irrespective of whether an air-raid warning has been received. This has caused much overcrowding in some shelters, while others have been relatively empty. Since such persons propose to spend the night in the shelters, many of them have taken beds, armchairs etc. to the shelters and have assumed an attitude of proprietorship in relation to a shelter which was intended for the use of persons caught in the street.
(Communal shelters were intended for the use of nearby residents. They were often supervised by local air-raid wardens.)

Councillor Tom Regan complained of the faulty workmanship of air-raid shelters. 'There are people in my ward who have backyard shelters and they have taken an umbrella in with them. These shelters are made of slabs of concrete, which have not been joined together but have simply been pointed with mortar. The result is that people are drenched when it rains."
(Councillor Regan represented Gorton North).

13/14/10.1940
In an air-raid on Manchester during the night, incendiary bombs were dropped in Openshaw and Gorton.

Openshaw
88 Vine Street, Riley's timber yard in Lees Street, Montana Street at its junction with Vine Street, 41 Ogden Street, 2 Rosina Street, 21 Ogden Lane, 144 Eastern By Pass, 49, 51, 61 Wetherby Street.

Gorton
3 and 5 Kenyon Street, 30 and 32 Sandown Street, Abbey Hey Lane, bakehouse Harrop Street.
(Manchester Fire Brigade Records).

1.11.1940 G.O.R.
There are complaints that the concrete seats in the school shelters at Spurley Hey, Old Hall Drive and Abbey Hey are very cold.

15.11.1940 G.O.R.
There are complaints about Anderson shelters in Gorton.

(Anderson shelters were made out of sheets of corrugated iron and were sunk in the ground. They gave protection against anything except a direct hit. The main drawback was that they were liable to flooding.)

6.12.1940 M.E.N.
Commenting on the increase in juvenile crime in Manchester, Mr Wright Robinson, a former chairman of the Manchester Education Committee, who presided over one of the juvenile courts, told the Manchester Evening News that it was largely out of the broken school life. There was, he said, a close association between truancy and juvenile delinquency.

20.12.1940 G.O.R.
Bags of sand have made their appearance in Gorton, Openshaw, Clayton and Bradford streets this week. They are for putting out fires and extinguishing incendiary bombs.

When war was declared, 50,000 children were evacuated from Manchester. By Christmas 1939 the number had fallen to 20,000. Now it has fallen to 5,000.

23.12.1940 M.E.N.
Bombs Shower on City : Shelterers Trapped in Wreckage
MANCHESTER BLITZ : MANY BUILDINGS FIRED
Manchester had its largest and most severe aerial bombardment last night. For many hours hundreds of incendiary and explosive bombs were dropped, and a pall of smoke hung over the city today.

The raid started shortly after dusk, when enemy raiders, apparently approaching the city from the south, spread fanwise over a wide area and adopted the familiar tactics of flare dropping, followed by incendiary bombs at various points.
Wave after wave of planes roared over the city every few minutes and targets for the later arrivals were made with the fires started.

Later high explosives and incendiaries dealt death to people and destruction to property.

Hospitals, shops, hotels and business premises were damaged.

Most of the fires had been got under control, thanks to the magnificent work of the firemen, who worked heroically hour after hour, regardless of the serious risk they ran in carrying on while the raiders were overhead.

When the attack started, many people were caught in the street.

Note
The Manchester Blitz began shortly after 6 p.m. on Sunday, December 22nd. The All Clear sounded about twelve hours later. The air attack was resumed the following evening and lasted until the early hours of the 24th.

Within one and a half hours of the onset of the Sunday attack, all available mobile fire units and sections were in action. *(Manchester Fire Brigade Records).* The Manchester Fire Services were unable to cope and fire engines came from Chester-le-Street, Cardiff and London to help.

The city was virtually defenceless, for although there were no R.A.F. night-fighters the barrage balloons were lowered early on the Sunday evening.

Gorton and Openshaw escaped with relatively little damage. An H.E. bomb fell in Delamere Street, damaging three houses and hurling a stone sett through the roof of Wood's, the bakers and confectioners, at the corner of Stanley Street and Abbey Hey Lane. The sett landed in a heavy well-sprung easy chair in one of the upstairs rooms - fortunately for the family, who were in the living room below. Another bomb fell at the rear of No. 2 Delamere Street but failed to explode. People living in the street were evacuated to the Alhambra Cinema.

On the same evening a stick of bombs fell on houses in Royal Street and Pink Street, Ardwick, causing severe damage to property and heavy casualties. These streets are on the opposite side of Ashton Old Road from Gorton Road.

271 and 152 German aircraft took part in the Sunday and Monday attacks respectively.

The Manchester casualties were 363 dead, 455 seriously injured and 728 slightly injured. 30,000 houses were damaged and 5,049 people were made homeless. *(Evening Chronicle, 15.10.1959).* It is not known how many of the seriously injured died later.

3.1.1941 G.O.R.
The response to the appeal to evacuate the children of Manchester has been disappointing. The numbers which will leave Gorton, Openshaw, Bradford and Clayton will not reach large proportions. Evacuation began yesterday and continued throughout today. The number registered in Manchester is 11,600 out of 80,000 who are eligible.

The recent blitz has had its effect in several ways on the life of the community. To begin with there was the wholesale cancellation of watch-night services, whilst churches and chapels which had steadfastly held evening services as usual have now responded to requests to cancel Sunday evening services and hold them in the afternoon.
The shopkeepers on the outskirts of the City had a busy holiday. More than one shop I went into was absolutely cleared out of stock. People would not risk going to Manchester and as they had been asked to stay away - well, local tradespeople reaped the benefit.

10.1.1941 G.O.R.
Centres for the homeless:
Brookfield Sunday School, Hyde Road
Crossley Lads Club, Ashton Old Road

17.1.1941 G.O.R.
The shopkeepers and business men of Higher Openshaw have agreed to form a firewatching section which would cover from the Gransmoor to the canal bridge. The main essentials of equipment are sand, stirrup pumps, buckets and supplies of water, electric torches, boiler suits and rubber boots.

14.3.1941 G.O.R.
There is a shortage of cigarettes in Droylsden.

21.3.1941 G.O.R.
Sunday opening of cinemas began on March 16th.

23.5.1941 G.O.R.
12,000 Morrison shelters have been sent to Manchester, but only 3,000 have been applied for.
(Morrison shelters were made of steel. They were shaped like a table and it was intended that they should be used as such during the day.)

6.6.1941 G.O.R.
Fewer churches in Gorton and Openshaw are observing the annual Whitsuntide. Rationing of clothing, cloth, footwear and knitting wool has been introduced. Each person will be issued with 66 coupons per annum. The number of coupons required is as follows:
one suit 26, one shirt 5, one pair of shoes 7, one coat 14, one dress 11, one pair of stockings 2. Hats are exempt. Rationing does not apply to second-hand clothing.

27.6.1941 G.O.R.
The residents of Kenyon Street, Abbey Hey, objected to the proposal to build brick air-raid shelters in the street. They said that they were eye-sores and blocked out the light. Finally they agreed that one shelter only should be built at the end of the street near the railway, where it did not shut out light.

4.7.1941 G.O.R.
There are more complaints from Gorton residents about public air-raid shelters. They said that they had enough shelter accommodation in their back yards. Public shelters were 'veritable death traps'.

24.10.1941 G.O.R.
Success of Morrison indoor shelters reported.

31.10.1941 G.O.R.
No. 4 Company (Gorton and Openshaw) of the Home Guard took part in manoeuvres to prepare for invasion. Regular troops invaded from Yorkshire and there was a mock battle in Openshaw.

The most realistic fighting was in a street that runs parallel with Ashton Old Road. A hose pipe was turned on the" invaders", who were attempting to force one entrance to a large works. The "invaders" sent for help and a Bren gun carrier charged the wielders of the hosepipe. There were two casualties: one Home Guard suffered a broken leg, another was shot in the side.
(The street in question was South Street and the works was Massey's.)

13.3.1942 G.O.R.
Permission for Sunday games in parks has been granted by the Manchester City Council, but no date when Sunday games begin has been given.

24.4.1942 G.O.R.
The Victoria Cross has been awarded to Rifleman John Beeley of 14 Ezard Street, Higher Openshaw. John Beeley, a member of the King's Royal Rifle Corps, was 23 years of age.

Rifleman Beeley died at his post at Sidi Rezegh in the Lybian Desert. On his own initiative he ran forward with a Bren gun and wiped out a strong enemy post which was pinning down his company.

Rifleman Beeley was a former pupil of Wheler Street school.

18.6.1943 G.O.R.
Efforts are being made to promote holidays at home. There are Sunday brass band concerts in Manchester parks including Debdale Park.

14.2.1944 M.E.N.
Children Sabotage City New Fire Guard Plan
Child "saboteurs", many of them under ten years of age, are wrecking the latest Manchester Fire Brigade Plan. Within a week of 500 - gallon emergency water tanks being erected for the use of wheelbarrow and light trailer pump fire-fighting parties, they have been filled with old bedsteads, wood, straw and tons of old bricks. In many cases the tanks have been half filled with this rubbish before officers of the National Fire Service have had time to fill them with water.

14.4.1944 G.O.R.
There were record Easter crowds at Belle Vue. 120,000 paid for admission.

9.6.1944 G.O.R.
Invasion Day services have been held at Gorton churches.

28.7.1944 G.O.R.
Children from the London area have been evacuated to Gorton to escape the Buzz Bombs (the V.1.s or pilotless planes).

13.10.1944 G.O.R.
The road blocks at Gorton bridge, Hyde Road, and Openshaw Bridge, Ashton Old Road, known locally as the "ramparts" have fallen after a short but sharp assault by workmen of the Manchester Corporation Highways Dept. The dangers of invasion have now passed.
(The road blocks were concrete blocks.)

24.12.1944
4 V.1.s - pilotless planes usually referred to as "buzz-bombs" - were dropped in and around the Manchester area. One fell in Didsbury near the Mersey. The others were at Oldham, Stockport and Worsley.

2.2.1945 G.O.R.
There has been skating on the Stockport canal for the first time within living memory.

9.2.1945 G.O.R.
2,000 workers - practically the entire day shift - marched out of the open gates of Vickers Armstrong's Works, Openshaw, at 10 a.m. on Wednesday. They marched to the Town Hall as a demonstration against the threat of redundancy.

11.5.1945 G.O.R.
Openshaw Went Gay on V.E. Day. Tea Parties in the Streets and Bonfires.
Openshaw had gone gay with a vengeance. The drabness of Ashton Old Road was hidden by a welter of red, white and blue. One of the biggest parties was in Grey Street, where 100 children and adults were the guests of No. 2502 Fire Brigade.

A piano was brought into the street and played by Mr Tomlinson.

Gorton's V.E. Day was Gay Day

V.E. Day in Gorton, compared with Armistice Day 1918, began in a subdued tone - probably because many local men are serving in the Far East and because of the general realisation that final victory had not yet been achieved. With the announcement that an important declaration was 'hourly expected', people began to put out flags and arrange bunting, and when the news came through of the unconditional surrender of the German forces, the district had undergone a transformation.

There were flags of all the United Nations - and even some of obscure origin! Women and girls came out with their hair in 'victory style' or tied with red, white and blue ribbon. Heavy rain did not damp the ardour of the residents in vying among themselves to have the best street in the district. When the King spoke over the radio in the evening, the streets were almost deserted, but after nine o'clock the revelry began and continued unabated till early on Wednesday. As night came on, bonfires flamed the victory message and fire-works were brought out. *(The official V.E. Day was Wednesday, May 9th.)*

17.8.1945 G.O.R.

In Openshaw the WJ celebration was the 'mixture as before' - bonfires, street parties, singsongs and impromptu dances. The residents showed more abandon than on V.E. Day and celebrated the end of the war with lightness of heart, but by no stretch of the imagination could it be described as Mafeking.

One of the biggest parties was in Abbey Street, Higher Openshaw, where there were 116 guests, children and adults.

Mr Thomas Torr's Victory V team in fancy costume complete with barrel organ made a tour of the Higher Openshaw district. *(The official V.J. Day was Wednesday, August 15th.)*

11.1.1946 G.O.R.

There is a proposal to replace the 'setts' in Vine Street.

22.3.1946 G.O.R.

Five men lost their lives and nine others were injured (five seriously) as the result of a cylinder of propane gas exploding in the erecting shop at the L.N.E.R. Locomotive Works, Openshaw (Gorton Tank).

31.5.1946 G.O.R.

Openshaw V.C. to attend V-Day parade.

Mr Stringer, who won his V.C. whilst serving with the Manchester Regiment in Mesopotamia during the last war, has been invited to attend the V-Day parade in London. He now lives at 12, Stanley Street.

8.2.1948 G.O.R.

The Cotton Mills of Openshaw Are Fighting the Crisis (Advert.)

Our mills are fighting Britain's battle - producing for a world that is waiting for cotton goods. We need more women back at work again.

(There were no cotton mills in Openshaw in 1948, but there must have been many women with experience in Droylsden's cotton mills.)

13.10.1950 G.O.R.

A number of street lamps have been broken in Abbey Hey and Openshaw.

23.2.1951 G.O.R.

An 86 ton electric locomotive no. 26020 has been built at Gorton tank. It is of the Bo-Bo class, i.e. it has two pairs of two wheel bogies. Locomotives of this type were used in Holland after the invasion for military purposes.

20.7.1951 G.O.R.

Wave of vandalism Sweeping the City.

Vandalism in city schools in the last two and a half years has cost nearly £6,000 in repairs.

7.12.1951 G.O.R.

John Norgan has been released from a Belgian gaol.

In June 1948, John Norgan of Henry Street, West Gorton, was sentenced to life imprisonment and fined a million francs by a military court at Bruges, Belgium, for alleged acts of treason committed during the German occupation.

When the German forces overran Belgium in the summer of 1940, John Norgan, a member of the Lancashire Fusiliers, was given shelter in a Flanders farmhouse. Here he spent the remainder of the war, marrying the daughter of those who had befriended him. The allegation against John Norgan, which he strenuously denied, was that he had denounced to the Gestapo a number of people who were on the run from the Germans. Mrs Norgan, on the other hand, had distinguished herself by her work for the resistance.

The sentence was later reduced to 20 years hard labour and a fine of 500,000 francs. A petition for his release with over 30,000 signatures was presented in October 1949. John Norgan has now been released from gaol.

8.2.1952 G.O.R.

George VI died on February 16th.

9.5.1952 G.O.R.

The pathway through Knutsford Vale, which connected Longsight, West Gorton and Gorton is now no more. The Vale, or Murder Lane as it is called, has been replaced by another path from Manby Road to Pink Bank Lane.

(See 10.7.1909 G.O.B.R.)

5.6.1953 G.O.R.

Rain damped the local Coronation festivities. Parties were held indoors and the streets were deserted. Yet in some parts of Openshaw it was tea in the rain. In Gorton floodlights had transformed some places into a miniature fairyland.

16.10.1953 G.O.R.

Rowdyism in Higher Openshaw by gangs of youths appears to be on the increase - especially in the Ashton Old Road - Fairfield Road area. Rival groups shout and scream at each other.

11.6.1954 G.O.R.

The electrified public rail service between Manchester (London Road), Glossop and Hadfield will be opened on June 14th.

21.2.1955 G.O.R.

The death of John Charles Whitelegg of 58, Gorton Lane, West

Gorton, has been reported. Mr Whitelegg, aged 76, was a former lamplighter. When on the round he carried a headlight on a pole and also a bamboo stick with a clip on the head, which was used to turn on the gas taps. Then with a flick of the wrist he would bring illumination.

22.7.1955 G.O.R.
The "Relief of Lucknow" was staged at Belle Vue with a cast of 200 and 400 colourful costumes.

6.7.1956 G.O.R.
Auburn House has now been pulled down. It was built in 1891 for a Mr Johnson at a cost of £6,000. The site of the house included Fairfield Wells, which were situated close to the gate of Auburn House nearest to the junction of Station Road (now Manshaw Road) and Ashton Old Road. The house was originally called 'The Thorns', taking its name from the nearby Seven Thorns Fields. Mr Johnson had the wells filled in.
Mr Johnson's family suffered a series of misfortunes, which led to the belief that the house was haunted and the family cursed because the wells had been filled in. First, Mr Johnson's son, a mining engineer, was victim of an accident in a pit in Ireland. Then his elder daughter died. His youngest child was playing on stilts, when she fell backward and was struck blind, remaining so for the rest of her life.

After the death of the first owner, the house was unoccupied for a number of years until it was bought by Mr Dale, whose daughter, Tessa, was well-known locally for singing. It was later used as a manufactory of children's novelty sweets. The site has now been purchased for the erection of a new Roman Catholic school.

31.10.1958 G.O.R.
Manchester Central Grammar School opened last week. It cost £289,000. It stands between Kirkmanshulme Lane, Stanley Grove and Pink Bank Lane.

12.12.1958 G.O.R.
Hula-hoop spinning is a dying gimmick.
(The hula-hoop had been a craze amongst children for some time. It was kept in motion about the waist by a swinging movement of the hips.)

6.2.1959 G.O.R.
A new bridge has been built at the Fenian Arches on Hyde Road because of the electrification scheme. *(See 17.9.1867).*

1.4.1960 G.O.R.
The Alhambra Theatre, Ashton Old Road, Higher Openshaw, closed its doors at the weekend.

26.5.1961 G.O.R.
Queen Elizabeth presented a new guidon to the Duke of Lancaster's Own Yeomanry at Belle Vue Stadium.

4.6.1962 G.O.R.
The Metropole Theatre and Cinema is being demolished.

10.5.1963 G.O.R.
Gorton Tank is to close on 31.5.1963.
(The eventual demolition of Gorton Tank ended the life of the footbridge which for years has been a feature of Gorton and Openshaw. This footbridge, known as the "Birdcage", because it was enclosed with wire mesh, ran through the works at rooftop height, linking Widnes Street in Openshaw with Railway Street in Gorton.)

31.5.1963 G.O.R.
The Valour dedication plate has been removed from the wall of the Gorton Tank iron foundry to St. Barnabas' Church, Openshaw.
(The plate was fixed to the perimeter wall of the church. It was stolen in the 1970s.)

2.8.1963 G.O.R.
The Christadelphian Hall and the old smithy on Vine Street have been demolished. For years the smithy faced the penny stall on the open market, now the site of a supermarket and offices.

4.10.1963 G.O.R.
Admiralty Gunnery Equipment Depot closed last Monday.

27.12.1963 G.O.R.
The smallest house in Gorton stands at the junction of Cross Lane and Kirk Street. It is occupied by Mr and Mrs Albert Rose, both old age pensioners. The rent for this 'two up two down' house is 7s 8d a week, but they haven't a bathroom, an indoor toilet or hot running water. However, Mrs Rose's only complaint is that the house is very damp.

The front door is only about 5ft 6in high. It opens into a room which is barely 8ft square, but the house is wider at the back than the front and the rear downstairs room is considerably larger.

5.3.1965 G.O.R.
Billy Barker died at his home, 18 Woodhouse Street, Gorton, on Friday last. He could jump the 9ft wide canal at Higher Openshaw. He had such control over his body that he could jump into the canal, touch the water in the middle with his feet, then spring to the other side.

12.3.1965 G.O.R.
The Gorton engineering works of Newage (Manchester) in Crossley Street will close down in May and most of its employees will become redundant.

19.3.1965 G.O.R.
Queen visits Manchester.
Gorton folk turned out in their thousands along Hyde Road, Mount Road and Stanley Grove to give the Queen a rousing cheer.

9.4.1965 G.O.R.
The death had been announced of Mr Ernest A. Betts, aged 94, of 65 Far Lane Gorton. He was Gorton's oldest farmer. He had a small farm in Far Lane.

23.4.1965 G.O.R.
Huge forging press leaves Messrs B. and S. Massey's works.

14.5.1965 G.O.R.
Grave in a garden *(caption of photograph)*
Miss Norah Presland of Gorton examines a gravestone which

was hidden in the garden of a house in the Ryder Brow area for nearly 150 years. The grave was the last resting place of a farmer and his wife.

'James Barlow, yeoman, March 15, 1826, 90 years and his wife Sarah, April 4, 1816, 77 years.'

24.6.1966 G.O.R.
Beyer Peacock ends production at the end of this month.

15.7.1966 G.O.R.
Crossley Brothers, Pottery Lane, have appointed a receiver. In the year ended April, 1965, the firm showed a loss of £392,000. They have a full order book but are short of cash.

16.9.1966 G.O.R.
The King's Theatre, Stockport Road, Longsight, has been damaged by fire. It was opened in October, 1905, converted to a cinema in 1933 and closed down in 1964.

14.10.1966 G.O.R.
Redundancies at English Steel.

21.10.1966 G.O.R.
The Crossley Bros. foundry in Welcomb Street has closed down.
Joseph Stubbs of Louisa Street has also closed down.

9.12.1966 G.O.R.
569 Houses in Openshaw are to be pulled down. The new clearance zone will run from Pottery Lane to Cornwall Street and will be bordered on one side by Ashton Old Road and on the other by Whitworth Street East.

13.1.1967 G.O.R.
Kendall and Gent's are closing down.

21.4.1967 G.O.R.
Cross Lane Methodist Chapel, Gorton, is coming down.

14.7.1967 G.O.R.
Crewdson Hall, Openshaw, is to be demolished. It is situated on Whitworth Street with a side entrance on Fielding Street.
(Crewdson Hall was originally a works canteen. It was bought and transformed into a place of worship in the 1920s and named after Isaac Crewdson, chairman of the Manchester City Mission years ago. It was replaced by a new church, the Beswick Evangelical Church, which stands off Grey Mare Lane.)

15.9.1967 G.O.R.
There has been a delay in completing the Wright Robinson School.

21.6.1968 G.O.R.
For the past four months vandals have defaced and ripped up headstones in the graveyard at Brookfield Church, Gorton.

6.9.1968 G.O.R.
Bradford Pit has now closed.

15.8.1969 G.O.R.
Whitworth Hall, erected over 80 years ago by Sir Joseph Whitworth, is to be closed. In addition to the main hall there are wash-houses, baths and a part that was used as a public library. During the war it housed service personnel and was also used as an air-raid shelter.

6.1.1970 G.O.R.
111 Houses in Aberdour Street, Manchester Street, Railway Street, Sheffield Street, Reed Street, Seymour Street and Chapman Street are earmarked for demolition. At present they are occupied by 309 people.

12.6.1970 G.O.R.
Gorton and Openshaw station has been pulled down. It was made of corrugated iron and wood.
(It was opened on 25th August, 1906, replacing one on Cornwall Street. In turn it has been replaced by the present building.)

31.1.1970 G.O.R.
A slum clearance scheme for Gorton has been announced, involving 1,557 houses and 146 shops. Several cottages on Far Lane and Tan Yard Brow are to form part of a conservation area.

Debdale Park is in process of development as a regional park. There have been complaints of rampaging gangs of so-called 'fishermen' and 'bathers', who take over the area by assault. Fences have been damaged, walls overturned. People trespass on the allotment and on the adjoining golf-course. Cars are taken to the nearest point on the Debdale estate and left for the day.

14.8.1970 G.O.R.
A wave of crime and wanton destruction engulfed Gorton at the week-end. A 10ft length of one inch thick copper lightning conductor was hacked away from St. James' Parish Hall roof.

14.8.1970 G.O.R.
Kenyon House, Wellington Street, is to come down. It was at one time the residence of the Buckley family. Their mill in Stelling Street still stands.

28.8.1970 G.O.R.
Described as part of 'Vulcan's Anvil' during the Industrial Revolution, Openshaw is now less than a shadow of its former self.

20.11.1970 G.O.R.
Commenting on the hardships suffered by residents in the Grey Street development area, Sir Richard Harper, chairman of the Housing Committee, said, 'If the people do not take what we offer, they will have to stay put until the Grey Street development area is complete.'

4.12.1970 G.O.R.
'The large scale slum clearance programme, which began in Openshaw 18 months ago, has turned Openshaw into a disaster area', claims Councillor John Gilmore. 'Rehousing has left the area with only about 140 families living between Openshaw bridge and the Ardwick boundary.'

29.6.1973 G.O.R.
Allegations of intimidation, stealing and filthy conditions were made by a party of angry Gorton housewives when they handed

a 1,200 - signature petition to Manchester's Lord Mayor protesting against squatters moving into empty houses near their homes.

31.1.1975 M.E.N.
The city's housing department wants to install solid fuel central heating in 568 houses on the Mount Road estate. Councillor Dennis Barker said that many residents want to retain their old gas appliances. 'Solid fuel was not as clean as gas and residents were having to use something they did not want.'

11.4.1975 G.O.R.
The disappearing face of Gorton.
Demolition has begun in Far Lane, once the main thoroughfare between Manchester, Denton and Hyde. Most of the Gorton Cross Street shops have gone.

16.5.1975 E.M.R.
The Gorton Morris Men was formed in 1974. The costumes are traditional. The dances are original but the routines are strictly traditional. Morris dancing in Gorton has been traced back to the 17th century, although the North West Processional Morris, as it is now known, probably did not evolve for another century. Gorton Morris men were a part of the annual rush-bearing ceremony at Gorton Chapel - now St. James' Parish Church - the last recorded instance of which was in 1874.
(The author of this book does not know of any evidence that Morris dancing was practised in Gorton in the 17th Century.)

31.12.1976 E.M.R.
The old Abbey Hey School (Rylands Mill) has now been pulled down. A single storey building, it stood on land adjoining Abbey Hey Lane and the west bank of the canal. An inscription on the building read 'Abbey Hey School 1876'.

3.6.1977 E.M.R.
The Jubilee (of Queen Elizabeth II) was celebrated in Openshaw with street parties, fireworks, bonfires and dancing. In Gorton there was floodlighting, transforming some places into miniature fairylands.

12.9.1977 E.M.R.
It was Noah's Ark in reverse at Belle Vue Zoo, today, as on a wave of nostalgia, the animals continued to leave two-by-two. After 141 years, financial problems forced the Zoo to close yesterday.

6.1.1978 E.M.R.
A skateboard spectacular has been drawing hundreds of youngsters to Belle Vue this week.

19.2.1980 M.E.N.
Work has started on a new £3 m shopping centre at Gorton, Manchester. The contract went to House of Orange Developments, whose proposals include a supermarket, a range of shops and kiosks and parking space - all grouped round the existing retail market bounded by Hyde Road, Garratt Way and Wellington Street.

1.1.1988 E.M.R.
On November 14 an era came to an end in Manchester, when the famous Belle Vue Stadium which had stood on Hyde Road for 59 years, closed for the last time.

The decision to demolish the Belle Vue Ace's Hyde Road stadium will have stirred up many memories among speedway fans both old and young, but can any of you remember the days when speedway took place at the Snipe in Audenshaw?

Mr Sam Mellor, of Sidley Place, Hyde, recalled: "As far as I am concerned, the first speedway in Britain took place at the Snipe. In the early days, individuals competed rather than teams. Racing took place on Sundays and this eventually led to the closure of the track. Sunday sport was largely outlawed in those days and the riders had to wear masks to prevent identification. Eventually some were named and the racing drew to a halt. However not long afterwards, the Belle Vue stadium opened".
(Speedway racing was resumed in March, 1988, at the Belle Vue greyhound track.)

ADVERTISEMENTS

J. TORKINGTON,
70, CHURCH LANE, GORTON,
GENERAL DEALER.
Glass, China, Tea Urns, &c., on hire at reasonable terms.
Lessons given on the Violin and Mandoline.

MRS. TYRER,
Feathers Cleaned, Dyed, Curled, and Altered.
Orders promptly attended to.
Note the Address
25, WILLIAMS ST., GORTON (Near Belle Vue Station).

MRS. McKEAN,
(WIDOW),
40, Ellesmere Street, Gorton.
KNOCKING-UP from 3 to 7.
All communications put in Letter Box promptly attended to.

Private Lessons in Shorthand, Typewriting, & Business Subjects.
848, Hyde Road, Gorton.
Terms, etc.—Mr. A. RALPHS, F. Inc. S. T.

Ici on donne des leçons particulières dans la langue Française.

From the Gorton Parish *(St. James)* Magazine, October 1905.

A prison van carrying two Fenian leaders was ambushed on its way to Belle Vue gaol under the railway arch on Hyde Road near Grey Street.
17.9.1867

Belle Vue Prison. Built 1850. Demolished 1890. It stood on the north side of Hunter's Lane.

Gortoncross Street in 1964 *(Courtesy Ashton Reporter)*

Cross Street *(Gortoncross Street)* before the First World War, viewed from Hyde Road.

CHAPTER II

From The Earliest Times to the Civil War

Manchester, during and after the Roman occupation
In A.D. 79, the Romans built a fort, which they called Mamucium, in the angle formed by the rivers Irwell and Medlock. A "vicus" or civilian settlement grew up nearby, in which metal working and pottery were the main industries. There is evidence that after the departure of the Roman garrison the settlement continued for a time. A road linked the vicus and fort with Stockport, following the line of Stockport Road.

The Nico Ditch
The Roman occupation of Britain ended about the year A.D. 410, but well before then the Anglo-Saxons had begun their invasions. To the people of south-east Lancashire the threat came from the Anglo-Saxons of Mercia. To meet this threat they constructed an earthwork fourteen miles long. This earthwork was later called the "Nico Ditch", which means the "Great Ditch". The line of the Nico Ditch forms Gorton's southern boundary.

According to popular tradition the Nico Ditch was dug in one night by the men of Manchester to keep out the Danes. It has been calculated that, assuming that each man dug six feet of ditch, the population of Manchester would have had to be about forty thousand. This is completely out of the question.

In 1954 an archaeological survey of the Nico Ditch was made by Dr. J.D.Bu'lock and Mr Frank Willets and the main findings were published in the Manchester Guardian on 19.10.1954. Originally it ran from the River Irwell in Flixton, crossed the Roman road in Stretford, went through Longford Park and Chorlton to Platt Brook near Wilbraham station and then left Platt Brook in Platt Fields and ran eastwards into Old Hall Lane. It then continued along Old Hall Lane and Matthews Lane and across Melland's playing field. From there it ran parallel with and slightly to the north west of Laburnum Road and across Hyde Road onto Denton golf course. Beyond there it ran beneath Audenshaw reservoir, turning northwards to join a subsidiary ditch that marks the Droylsden boundary and from there entered Ashton Moss towards the Medlock.

Originally the ditch was fifteen feet wide and behind it a bank of earth rose about 12 feet above the ditch bottom. It is probable that the bank, which was on the north side of the ditch, carried a palisade.

The Nico Ditch was one of what are termed "linear earthworks", of which the greatest example is Offa's Dyke. The Nico Ditch was too long and too weak to be continuously manned, but it was an obstacle to small bands of raiders laden with plunder or driving cattle before them.

In 625, Cerdic, the king of the British kingdom of Elmet which covered much of the West Riding, was driven out by Edwin, the Saxon king of Northumbria. British power in Lancashire collapsed and the Nico Ditch fell into disuse. A small portion of it can be seen in Melland's playing fields, Mount Road.

Gorton's name and the first settlement
The name "Gorton" is probably derived from the Anglo-Saxon word "gor", meaning mud or damp ground, and "ton", meaning a settlement. If this is so, it is likely that Gorton was first settled by the Anglo-Saxons. The earliest appearance of the place-name is in a list of townships which between 1237 and 1238 paid a tax known as the "30th", presumably because they paid 1/30 of the annual value of their produce. Gorton paid 14s 8d.

The boundaries of Gorton
The Corn Brook forms almost the whole of the Gorton-Openshaw boundary. A North West Water Authority map shows its source to be in or near Toxteth Street on the north side of Ashton Old Road. Shortly before the Corn Brook reaches Pottery Lane it is joined by Clayton Brook. However, in Gorton Local Board minutes the Corn Brook is sometimes called the 'Black Brook'.

The Gore Brook was the boundary between Gorton and Audenshaw until 1823, when Debdale *(deep dale)* was flooded to make a reservoir. That length of the Gore Brook which flowed through Debdale was diverted and culverted so that it now flows along the east bank of the Gorton and Audenshaw reservoirs.

To the south, the Nico Ditch separates Gorton from Levenshulme, Reddish and Denton. Old Hall Lane and Matthews Lane mark the line of the Ditch. This length is for the most part used as a drain and is culverted.

To the west, Stockport Road is the principal boundary, but, according to the Victoria County History *(vol. 4, p. 277)*, only since 1609, when it was decided that Greenlow Marsh was in Gorton and not in Chorlton or Greenlow Heath.

Kirkmanshulme or Newton detached
The name "Kirkmanshulme" means "Churchman's hulme", "hulme" being a piece of land near to water. It was part of Gorton until some time between 1154 and 1162, when Albert Grelley, Lord of the Manor of Manchester, bestowed it upon the parish church of Manchester.

From time immemorial Newton had been part of the endowment of the parish church of Manchester, so that, when in 1853 a Local Board for the township of Newton was formed, Kirkmanshulme was administered jointly with Newton and was known as "Newton detached". In 1859 Kirkmanshulme was separated from Newton.

Gorton, Longsight
There is a triangle of land, bounded in the east by Kirkmanshulme and in the west by Stockport Road. On the 1844 tithe map it is marked as "Gorton detached". The same piece of land is also known as "Gorton, Longsight". In the 13th century Longsight was part of Grenlawemore, which later became known as Grindlow. In the course of time, portions of it were appropriated by the surrounding townships of Gorton, Moss Side, Newton and Chorlton on Medlock. "Longsight" is probably a corruption of "Longshut", a field name.

Openshaw
The place-name "Openshaw" means "open wood". The earliest mention of Openshaw is in the list of townships which between 1237 and 1238 paid the tax known as the 30th. Openshaw, spelt "Openshae", paid 12s 10d. The name is of Anglo-Saxon origin, indicating an Anglo-Saxon settlement.

Little Droylsden
Little Droylsden was the name given to a small triangular piece of land, which lay approximately between Abbey Hey Lane, Capital Road and Ashton Old Road. Until 1889, when it was incorporated in Openshaw, it was administered by the township of Droylsden.

The Manor of Manchester
In the years immediately following the Battle of Hastings the Manor of Manchester was formed. It was roughly identical with modern Manchester with the addition of Ashton-under-Lyne, Droylsden, Heaton Norris, Denton, Reddish and Haughton but without Wythenshawe and Northenden. The hall of the Lord of the Manor was where Chetham's School of Music is now, i.e. in Long Millgate.

The Surveys of 1282, 1320 & 1322

A survey of the Manor of Manchester was made in each of the following years: 1282, 1320 and 1322. The surveys were in Latin, the language used for official documents. In 1861 John Harland published a translation in a book entitled Mamecestre, the medieval name for Manchester.

The only important fact about Gorton in the 1282 survey is that there was a grain mill there, where corn was ground into flour. Openshaw had only one mention: "And there is a certain plot, near the cross of Opyn-sawe, which is worth yearly 6s 8d".

GORTON IN 1320
The survey of 1320 is detailed in its description of Gorton. It gives the names of five men and one woman who were living in Gorton at that time and also the duties they had to perform for the Lord of the Manor in return for their land. They were all described as "nativi", i.e. born villeins. Villeins belonged to the class of unfree men and women known generally as serfs. They were superior in status to the bondmen and bondwomen. The names of the six were:

Henry the Reeve. He was the most important. As a reeve or bailiff, it was his duty to see that the Lord's commands were carried out. Henry was the illegitimate son of John de la Warre, the Lord of the Manor. He had one oxgang for which he paid 8s 4d per annum. An oxgang was an area of land which was calculated in the following manner. A plough was drawn by a team of eight oxen. The area which a team was capable of ploughing in a year was equal to eight oxgangs. An oxgang was therefore one eighth of this area. As soil varied in texture from one place to another so the oxgang varied in area between 10 and 18 acres.

Geoffrey of the Abbey. Geoffrey had one oxgang of land for which he paid 4s 5d per annum. The Abbey was probably the Abbey of Dore in Hereford, for about this time the Manor of Manchester was transferred to the Abbey of Dore for a period of sixteen years. Geoffrey probably acquired his name because he came from the Abbey. It is also probable that the land he farmed was in that part of Gorton which is now known as Abbey Hey.

Thomas of the Olres (Alders). Thomas had one messuage (a house with land attached) and one oxgang of land in addition, for which he paid 13s 4d.

Hugh of the Abbey. Hugh had one messuage and one oxgang of land for which he paid 4s 5d per annum. Like Geoffrey he probably had a connection with the Abbey of Dore.

Emma the Widow. Emma had one messuage and one oxgang for which she paid 10s 8d per annum.

Hugh, son of Richard. Hugh had half an oxgang of land, for which he paid 5s per annum.

The duties of the six villeins
In addition to paying an annual rent for their land the six villeins had to perform a number of duties for the Lord of the Manor of Manchester. Although these duties were burdensome, they were less so than those of villeins elsewhere. Because they paid a rent they were excused "weekwork", whereby one day per week had to be spent working on the land of the lord without pay. Whereas the Gorton villeins were paid for carrying out such duties as ploughing, harrowing and reaping, in other manors villeins were not paid. The duties of the six are given below:

1. They had to do one day's ploughing each year on the lord's land in Gorton using their own ploughs. For this service they received one meal and 2d.
2. They had to harrow for the lord one day each year on his Gorton land. For thus they received one meal and 1d. If they harrowed for half a day they received 1d but no meal. A harrow is a frame for pulverising and smoothing soil.
3. They had to reap for the lord on his Gorton land for one day each year. For this they received 1d and one meal.
4. They had to carry the lord's corn. For this they received 2d and one meal.
5. They had to grind their corn at the lord's mill in Gorton, for which they paid the miller one sixteenth of the flour produced.
6. They had to fetch millstones for the mill from "wheresoever they may be found". For each pair of millstones they were paid 4d for loading and "3s or other sum for carriage in proportion to the distance of the quarry from the mill".
7. If they had a daughter who "married out of the house", i.e.

a man from another manor, a payment had to be made. This was because her services were lost to the lord.

8. If they had a son who was "placed out at a free handicraft" (put to a trade), a payment had to be made.

9. When one of the villeins died, the lord would inherit a proportion of his or her property. The proportion was 1/3 if there was a surviving wife and son and 1/2 if there was only a surviving son or wife. If there was no surviving wife, son or daughter, the lord would inherit all the property.

Other inhabitants of Gorton in 1320
The six villeins were not the only inhabitants of Gorton. It is reasonable to suppose that some of them had families. In addition there were a number of men and possibly women whose status was higher than that of a villein but lower than that of a freeholder, who had to plough, harrow and reap etc. for the lord. These are mentioned in the survey.

Fishing in the Gore Brook. The Lord of the Manor held the fishing rights in the Irk and the Gore Brook, as by law the banks of these streams belonged to him. Fishing licences brought in a total of 12d.

The Gorton flour mill. The people of Gorton had to take their corn to the mill on the Gore Brook, paying one sixteenth of the flour to the miller for the service. There is no record of when the mill fell into disuse or of its site, although it has been suggested that it stood on or near the site of the old tannery.

Openshaw in 1320
There are fewer references to Openshaw in the 1320 survey than there are to Gorton. None of the inhabitants are named, but the following passage makes it clear what their duties were:

"....... the tenants of Gorton .... shall perform the same customs of ploughing, harrowing, reaping and carrying corn or millstones as .... the tenants of Opon-schaghe".

In addition the people of Openshaw had to take their corn to be ground in the lord's mill, not the one in Gorton but one on the River Irk. The site of the mill is below Victoria Station. Payment for grinding the corn was as at the Gorton Mill.

There was a peat bed in Openshaw one hundred acres in extent,"....... in which the tenants of the Lord of Gorton, Oponschaghe and Ardwycke have a common of turbary". Common of turbary means the right to take peat without making any payment. The Openshaw peat moor is believed to have been in the vicinity of Fairfield Road, which up to the 19th century was called Moor Lane. It was part of a huge bed of peat which included Ashton moss.

Number of houses and estimated population in 1322
In the 1322 survey there is a list showing the number of messuages in the various hamlets of the Manor of Manchester. Assuming four people to each house an estimate can be made of the population of Gorton, Openshaw and two neighbouring hamlets.

In:	Openshaw	4 messuages	16 inhabitants
	Denton	1 messuage	4 inhabitants
	Gorton	15 messuages	60 inhabitants
	Ardwick	8 messuages	32 inhabitants

Farming in medieval Gorton and Openshaw
In the middle ages the "common or open field" system of agriculture was practised throughout the greater part of England and Wales. This means that all the arable land around a village was divided into a number of large, unfenced fields, which were cultivated communally by the peasants. Each field was again divided into long, narrow strips, each approximately 220 yards by 5 yards. The strips of an individual peasant were scattered throughout the open fields, possibly to permit a fair distribution of good and bad land.

In the midlands and the south there were usually three fields around each village, which were cultivated on a rotary system of autumn wheat and spring barley, with each field lying fallow every third year. There is evidence that in Lancashire the period of fallow was confined to the winter by sowing spring crops only.

GORTON AND OPENSHAW AT THE TIME OF THE CIVIL WAR

By 1641 the conflict between Charles 1 and Parliament had brought England to the brink of civil war. Whilst the main cause was Parliament's desire to play a greater part in ruling the country, fear of a Roman Catholic revival also played a part. Parliament drew up a "Protestation" expressing their support for the Protestant religion and their opposition to Roman Catholicism. A letter was sent to the sheriffs and mayors recommending that the Protestation should be signed by all men above the age of eighteen and that a list should be made of all names, "both of those that do take it, and do refuse to take the Protestation".

From the Gorton and Openshaw lists a rough estimate of the populations of the two townships can be made, by assuming that there was an equal number of males and females both above and below the age of eighteen and that the number of men and women above the age of eighteen made up 60% of the population. It is also assumed that all the men above the age of eighteen took the Protestation.

96 men above the age of eighteen in Gorton signed the Protestation including witnesses
96 women above the age of eighteen

192 60% of the population
128 40% of the population - males and females below the age of eighteen

320 estimated population of Gorton in 1641

35 men above the age of eighteen in Openshaw signed the Protestation including witnesses
35 women above the age of eighteen

70 60% of the population
47 40% of the population - males and females below the age of eighteen

117 estimated population of Openshaw in 1641

The Gorton Protestation
The Certificat of the minister and Constables of Gorton of all that have taken the protestation with the townshippe of gortn.

Imps	Thomas Strangeways gent	William Birtinshawe
	Phillipe Strangeways	John Robertson
	Edmund Tomlinson	Nicholaus Sommester
	Fromnchnis Wood	James Sommester
	John Hibbart	Nicholaus Sommister
	John Jackson	James Sommister
	Raphe Graner	George Wright
	William Hibbart	Hugh Bordman Sen
	Raphe Hibbart	William Andrew
	Isaac Hibbart	James Worthington
	Robert Andrew	Roger Lyne
	John Townley	Edmund Knowles
	John Andrew	William Knowles
	John Rider	Robert Strengfellowe
	Raphe Rider	George Pomfret
	George Andrew	James Taylior
	Thomas Rider	James Taylior
	Robert Wildinge	Richard Taylior
	Thomas Graner Senior	George Taylior
	Thomas Graner Junior	John Platt
	Thomas Asston	James Dycen
	Richard Beswicke	Samuell Clough
	James Worthinton	Raphe Small
	Edumnd Grundie	Raphe Small
	James Worthinton	Robert Small
	Robert Kenion	George Small
	Raphe Hall	Allexander Herd
	James Prestwicke	Hugh Bordman
	John Scott	John Hill
	Franchis Williamson	Thomas Taylior
	Thomas Bexwicke	Nicholaus Wortencroft
	Thomas Beswicke	John Cocke
	Thomas Shelmerdine	James Cheetham
	Ambrose Rider	John Bordman
	William Rider	Edmund Walker
	Robert Prestwicke	Stephen Shalcross
	Samuell Prestwicke	Peeter Hall
	Robert Prestwicke	Samuel Hage
	Robert Beswicke	Edward Beswicke
	George Sommester	Raphe Prestwicke
	Adam Sommester	John Wilkinson
	John Townleye	Samuel Parcival
	William Ouldam	Raphe Pycroft
	George Greaines	Thomas Sommester
	Joseph Greaines	George Sommester
	Thomas Oldham	Jarves Leigh
	John Oldham	

All these whose names are above written have taken the protestation and they are all the men wthin Gorton that are above eighteene yeares of age.

Preste Jo:wwigan minitr
Raphe Shellmerdyne
William Booth }
James wroe } Constables

Imps is an abbreviation of "Imprimis", meaning "First of all". Thomas and Phillipe Strangeways were members of the Strangeways family who for many years had lived in the district of that name. A Thomas Strangeways, probably the one who signed the Protestation, sold the estate in 1648 to John Hartley. According to John Higson he was the lay member for Gorton in 1646.

The Openshaw Protestation

The names of such as have taken the protestation in Openshaw februarie the 20th 1641 // William Strenfeelowe
Thomas Busche
Constables Openshaw
Jo : Wigan minister at Gorton

Thomas Campynot (Campyon?)	Richard Ellor senior
John Jackson	Richard Ellor Junior
John Ellor	Edward Besswick
Hugh Bordsell	Cornelius Besswick
Robert Walwork	Thomas Besswick
john Bordman	Thomas Bertch senior
william Strenghfelow	Thomas Bertch junior
Thomas Besswick	Samull Bertch
nathaniull Besswick	John Bertch
John Worthington	Charles Hunt
James Ellor	James Hunt
william Haughton	John Grounshaw
John Bertch	Henry mather
nathan Hobson	william Tonge
James Besswick	George kenion
Thomas Smith	Raphe Ellor

Apparently no-one refused to take the Protestation. The reason for this unanimity is easy to explain. Most men probably approved of the Protestation and any who disapproved would find it wiser to follow the majority. Dissent was in fact strong in Gorton and Openshaw and dissenters supported the cause of the Puritan parliament.

CHAPTER III

THE 18TH AND EARLY 19TH CENTURIES

Occupations of Gorton and Openshaw people up to the end of the 18th century

The survey of 1320 shows that Gorton and Openshaw were agricultural communitites. In the centuries that followed new industries developed and by the 18th century agriculture played only a minor role in their economy. The baptism register of the Gorton parish church provides evidence of this change. Below is an analysis of the occupations of Gorton and Openshaw fathers between 1742 and 1773.

	Gorton	Openshaw	Total
Weavers	66	31	97
Whitsters	47	11	58
Hatters	19	4	23
Feltmakers	18	7	25
Cordwainers	10	6	16
Husbandmen	11	19	30

"Cordwainer" is the old name for a shoemaker. A "husbandman" was a working farmer. A "whitster" was a bleacher. There were other trades, but the numbers employed were insignificant.

The expansion of the clothmaking industry

Until the 18th century cloth in this country was made almost exclusively from wool and linen. Clothmaking was a domestic industry, the yarn being spun on spinning wheels and the cloth woven on handlooms in the cottages of the labouring class. Spinning was a task for the women in their spare time. Presumably that is why spinning does not appear in the above list of occupations. Weaving was done by the men.

In the 18th century the demand for cloth and particularly cloth made of cotton increased rapidly. This was due to an increase in the population and the opening of markets overseas. Expansion of the textile trade was held up by a shortage of yarn:it took eight spinners to produce sufficient yarn to keep one weaver in work. The solution to the problem began in 1767 with the invention of the spinning jenny by James Hargreaves. This could spin a number of threads simultaneously. It was followed in 1769 by Richard Arkwright's water-frame and in 1779 by Samuel Crompton's "mule". Now there was an abundance of good quality yarn.

A new problem then arose: the handloom weavers could not cope with the demand for cotton cloth, although more and more men were attracted to the trade by the good wages that could be earned. The demand for weavers led to Edmund Cartwright, a clergyman, building the first powerloom in 1787. It was a clumsy and inefficient machine, which posed no threat to the handloom weavers. In the course of time there were improvements, four of them by William Radcliffe, a Stockport manufacturer, and his mechanic, Thomas Johnson, in 1803-04.

Gorton and Openshaw weavers

There can be little doubt that the clothmaking industry in Gorton and Openshaw followed the national trend, although the baptism register for the period before 1741 provides little information about occupations. Before 1681 occupations were not recorded and only infrequently between 1681 and 1740. Up to 1768 weavers were classed as "websters", "weavers" or "linen weavers". From 1768 they were all classed as "weavers". Possibly they were now all engaged in the manufacture of cotton cloth. By 1788 they almost certainly were for in that year William Radcliffe, a Stockport manufacturer wrote, "Cotton, cotton, cotton has become the almost universal material for employment".

The decline in handloom weaving

For some years after the powerloom had become an efficient machine, the number of handloom weavers continued to increase, so great was the demand for cotton cloth. Nationally the decline began in 1820. In Gorton and Openshaw it began in 1825 when Gorton Mill was opened at the side of the canal, but as late as 1851 there were still three handloom weavers on Far Lane: Mary Hibbert, her daughter Ellen and her sister Betty.

The whitsters

In the early years of the industrial revolution bleaching took eight months. First, the cloth or yarn was exposed to the action of sunlight and water by laying it out in a field - this was called "crofting". Then came "bowking" - immersion in a solution made with the ashes of trees and plants. Next, there was "souring" in buttermilk. Finally came washing by hand in streams.

In the 18th century a number of discoveries speeded up the bleaching process. The use of dilute sulphuric acid for souring reduced the time by half. Chlorine enabled the bleaching process to be completed in a few days.

The feltmakers and hatters

The making of felt hats is associated with Denton and Stockport. In the 18th century the industry was widespread throughout Lancashire and Cheshire. Locally it provided employment not only in Denton and Stockport, but also in Gorton, Openshaw, Audenshaw and Droylsden.

The names of local feltmakers are recorded in the baptisms register of Gorton chapel from 1681, but no hat-makers appear before 1741. There is however evidence that hat-making was carried out locally well before the latter date. John Dyson (died 1710) was a hat-maker and the inventory of his goods includes Tooles and Implements for hatting trade £4 4s".

Felt-making could be a profitable trade. Zachariah Peacock of Denton, feltmaker, in his will dated 1791 left eight dwelling houses and lands situated at Hooley Hill and Crown Point. *(It is highly likely that Crown Point takes its name from a fort in Canada, which during the Seven Years War (1756-63) was strategically situated at an important cross-roads. It has been established that a cross-roads in the Burnley area, another Crown Point, was named after the Canadian fort.)*

The first process in hatting was making the felt. This was done in a "bow-garret". Here there was a long table partitioned by hurdles. At each section a man worked a hatter's bow, which was suspended over the bench on which the wool and fur fibre was laid. The cat-gut string was plucked with a wooden pin and the vibration caused the fur and wool to scatter and settle in a layer. The material was then pressed into the shape of a hood, twice the size of the hat which would eventually be made.

The next stage was planking. In the planking shop four to eight hardwood planks were arranged around an iron or lead kettle or cauldron kept full of nearly boiling water with a wineglass of vitriol added to aid shrinking. By constant dipping and working the hood with a wooden roller on the planks it was shrunk to the correct size.

After planking the hat was shaped on a cylindrical wooden block. It was then dried and dyed. Blocking produced the final shape by pulling and pressing on the appropriate wooden block.

Next came stiffening and waterproofing and then the highly skilled process of finishing, softening and reblocking and raising the nap. This was followed by binding, lining and trimming and finally shaping with irons in the most fashionable style. *(see p114, The Hatting Industry by P.M. Giles, Lancs. and Chesh. Antiquarian Society, Vol LXIX)*

The Gorton hat-shops and the Gorton House hat works
Hatting survived in Gorton until the 1840s. On the Gorton tithe map the hatters' workshops are marked as "hat-shops". Locally they were probably known as "planking shops", a workshop where the planking process was carried out. In Denton, where the hatting trade survived until after the 1939-45 war, the planking shops were small brick buildings at the back of the houses. The master hatter, who supplied the workers in the planking shops with felts, was called a manufacturer. He supervised all the hatting processes and arranged for the sale of the hats.
There were two hat manufacturers in Gorton during the first half of the 19th century: Joseph Gillham and Nathaniel Denton. In 1841 both were living in Gorton House together with their families and servants. Hat workers lived in cottages in the grounds of the house.

According to the Gorton rate book of 1848, Mr Denton was the proprietor of a "warehouse, shops (i.e. workshops) and a hat works" all within what was called Gorton House yard. It is likely that he would supply the Gorton hat-shops (i.e. planking shops) with felts and that after planking the hats were taken to Gorton House works for further processing.

Hats made of coarse wool were known as "cordies". If there was a proportion of fur they were known as "stuff hats". As only a few Gorton hatters described themselves as "stuff hatters", it is likely that the majority were makers of low quality hats.

By 1850 the hat works was taken over by Samuel Howarth and Sons. By 1855 it had closed down, probably due to a depression in the hatting industry brought about by a change in fashion from felt hats to silk hats.
(See Hatting in Denton by H.C. Caffrey).

Gorton Tannery
The earliest reference to the tannery on Tan Yard Brow is in the deeds of Gorton Old School, dated 1812, where the name of Thomas Pownall, tanner, appears. In the late 19th century the tannery was acquired by John Ashton. It was worked by John Ashton and Co. until about 1933 when it closed as a tannery and specialised in the manufacture of leather goods. *(Manchester Evening News, 26.2.1953)* The works closed down in the 1960's.

The Manchester and Stockport Canal
In 1792 the Ashton Canal Act authorised the building of a canal from Piccadilly, Manchester, to Ashton. The canal was opened in 1796. An extension, from Clayton to Heaton Norris, through Openshaw, Gorton and Reddish, was opened in 1797. It ceased to be used by commercial traffic in 1933 and was abandoned in 1962.

The Clayton-Heaton Norris branch, marked on maps as the Manchester and Stockport Canal, played an important role in the development of industry in Gorton and Openshaw. The coal, used in Gorton mill on Abbey Hey Lane, was brought by canal, presumably from the Ashton and Oldham mines.

Filtered canal water was used extensively in manufacturing, particularly in the early years of the 19th century, before a supply of water could be obtained from Manchester Corporation Waterworks or its predecessor, the Manchester and Salford Waterworks Company. Gorton Tank had a 30,000 gallon tank, filled with water pumped from the canal, on the top of the canal maintenance workshop in Cornwall Street.

The Gorton Reservoirs
At the beginning of the 19th century water to Manchester and Salford was supplied by the Manchester and Salford Waterworks Company, which was privately owned. An Act of 1823 authorised them to construct two reservoirs in the Debdale Valley in Gorton. The works was completed in 1826 and the water was conveyed to a reservoir in Beswick. In 1845 the company began sinking a well to secure an additional supply of water. Nevertheless the supply was inadequate. In 1851 the Corporation bought out the old Waterworks Company. In 1963 the reservoirs ceased supplying water to the Manchester area.

John Dyson, a Gorton hatter
John Dyson died in 1710, presumably shortly before July 6th, the date of the inventory of his goods.

July 6th 1710 Ann Inventorie of the goods and Chattels of John Dyson of Gorton Deceased ....

	£	s	d
Imprimis three mild cows	09	00	10
Two calves	00	13	04

One mare and one Geldinge	08	00	00
In the fire houe			
One Cupboard	00	05	00
In pewter	00	10	00
In brass	00	05	06
In Table and forme	00	03	00
In a Coffer	00	05	00
In five white wood Chairs	00	02	06
In nine Stooles	00	02	03
In Three boards or shelves	00	02	00
In one old Table and Three Trests	00	02	00
In fire Iron Crow Tongues fire shovell and bread Iron	00	06	00
In one spitt goolbeards A pair of Tonges and Toasting Iron	00	02	06
In frying pann	00	00	08
In fallboard saltpie and bellows	00	01	04
In one Iron pott	00	05	00
In the Butterie			
In one Churne	00	03	00
In Treene Ware	00	05	00
In foure Little Chessfords	00	01	00
In Trenchers with one Churne Lidd	00	01	08
In Earthen ware	00	03	06
In milk boards with one Iron Ladle	00	03	00
In the parlour			
In a pair of bedstocks with beding Thereupon	00	12	00
In Two Coffers	00	05	00
In one Chaire Kneading Turnell and peel	00	01	00
In the Chamber over The parlour			
In Two Coffers and one box	00	04	00
In Two bords or shelves	00	01	06
In The Little parlour			
In a pair of bedstocks with beding	00	06	00
In one Kinlett	00	01	04
In one shelf	00	00	04
In one Axe A pair of mittens and old shoeell	00	02	06
In the Kitchin			
In one Cupboard Table	00	02	00
In Three Sheves	00	01	00
In Two Hackney saddles	00	05	06
In the out houseing			
In Two packsaddles with orleys and wonleys	00	06	00
In A pair of white wood bedstocks	00	03	00
In four soals and four framphołds	00	01	04
In one Coffer	00	02	00
In one Cheess press	00	02	00
In four Rakes and Three pitchforks	00	01	05
In Tooles and Implements for Hatting Trade	04	04	00
In weaing Apparrell	00	10	00
In Husslement	00	01	03
	24	17	05

Edward Hartley
John Knight

bedstocks	bedsteads
chessfords	cheese dishes?
crow	a hinged iron frame fastened to the side of the grate. When lowered onto the fire, it served as a platform for a pan.
bread iron	probably an appliance consisting of a thin iron plate at the end of a long handle, used for removing bread from an oven.
fallboord	possibly a hinged board fastened to a wall and used as a table
fire house	fire house - the room in which a fire was usually kept burning. In John Dyson's house it served as a living room and kitchen. The room which was termed "The Kitchin" was almost empty.
fire iron	This does not appear to be a separate iron, but a description of the four items that follow.
forme	bench
goolbeard	a iron rack in a chimney used to support the pothooks
husslement	household odds and ends e.g. needles, thread, pins.
Imprimis	first
orleys	overlays
saltpie	salt box
sheves	shelves
shoeell	shoe heel
soals	soles
treene	wooden
trenchers	plates
trests	trestles
turnell	bowl
weaing Apparrell	wearing apparel
wonleys	girth used to secure a load on a packhorse

(The original inventory of the goods left by John Dyson is in the Lancashire County Records Office, Preston)

Openshaw in the late 18th and early 19th centuries

"John Ogden of Openshaw, born 13.1.1773, recollects that when he was about ten years of age, there were only thirteen dwelling-houses close to the Ashton Road, with three others standing a little aback, between where now exists the canal bridge, Openshaw, and the New Cross, Manchester."
(John Higson in the Droylsden Journal for August 1854).

It is likely that John Ogden's memory was at fault, for there must have been far more that thirteen houses between the two points mentioned. Perhaps he meant within the Openshaw boundary. Johnson's map of 1819 shows approximately thirteen houses.

Higson, quoting John Ogden, said that the first house on the right-hand side was known as "Sheepshouters" or "Walker's tenement", and that its present name was the Drover's Inn. Further along in Bradford was the Plough Inn, with a wooden representation of a plough swinging over the door. It was, said Higson, now known as the "Gray Mare".

At the junction of Gorton Lane with the main road was Gorton

Lane End Farm, occupied by Mrs Aldred and afterwards by Robert Chapman.

John Selby, an old Openshaw character

"1822. The locally celebrated John Selby interred at Gorton Church. May 28, Aged 55. He was very eccentric."
(John Higson's Gorton Historical Recorder.)

This same John Selby was the subject of an article in the Ashton Weekly Reporter of 29.5.1858. The title of the article was: *"Jack Selby a character"*. The greater part of it is given below.

"Jack Selby and his father, James Selby, lived at an old cottage, adjoining the farmhouse, Rushcroft, held by Robert Turner. Both were Methodists. They were frequently plagued by mischievous youths of Openshaw and Little Droylsden. *(Little Droylsden was a triangular piece of land on the Openshaw side of the point where Abbey Hey Lane crosses the Manchester to Sheffield railway.)*

When the family resided at Ryder Brown, owing to some real or fancied next-of-kinship, a large fortune was supposed to be on the eve of possession. One of the daughters, buoyant with anticipation of the good time coming and thinking it disgusting to rich folks, carried the pinwheel (spinning wheel?) out of the house. But she counted her chickens before they were hatched. Fortune, fickle goddess, unveiled her golden favours elsewhere and the poor despised machine was again reinstated in the corner.

In stature, says a friend of the old school, Jack Selby was a stout "withering" fellow, as big as two ordinary fellows of the present day. He was clad in a rude fantastic costume, the place of a hatband being supplied by a strong iron hoop, from whence rose an iron arch over the crown, to the centre of which a bell was suspended, consequently whenever on a tramp its jingling heralded forth Jack's approaching steps.

His loins were girded with a belt formed of a twisted hayband, where were dependent pig-rings, a key, hammer and pincers. So accommodating was the wearer that for the sake of a draught or two of ale, Jack would have rung all the swine in the country.

He would never settle down to any fast job of work, but subsisted on allowances from the poor rate and contributions of his friends. In fact, 40 years ago he was accounted the only independent gentleman that Openshaw could boast of."

Bow-garret

The Hat Battery: hatters working at the plank round the kettle, which is heated by a coal-fire.

CHAPTER IV

FAR LANE IN 1841 THE 1844 TITHE MAPS

Far Lane in 1841

In 1841 census returns gave for the first time detailed information about the occupiers of dwellings i.e. name, age within five years, occupation where applicable, and whether born within the county of residence. The relationship of the members of a household to each other was not given, although in most cases it can be inferred.

Below is a copy of the census returns for Further Lane, the old name for Far Lane, and for Bottom of the Brow, which was a continuation of Further Lane. Bottom of the Brow eventually changed its name to Far Lane. It is not possible to identify any individual house except the Black Horse Inn, which in 1841 was occupied by James Fletcher and his wife, Caroline, and their three children. In its hey-day the Black Horse had been a well-known coaching inn on the main road from Manchester to Denton and Hyde. With the building of Hyde Road it had lost its importance and had degenerated into a beer-house. It lost its licence in the early years of the 20th century and was demolished some time after the Second World War.

Except where marked with the letters NBIL (Not born in Lancashire) residents were natives of Lancashire. Repetition of surnames has been avoided. Thus Mary in the first line is Mary Worthington. Thomas, James etc. all have the surname Worthington. Hannah on line four is Hannah Hall.

The term "inmate" is used to describe Joseph Taylor, Joel Whittaker, Samuel Beswick, Lucy Barlow and Michael Smith. It may mean that they had been inmates of the Wellington Street workhouse, by 1841 apparently no longer in use, and that as they were receiving outdoor relief they continued to be classified as inmates. There was considerable distress in the district at the time brought about by the closure between 1840 and 1844 of Gorton Mill. This is not apparent in the census returns, which give the occupation of an individual but do not always state whether or not he or she is working.

James Worthington, 50, hatter Mary, 50
Thomas, 25, hatter James, 21, mechanic George, 15, hatter Charles, 15, hatter Sarah, 8

Hannah Whittaker, 50, silk weaver Esther Hall, cotton weaver, 35 Hannah, 10

Samuel Lee, 30, hatter Sarah, 30
Hannah, 11 George, 10 Mary, 8 James, 6
William, 4 Sarah, 3 months.

Martha Arderne, 45, cotton weaver Alice, 40 James Beswick, 84, independent

Charles Taylor, 25, spinner Mary, 25, cotton weaver
Mark, 3

Peter Ashton, 50, hatter Ann, 50
Anne, 20, cotton weaver Caroline, 20, cotton weaver
Sarah, 15, cotton weaver
Peter, 15 William, 10 Jane, 75

William Tatton, 40, hatter Elizabeth, 35
James, 12 Charles, 12 Elizabeth, 9 William, 6
Ephraim, 4 Thomas Green, 30, hatter

George Bradley, 35, hatter Ann, 35
James, 15 William, 12 John, 12 Luke, 8
Mark, 4 George, 1

James Walker, 55, warper Ann Whittaker, 70 Elisha Hibbert, 25

John Smith, 50, tanner (NBIL) John, 20, carter
Catherine Howard, 45, female servant (NBIL)

Stanley Wood, 30, surgeon Emily, 9

George Taylor, 30, labourer (NBIL) Frances, 25 (NBIL)
George, 3 (NBIL) Thomas, 1

James Eshworth, 40, labourer (NBIL) Thomas Moody, 20, labourer (NBIL)
John Pimlow, 15, labourer (NBIL) John Jones, 20, labourer (NBIL)
John Holland, 15, labourer (NBIL) Robert Hoskinson, 15, labourer

James Greenlees, 25, mechanic Charlotte, 20
Elizabeth, 4 Edwin, 2 Ann Piddington, 50, female servant (NBIL)

Elizabeth Ingham, 35 Maria, 15 William, 11
William Hardy, 20, male servant Sarah Daniels, 15, female servant

Samuel Taylor, 25, joiner Elizabeth, 25

John Birch, 30, hatter Alice, 25

John Williamson, 55, hatter Kitty, 55
Jane, 20, cotton weaver Betty, 20, cotton weaver
Joseph, 20, hatter
Mary, 15, cotton weaver James, 13 Aaron, 10

John Nicholson, 45, hatter Alice, 45
Alice, 22, weaver Ann, 20, weaver John, 19, hatter
Elizabeth, 17, weaver
Joseph, 25, weaver Frances, 13, weaver Mary, 7
George, 5 William, 3

Ann Barrett, 40, widow George, 20, unemployed
John, 18, labourer
James, 15, labourer William, 9 Thomas, 6 Ann, 4
Samuel, 1

Isaac Walker, 70, army pensioner Parnell Walker, 65 (Female)
Esther, 20, cotton weaver James, 15, cotton weaver
Ann, 15, cotton weaver John, 14, apprentice

Charles Tatton, 35, hatter Rowena, 35
Samuel, 8 John, 5 James, 2 William, 2 months
James Tatton, 45, lodger

John Hibbert, 50, tanner Martha, 50
John, 25, hatter Mary, 20, weaver Joseph, 20, spinner
Samuel, piecer, 15
Eliza, 12 Thos, 9

Joseph Taylor, 30, spinner (inmate) Martha, 25
Hannah, 7 John, 5 Joseph, 2

John Moors, 40, tanner Hannah, 35
Mary, 15, cotton weaver Ellen, 14, cotton weaver
Ralph, 12 Nancy, 10
Sarah, 8 John, 4 Charles, 1 month

Mary Hibbert, 35, weaver Ellen, 35, weaver Betty, 30, weaver

Richard Piddington, 25, tanner Betty, 25
Richard, 3 Ann, 1 Abram, 15

James Nicholson, 35, hatter Ann, 35
John, 2

Thomas Nicholson, 50, hatter Dinah, 50
George, 20, dyer Thomas, 15, labourer James, 13
Sarah, 8
George, 40, hatter (lodger)

James Birch, 25, hatter Elizabeth, 25
James, 4 John, 11, apprentice

Richard Piddington, 25, dealer Mary, 25
Jane, 6 Thomas, 1
William Wood, 45, labourer Sarah, 55 James Howarth (lodger)

James Fletcher, 30, beer seller Caroline, 25
Elizabeth, 5 Frances, 3 Emma, 2

Deborah Holt, 60, widow Martha, 20, female servant
Joel Whittaker, 35, inmate

Bottom of Brow
Thomas Lee, 35, dyer Mary, 35
William, 15, labourer Sarah, 15, cotton weaver Joseph, 10 Alice, 2

James Grimshaw, 50, hatter Ann, 50
Nancy, 26, cotton weaver Rebecca, 20, cotton weaver
James, 15, hatter Samuel, 15, hatter

George Standring, 40, silk weaver Mary, 46
Betty, 26, cotton weaver Mary, 15, cotton weaver
Anne, 15 Sarah, 11
Samuel, 7 William, 6 Jane, 2 Samuel Beswick, (inmate)

John Schofield, 40, hatter Alice, 40
Ann, 15, cotton weaver John, 13 Caroline, 8
Samuel, 6

George Aspinall, 45, hatter Alice, 50
John, 25, hatter Anne, 20 Thomas, 18, porter
James, 16, hatter William, 14

Mark Knight, 55, hatter Anne, 55
George, 25, hatter

John Gresty, 25, hatter Sarah, 25
Elizabeth, 2 Abraham, 6 months

Joseph Robinson, 30, hatter Mary, 30
Ann, 5

John Macdonald, 35, tanner Helen, 35
Mary, 5

Edward Aspinall, 50, hatter Mary, 50
Mary (junior), 30 Sarah, 20, cotton spinner Charles, 15, hatter Samuel, 15, hatter
Edwin, 15, hatter Amy, 5 Lucy Barlow, 25 (inmate)
Mark, 4 William, 2

John Fisher, 25, excavator Hannah, 30
Gaziah, 4 (girl) Thomas, 1 Michael Smith, 25, (inmate)
Mary Smith, 25 (NBIL)
James Smith, 5 (NBIL)

William Walton, 30, joiner Sarah, 31

Chris Carolin, 25, hatter (NBIL) Sarah, 25 (NBIL)
John Houseman, 25, hatter (inmate) (NBIL) Janet Houseman, 20, (NBIL)

Augustus King, 35, tanner (NBIL) Mary, 35 (NBIL)
Sarah, 9 (NBIL) Robert, 7 (NBIL) Frederick, 8 months (NBIL)

John Worthington, 30, hatter Elizabeth, 30
William, 6 James, 5

The Tithe maps of Gorton and Openshaw
Up to 1837 the farmer had to pay to the church one tenth of the annual produce of his farm. This tax was called a "tithe", the word being derived from the old English "teotha", meaning tenth. Every kind of produce was subject to tithes, both animal

and vegetable, including the natural increase of all farm-stock.

In 1836 Parliament passed the Tithes Commutation Act, whereby an equivalent money payment was substituted, based on a scale depending on the septennial average price of corn. To calculate the money value of the tithes, a map of each township had to be drawn up, showing the boundaries of each plot of land. The plots were marked on the map with a reference number. Accompanying the map was a schedule, which using the reference numbers gave all the necessary information about each plot: the area, the owner, the occupier, a description of the plot e.g. cottages, road, meadow, pasture.

The tithe maps of Gorton and Openshaw, drawn up about 1844, show that the greater part of the townships was open country but that only a small proportion of the population had any land at all and of these only a minute proportion had sufficient land to make a living. In fact those who held the most land employed workers to farm it and derived most of their income from other sources e.g. John Rylands, Robert Bennett and George Grimshaw of Gorton and George Whyatt of Openshaw.

Gorton

Land usage	Area in acres	Number of occupiers	Area in acres
Arable	30	16	under 5
Meadow and pasture	1310	7	5 - 10
Sites of buildings	70	10	10 - 20
Woodland	10	7	20 - 30
Not subject to tithe	69	6	30 - 40
Total area	1489	6	40 - 50
		2	50 - 60
		5	60 - 70
		0	70 - 80
		1	80 - 90
		60	

Openshaw

Land Usage	Area in acres	Number of occupiers	Area in acres
Meadow and pasture	523	10	under 5
Buildings	30	8	5 - 10
Not subject to tithe	26	7	10 - 20
		4	20 - 30
		5	30 - 40
Total area	579	1	40 - 50
		35	

Field names

The oldest field name, "Seven Thorns", is used for eight fields in what at one time was the Fairfield area of Openshaw. The name is an old one, appearing in a 1587 inventory of the possessions left by Robert Birkenshaw of Gorton:

A certen tack of ground of ii acres and a roode for ii years and also other ii acres called Senthorns (Seven Thorns).

The circumstances in which the name "Seven Thorns" came to be used is a matter of conjecture. Either the eight fields originally formed one large field in which grew seven hawthorn trees or the fields were named individually after a group of hawthorn trees growing in the area.

Yarn croft may have been a field used for bleaching yarn. It lay in Openshaw immediately to the north of Corn Brook

Toad Lane Hey was to the north of Abbey Hey Lane. "Toad" may have been the dialect word for "the old", the lane in question being Abbey Hey Lane. There is a reference to a "Little Toad Lane Field" in deeds dated 1631 - 1658.

The Town Croft was at one time the village common. It is mentioned in Gorton deeds of 1658.

The Gore brook forms the northern boundary of Whitley field. This field was mentioned in Gorton deeds 1690 - 1708.

Cottages on Far Lane.

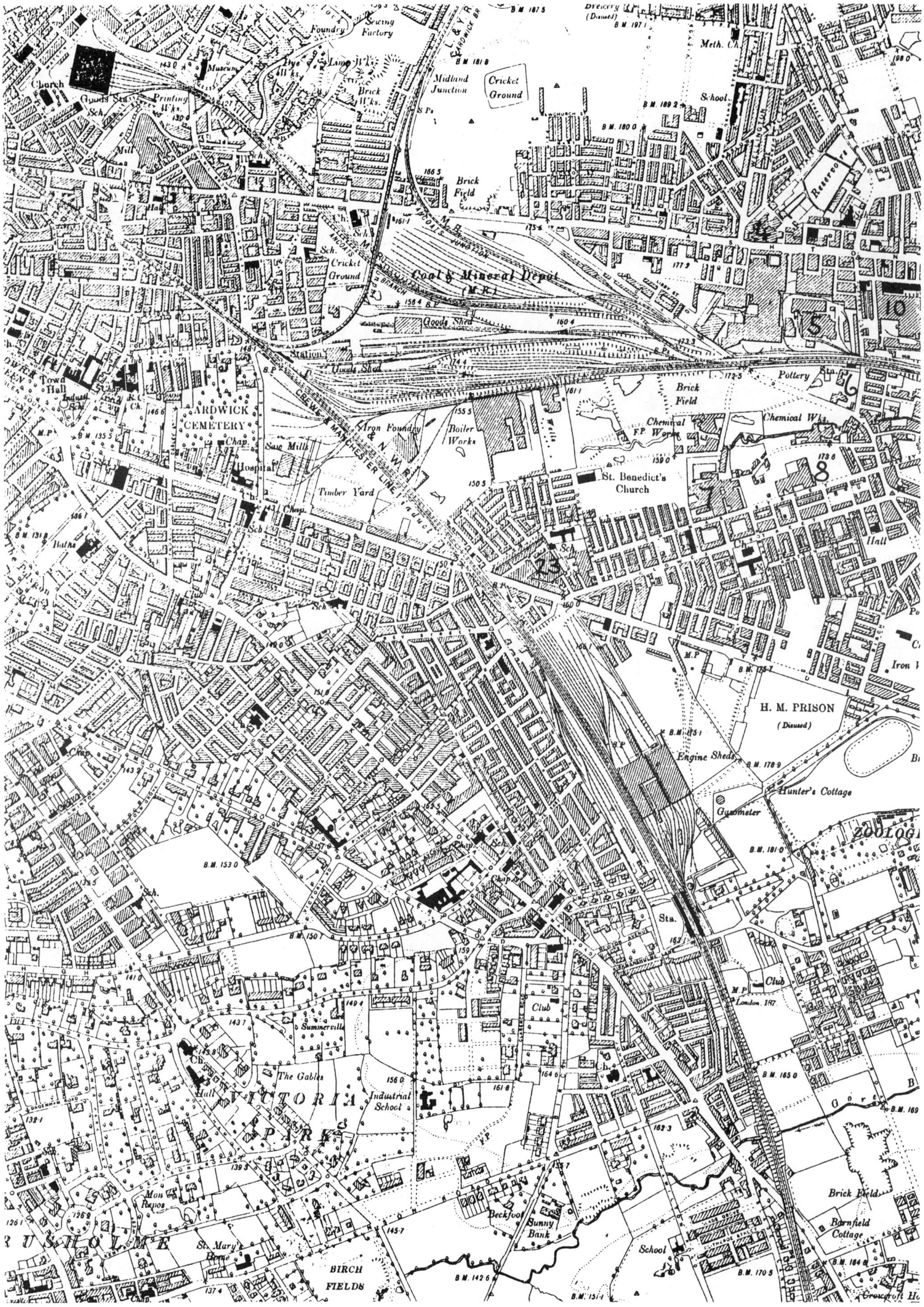
Foundry
Sewing Factory
Museum
Church
Goods Sta.
Sch.
Printing Wks.
Dye Wks.
Lime Wks.
Brick Wks.
Midland Junction
Cricket Ground
Brick Field
Meth. Ch.
School
Reservoirs
Cricket Ground
Coal & Mineral Depot
(M.R.)
Goods Shed
Station
Goods Shed
Town Hall
Industl. Sch.
ARDWICK CEMETERY
Chap.
Hospital
Saw Mills
Iron Foundry
Boiler Works
Timber Yard
CREWE & MANCHESTER LINE
L. & N. W. R.
Brick Field
Chemical F.P. Works
Chemical Wks.
Pottery
St. Benedict's Church
Baths
Hall
H. M. PRISON
(Disused)
Engine Sheds
Hunter's Cottage
Gasometer
ZOOLOG
Sta.
Club
Club
Summerville
The Gables
Industrial School
VICTORIA PARK
Mon Repos
Beckfoot
Sunny Bank
School
Brick Field
Barnfield Cottage
RUSHOLME
St. Mary's Home
BIRCH FIELDS
5
6
8
10
23

Clayton Mill
Brooks Street
Ivy Cottage
Reservoirs
Weir
Dye Wks.
Clayton Brook
Brick Wks.
Magazine
Clayton Gardens
Iron Foundry
Parly. Co. Div. & Union By.
Co. Boro. By.
Acres 579·274
OPENSHAW
25
Church
3
Engineering Wks.
Victoria Mill
Hall
Club
Saw Mill
10
11
12
2
Chap.
Sch.
13
14
15
16
MANCHESTER SHEFFIELD & LINCOLNSHIRE RY.
Engineering Works
Gorton Yard
West Gorton
Mill
Corn Brook
Engine Shed
School
Canal Depot
Iron Wks.
Hotel
Gorton Station
ASHTON UNDER LYNE CANAL (STOCKPORT BRANCH)
Co. Boro. By.
L.B.D. By
R.C.C.
Gorton Foundry
17
18
Engineering Wks.
Cricket ground
Hall
Rectory
Church
Police Sta.
Chap.
22
Iron Wks.
Club
Hope Farm
Gum Wks.
Schools
New Mills
Gorton Villa
19
Field Farm
St. James's Church
20
School
Bridge
Brewery
Rectory
BELLE VUE ZOOLOGICAL GARDENS
Co. Boro. By.
L.B. Offices
Cateknowl
Chatsworth Mills
21
Belle Vue Station
Sunny Brow
GORTON
Club
Saw Mills
Church
GORTON L.B.D.
Maiden's Br.
Parly. Boro. Parly. Co. Div. By.
L.B.D. By.
Nutsford Vale
Chemical Wks.
Dye Works
Iron Works
SHEFFIELD & MIDLAND JOINT
Rider Brow
GORTON
Acres 1488·715
Mount Farm
Union By.
Saw Mill
MANCHESTER CENTRAL STATION LINE
M. S. & L. R.
Brick Field
Barnfield Cottage
Pink Bank Cottages
Pink Bank Lane
Parly. Co. Div. Union & B.D. By.

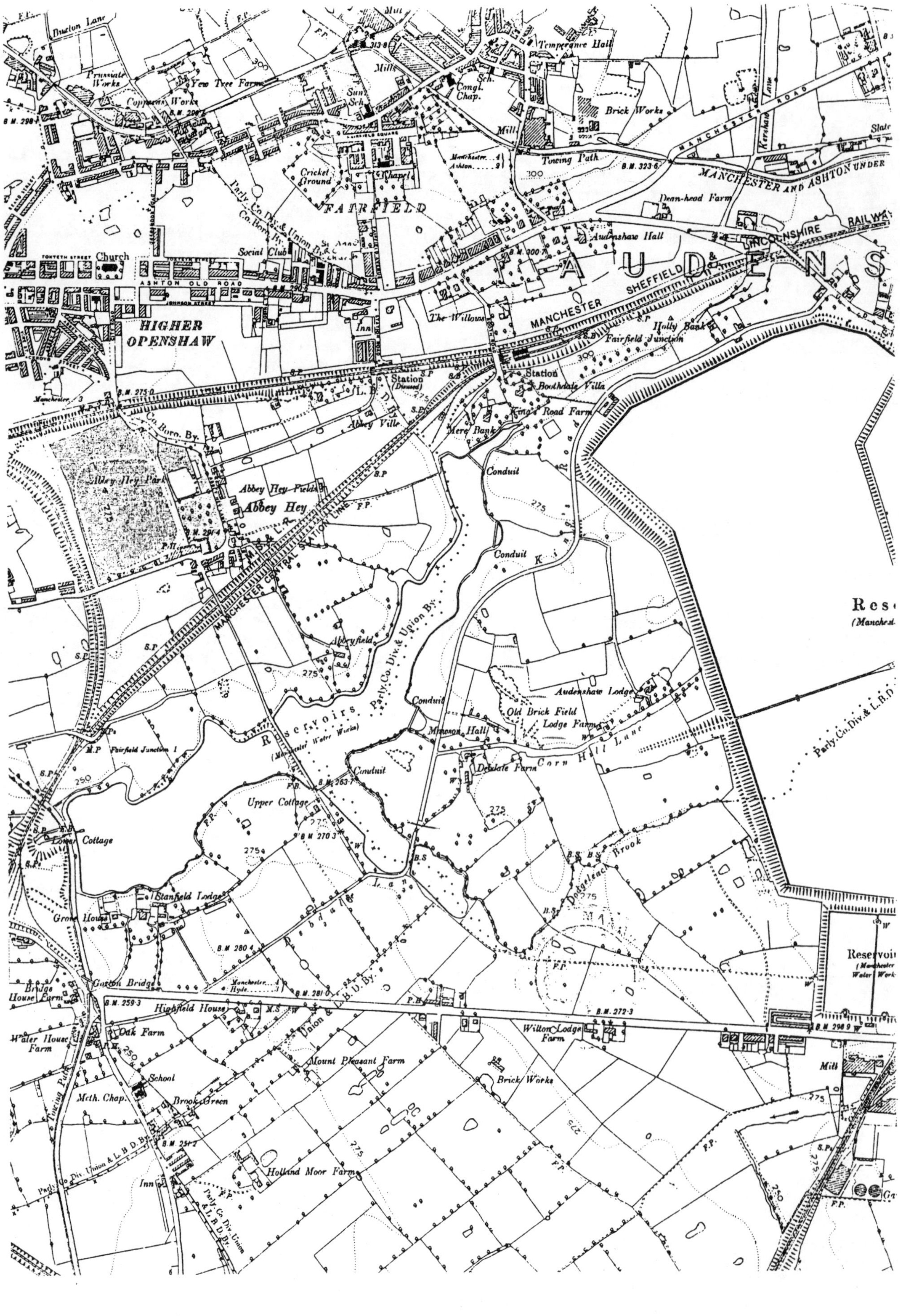
Droylsden Lane
Prussiate Works
Yew Tree Farm
Copperas Works
Temperance Hall
Congl. Chap.
Sun. Sch.
Mill
Brick Works
Towing Path
Manchester and Ashton under
Manchester Road
Kershaw Lane
Slate
Cricket Ground
Chapel
Fairfield
Dean-head Farm
Audenshaw Hall
Social Club
Church
Ashton Old Road
Higher Openshaw
Audens
Manchester Sheffield & Lincolnshire Railway
The Willows
Inn
Holly Bank
Fairfield Junction
Station
Boothdale Villa
King's Road Farm
Abbey Villa
Mere Bank
Co. Boro. By.
Abbey Hey Park
Abbey Hey Fields
Abbey Hey
Conduit
Manchester Central Station Line
Kings Road
Abbeyfield
Res
Reservoirs
(Manchester Water Works)
Parly. Co. Div. & Union By.
Audenshaw Lodge
Old Brick Field
Lodge Farm
Mimoson Hall
Corn Hall Lane
Dogdale Farm
Fairfield Junction 1
Upper Cottage
Lower Cottage
Dogdale Lane
Dogleach Brook
Stanfield Lodge
Grove House
Gorton Bridge
Bridge House Farm
Highfield House
Willow Lodge Farm
Reservoir
(Manchester Water Works)
Water House Farm
Oak Farm
Mount Pleasant Farm
Brick Works
Mill
School
Meth. Chap.
Brook Green
Towing Path
Holland Moor Farm
Inn
Parly. Co. Div. Union & L.B.D. By.

CHAPTER V

The Industrial Development of Gorton and Openshaw in the 19th and 20th Centuries

Key to the maps showing the principal industrial firms in Gorton and Openshaw at the end of the 19th century

1. Hampson Wrigley, cloth raisers and finishers, Ashton Old Road, Openshaw.
2. B. and S. Massey, steam hammers, Ashton Old Road, Openshaw.
3. George Saxon, steam engines for driving textile machinery, South Street, Openshaw.
4. George Whyatt, dressers, fustian shearers and finishers, Ashton Old Road, Openshaw.
5. Ashbury Railway Carriage Co., Pottery Lane, Openshaw.
6. Gorton Brook Pottery, Pottery Lane, Openshaw.
7. Brooks and Doxey, Union Iron Works, manufacturers of textile machinery, Thomas Street, West Gorton.
8. Frank Pearn, pump manufacturers, Thomas Street (now called Wenlock Way), West Gorton.
9. The Vaughan Crane Co., Royal Iron Works, Ambrose Street, Openshaw.
10. Crossley Bros., manufacturers of the Otto Gas Engine, Pottery Lane, Openshaw.
11. Joseph Whitworth and Co., engineers, Whitworth Street, Openshaw.
12. Gorton Locomotive Works (Gorton Tank), Ogden Lane, Openshaw.
13. John Smith and Co., iron founders, Tamworth Street, Openshaw.
14. The Steel Nut and Tube Co., High Bank Street Works, Openshaw.
15. The High Bank Mill, cotton manufacturers, Ogden Lane, Openshaw.
16. Harrison Naylor and Co., Eagle Iron Works, Lees Street, Openshaw.
17. Beyer Peacock and Co., locomotive manufacturers, Gorton Lane, Gorton.
18. Follows and Bate and Co., manufacturers of paint machinery, agricultural and horticultural machinery, Froxmer Street, Gorton.
19. John Rylands and Co., Gorton Mill, cotton manufacturers, Abbey Hey Lane, Gorton.
20. John Buckley, Gorton New Mill, cotton manufacturers, Croft Street, off Wellington Street, Gorton.
21. Robert Williams and Sons, Chatsworth Mills, finishers, waterers, embossers, shearers and hot pressers, Hyde Road, Gorton.
22. Higginbottom and Mannock, Crown Iron Works, Fenton Street, Gorton.
23. Holden and Brooke and Co., Sirius Works, Heywood Street (now renamed Haverford Street) off Clowes Street, West Gorton, pump manufacturers.
24. J.W.Gill, cotton manufacturers, Union Mill, Tamworth Street, Openshaw.
25. John Hall Underwood, Churchfield Rope Works, Openshaw.

The Industrial Revolution
During the 18th and 19th centuries British industry underwent changes so great that the term "Industrial Revolution" has been used to describe them. The manufacture of cloth moved from the cottage to the factory. New processes for making iron and steel were invented. James Watt built his steam-engine. Following the success of the Manchester-Liverpool Railway, completed in 1830, a network of railways was constructed to link the important towns.

The 19th Century

Gorton's first factory - Gorton Mill
In August, 1825, Messrs John Lees and Sons commenced spinning and weaving in their new mill on Abbey Hey Lane at the side of the canal. The site was chosen because the canal linked the mill with the coal-mines of Ashton and Oldham. Probably canal water, filtered, was used in the mill until the 1850s when mains water beame available.

A steam-engine provided the power for working the looms and spinning machines. The total number of hands employed in 1832 was 711, a figure which included 190 girls under 18 and 220 females aged 18 and over. There were 137 males under 18 and 156 aged 18 and over.

A slump brought about the closure of the mill in 1840 and all the mill property was bought by John Chapman of Glossop, Member of Parliament for Grimsby. In 1843 John Rylands took it on lease. In 1864 he bought it from John Chapman.

John Rylands enlarged the mill, installed new machinery and made every effort to make the buildings fireproof. A private telegraph connected the mill with the firm's offices in High Street. *(Manchester City News 15.4.1865)* It closed down in 1919.

Gorton New Mill, better known as Buckley's Mill
Gorton New Mill stood on Croft Street (Stelling Street) off Gorton Lane. It was opened in 1858 by John Buckley. John Buckley was born in Staley, Cheshire, in 1803. He settled in Gorton and became the proprietor of the Chapel House Tavern, Croft Street. In 1832 he built a brewery at the side of the tavern.

Buckley's mill was eventually sold to Messrs James Moorhouse and Son, cotton manufacturers, when it employed 200 workers, including 150 women. In September, 1928, it caught fire and was almost completely destroyed. *(Gorton and Openshaw Reporter, 8.9.1928)*

George Grimshaw's High Bank Mill

In 1861 George Henry Grimshaw of High Bank, Gorton, built a cotton mill on Ogden Lane, Openshaw. It was named High Bank Mill after Mr Grimshaw's own residence. It closed down during or shortly after the First World War and the building was sold to Messrs Hugon, who converted it into a suet works.

There were other textile mills in Gorton and Openshaw of whose history little or nothing is known. There was the Union Mill of J.W.Gill in Tamworth Street, Openshaw and the Gorton Spinning Company in Thomas Street, Gorton. In Victoria Street, Openshaw, was Victoria Mill. Behind Hampson, Wrigley's works was the Imperial Oil Cloth Co's Mill, usually known as Orrell's Mill.

George Whyatt and Son

George Whyatt and Son were already established in Openshaw in 1849. In 1882 they advertised themselves as dressers, fustian shearers and finishers. This type of fustian was a coarse cotton cloth, which at the shearing stage was stretched over a long table. The fustian shearers walked back and forward all day, cutting the cloth to form a pile.

Whyatt's dyeworks was demolished in 1890 and the Metropole Theatre built on the site. There is a reminder of the works in the name of the nearby Dyer Street.

Henry Crabtree and Sons

On Ashton Old Road at the corner of Old Lane stood the Bank Dyeworks of Henry Crabtree and Sons. It was pulled down in 1910 to make way for the Alhambra Theatre.

The Manchester and Birmingham Railway Co.

On the 4th June, 1840, the Manchester and Birmingham Railway was opened to the public as far as Edgeley, Stockport.

The Sheffield, Ashton-under-Lyne and Manchester Railway, Gorton Tank and Richard Peacock

In 1825, when Messrs John Lees and Sons opened Gorton Mill, it might have seemed that Gorton's future lay in the manufacture of textiles. However, a series of events in the 1840s exercised such a profound effect on her development and that of her neighbour, Openshaw, that by 1854 the two townships were well on the way to becoming one of the great engineering workshops of the world.

In 1838 the Sheffield, Ashton-under-Lyne and Manchester Railway Company began building a line between Sheffield and Manchester. In 1845 the board of the railway decided to build a permanent locomotive and carriage depot in Openshaw. The site was chosen for two reasons. First, local taxes were low compared with those levied in Manchester. Second, linking the depot with the main line of the railway presented no engineering problems. Had a site been chosen further to the east, where the land began to rise and the railway ran in a cutting, an additional cutting would have been necessary.

Responsibility for the planning and design of the depot was given to a remarkable man, Richard Peacock, who in 1841 had joined the company as "Engine Driver No 1". He was then only twenty years of age. In 1847 the company became by amalgamation the Manchester, Sheffield and Lincolnshire Railway. The Openshaw depot was completed in 1848. It was usually known as Gorton Tank. *(See Great Central by Dow, Vol.1, pages 106, 211-223)*

According to tradition the "Tank" part of the name is derived from a water-tank near the depot, which was used for filling the boilers of the locomotives. A different explanation was given by Richard Peacock in the Gorton and Openshaw Reporter of 22.12.1883. He pointed out that the name "Tank" was used to describe all large railway engineering works and gave as additional examples "Longsight Tank" and "Miles Platting Tank". The word "Tank" acquired its specialised meaning at the Longsight Depot of the Manchester and Birmingham Railway. Wooden sleepers were impregnated with a liquid preservative which was contained in tanks. Hence the name "Longsight Tank". From that time it became customary to describe any railway depot as a "Tank".

Although the official title of the depot was "Gorton Loco Works", it was in fact in Openshaw. The confusion may have arisen because in 1846, when work on the depot was beginning, the nearest station was known as "Gorton Station".
So, an accident of topography and low taxation led to the building of a railway repair shop in Openshaw. A man of exceptional talent, Richard Peacock, was put in charge of it. He later formed a partnership with Charles Frederick Beyer and together they founded the firm of Beyer, Peacock. The foundations of Gorton and Openshaw's engineering industry were now laid.

The later history of local railways

The branch of the Great Central and Midland Joint Railway between Ashbury East junction and Romiley junction and through Belle Vue, Reddish North and Bredbury was opened for goods on 14.5.1875 and for passengers on 2.8.1875. Belle Vue station was opened on 1.9.1875. *(History of Manchester Railways by William Harrison)*

In 1892 the Manchester Suburban Railway was completed. Its purpose was to connect the Midland Railway at Central Station with Fairfield and Gorton on the Manchester, Sheffield and Lincolnshire Railway. Fairfield Station was rebuilt a little to the east of its old site and a track was laid across what are now playing fields and a golf course to join a line from Gorton Station near Tan Yard Brow. From Manchester Central to Fairfield via Chorlton-cum-Hardy, Wilbraham Road, Fallowfield, Levenshulme and Hyde Road took thirty one minutes.

In 1897 after amalgation the Manchester, Sheffield and Lincolnshire Railway became the Great Central Railway. In 1923 following reorganisation the Great Central was renamed the London North Eastern Railway. In 1947 the L.N.E.R. became part of the British Railways.

Beyer Peacock, Gorton

In 1854 Richard Peacock resigned his position with the Manchester, Sheffield and Lincolnshire Railway and with Charles Frederick Beyer and Henry Robertson formed the company of Beyer, Peacock. Beyer, the son of a poor weaver, was born in Saxony in 1818. The works known as Gorton

Foundry, stood on Froxmer Street, off Gorton Lane.

The most famous of the Beyer Peacock locomotives are the "Garratts", named after their inventor, Herbert William Garratt, an Australian engineer. The locomotives ran on bogie wheels and so were particularly suitable for winding tracks in mountainous areas. *(See Beyer Peacock by R.L.Hills and D.Patrick)*

Brooks and Doxey, Gorton
The firm of Brooks and Doxey, textile machinery manufacturers, was established by Samuel Brooks in 1859 in the Union Mills, Manchester. In 1864 he moved to new premises in Thomas Street, West Gorton, naming the new works the Union Iron works. It then employed 70 men. In 1909 there were 2,600.

The Lancashire Steel Company, Gorton Lane, Gorton
It was one of the first firms to use the Bessemer process for converting pig-iron into malleable iron and steel. It closed down in 1871.

Bolckow Vaughan, steel manufacturers, Gorton Lane, Gorton
In 1871 Bolckow Vaughan took over the works and plant of the Lancashire Steel Company. There is a reference to it in a street directory of 1876 but not in later directories.

Messrs Harrison, Naylor and Co., Lees Street, Openshaw
The Gorton and Openshaw Reporter of 5.10.1872 reported that the staff of Messrs Harrison, Naylor of the Eagle Iron Works had held a dinner at the Halfway House to celebrate the installation of a new steam-hammer.

Follows and Bate, Froxmer Street, Gorton
Follows and Bate moved to Froxmer Street in 1890 probably from Deansgate. They manufactured paint machinery and agricultural and horticultural machinery.

George Scott, Heywood Street, Gorton
In an 1876 directory George Scott is shown as the proprietor of the Crown Iron Works, Heywood Street.

Hampson, Wrigley and Co., Ashton Old Road, Openshaw
Hampson, Wrigley and Co. were cloth finishers and raisers. Their works was at the side of the canal. The firm began in 1877 as A.Hampson and Co.

The Imperial Oil Cloth Company, Ashton Old Road, Openshaw
The factory of the Imperial Oil Cloth Company was next to Hampson, Wrigley's works. It is shown in an 1891 directory. It was also known as Orrel's Linoleum works. It caught fire and does not appear to have reopened.

The Ashbury Railway and Carriage Company, Openshaw
According to Hills and Patrick in their history of Beyer Peacock, Richard Peacock persuaded Jack Ashbury to build his works in Openshaw. It was opened shortly after the completion of the Openshaw section of the Sheffield, Ashton-under-Lyne and Manchester Railway. Early in this century it was known as the Gorton Carriage Company.

George Saxon Ltd., Openshaw
In the Openshaw rate book of 1859 a George Saxon is shown as the owner of a "Machine Shop Smithy" on Ashton Old Road. He was presumably the founder of George Saxon Ltd., builders of steam engines for driving textile machinery. The works was on South Street.

B. and S. Massey Ltd., Openshaw
The founders of B. and S. Massey were Benjamin and Stephen Massey, the sons of a wealthy Old Trafford slate merchant. After they had served their apprenticeship in engineering, their father bought for them a plot of land on the north-east side of Openshaw canal bridge. Here in 1861 was built their first workshop known as the Openshaw Canal Iron Works.

The brothers intended to build steam engines for use in cotton mills, but the cotton trade was slack because of the American Civil War and no orders were forthcoming. They were advised by a Mr Lewis of Gorton to specialise in steam hammers. Within a few years Massey hammers had found a profitable market in this country, in most European countries and in Argentina, Brazil, "Russian Poland", Canada, India, Australia and Ceylon.
(See "B. and S. Massey 1861-1971" by Hurford Janes)

Rope Making
Up to the end of the 19th century rope was made in long narrow yards called "rope walks". A rope walk in Knutsford Vale, Kirkmanshulme, is shown on the 1844 tithe map. It was owned by John Scott. There was another in Rylance Street, which appears to have been the property of the Ancoats Flax and Hemp Spinning Company. A third rope walk is marked on a large scale Ordnance Survey map of 1895 on the east side of St. Barnabas's church. In an 1865 street directory it is called the Churchfield Rope Works. It was owned by John Hull Underwood.

Frank Pearn and Co, West Gorton
In 1872, Frank Pearn, aged 21, an apprentice with a firm of pump makers, set up in business on his own. The works was in Hulme. In 1878 he moved to Thomas Street. In 1936 the firm was supplying pumps for the Anglo Iranian Oil Company. In 1942 they designed and produced pumps for PLUTO (Pipe Line Under The Ocean), which following the Normandy invasion was used to supply fuel to the allied forces. In 1950 Frank Pearn and Co. joined Holden and Brooke. *(See Ken Lilley, Gorton Heritage)*

Joseph Whitworth, Openshaw
Joseph Whitworth was born in Stockport in 1803. He served his apprenticeship in the engineering works of Maudslay and Clements of London. In 1833 he started as master mechanic in Manchester and in the following year commenced business in a mill at the side of the Rochdale canal. The site of the mill is now occupied by the hall of the Shena Simon College.

Among Joseph Whitworth's achievements were the standardisation of screw threads, the "Whitworth Thread", the construction of a machine which could measure to a minute fraction of an inch and the invention of the modern machine tool.

In 1880 Joseph Whitworth moved to Openshaw on what

is now Whitworth Street. In 1897 his firm amalgamated with W.G.Armstrong and Co. to form Armstrong, Whitworth and Co. In 1890 Joseph Whitworth built for the people of Openshaw the Whitworth Hall on Ashton Old Road, comprising wash-houses, baths and a library.

Crossley Brothers
In 1866 Francis William Crossley purchased the business of John Macmillan Dunlop, a manufacturer of machinery for working india rubber. The works was in Great Marlborough Street, Manchester. On the retirement of Mr Dunlop, William John Crossley joined his brother and the firm became known as Crossley Brothers.

In 1869 the firm took up the manufacture of atmospheric gas engines under the patents of Otto and Langen, two German engineers. In 1876 they sold to Crossley Brothers the right to manufacture their new Otto gas engine. In 1882 all production was transferred to a new works on Pottery Lane.

Francis William and William John were extremely religious and insisted that all workmen should attend a place or worship. For those who had no place of worship a church was built within the factory and a minister of religion was engaged to conduct sevices. The church building is still in existence. The brothers supported the Salvation Army in its campaign against drink and in their early years would not supply Crossley engines to breweries.

In 1888 they established the Crossley Lads Club, using a room in the works as a club house. In 1912 the Club took over the building occupied until then by the Home of Peace for Persons in Consumption on Ashton Old Road. This hospital had been founded and maintained by the two brothers. The Crossley Lads Club house is now used by the Crossley House Youth Centre. There was also an annual camp at Wray Castle on Lake Windermere.

Higginbottom and Mannock
Higginbottom and Mannock of the Crown Iron Works, Fenton Street, Gorton are listed in an 1882 street directory. They manufactured overhead cranes.

Kendall and Gent
The firm of Kendall and Gent, machine-tool manufacturers, was founded by William Kendall and George Gent in 1847. Their works, the Victoria Works, was in Dickinson Street, Salford. Between 1889 and 1900 they built a new Victoria Works near Belle Vue station.

Robert Williams and Sons Ltd., Gorton
In an 1879 directory Robert Williams was described a a finisher, waterer, embosser, shearer and hot processor. His works was in Fairfield Street, Manchester. By 1890 he had moved to the Chatsworth Mills, Hyde Road, Gorton, near Belle Vue Station. An 1890 directory describes the company as being waterers, embossers, finishers etc. of textiles and manufacturers of every description of fancy papers.

John Smith and Sons, Openshaw
The firm of John Smith and Sons, iron founders, of the Openshaw Bridge Works, was established in Tamworth street by 1890. They were manufacturers of domestic fire grates.

Joseph Stubbs, Openshaw
Joseph Stubbs, iron founders, moved from Ancoats to Louisa Street between 1890 and 1900. They described themselves as "patentees of special machinery for winding, clearing and warping yarn". Later, with the decline of the cotton trade, they ceased to specialise and made castings for all purposes.

Abbey Hey Pottery, Gorton
In or about 1893 Slack and Brownlow built a pottery in Abbey Hey on a piece of open ground between Jackson (Jetson) Street and Abbey Hey Lane. The main product was jam jars.

Holden and Brooks and Co., Gorton
In 1883 Robert Brooke and Harry Holden, employed by the Manchester Locomotive Manufacturers, Sharpe, Stewart and Co., set up business on their own account, basically as manufacturers of the Boiler Feed Injector. This was a pump for feeding water into steam boilers. Their works was in Simon Street, Salford. In 1897 they moved to the Sirius Works, Heywood Street, now renamed Haverford Street, West Gorton.

The Vaughan Crane Company, Openshaw
In 1872 Henry Vaughan of Lincoln and Mr J.S.Stubbs set up an engineering works, known as the Royal Iron Works, in Openshaw for the manufacture of millwright equipment and other small engineering supplies. The site was between Ambrose Street and the railway. The partnership broke up in 1879.

In 1886 William Henry, a son, joined Henry Vaughan at the Royal Iron Works. In 1890 an associate company, the Vaughan Pulley Company was formed. Vaughan and Son Ltd., were soon manufacturing overhead travelling cranes, both electric and hand operated.

1900 to 1945

The pattern of Gorton and Openshaw's industrial development, shaped in the second half of the 19th century, lasted for approximately 100 years, and by and large the industrial scene continued to be dominated well into the second half of the 20th century by the old household names, such as Gorton Tank, Beyer Peacock, Brooks and Doxey, Kendall and Gent, Holden and Brooke, B. and S. Massey and the Vaughan Crane Company.

Rylands' Mill
Rylands' Mill closed down in 1919.

Crossley Motors
In 1906 Crossley Bros. began the manufacture of motor cars at their Openshaw works and then in 1910 transferred production to their gas plant works on Gorton Lane, Gorton, and a new company, Crossley Motors, came into existence. Their cars were large, hand-built and expensive. They included the 20.9 h.p. "Super Six" and the 15.7 h.p. "Six".

When in the years following the Great War there was an increasing demand for a small, cheap car, Crossley Motors attempted to break into this new market with the manufacture of a small 10 h.p. car. Commercially the car was unsuccessful. They were, however, successful in their manufacture of motor buses.

In 1917 Crossley Bros. built DH9 aeroplanes at their National Aeroplane Works on Crossley Road, Heaton Chapel.

Electromotors, Openshaw
Electromotors had a works in Louisa Street, Openshaw, as early as 1914. Between the two world wars they amalgamated with Laurence Scott under the name of Laurence Scott and Electromotors.

Ferguson, Pailin Electrical Engineers
Ferguson, Pailin Ltd. appear to have been established in Buckley Street and Edward Street shortly after the Great War.

Hugon and Co., suet refiners, Ogden Lane, Openshaw
Hugon and Co. of Pendleton acquired the High Bank Mill some time between 1914 and 1921 for the manufacture of Atora suet.

Lindsay and Williams, cable manufacturers supplies, Openshaw Bridge Works
Lindsay and Williams began in Bennett Street, Ardwick. In the early 1920s the company moved to Openshaw and took over the old horse-tram depot at the corner of Ashton Old Road and Louisa Street.

Abbey Hey Pottery
Abbey Hey Pottery closed down in the 1920s because their stone jars could not complete with the glass jars that were now on the market.

Armstrong Whitworth and English Steel
In the years following the Great War, a fall in the home demand for armaments and the loss of foreign markets brought about a recession in the iron and steel industries. Armstrong Whitworth began to reduce its workforce. In 1926 the machine tool department was closed down and the machinery sold to Craven's.

In 1929 Armstrong Whitworth, Vickers and Cammell Laird merged to form the English Steel Corporation. As part of a plan of rationalisation the small-tool and the steel tool business of the Corporation was concentrated at Openshaw in the North Street works of Armstrong Whitworth. The works became known as English Steel. The work carried out on the Whitworth Street side of Ashton Old Road was transferred to the Elswick works of Armstrong Whitworth. The transfer was completed in 1934 and most of the buildings were demolished.

In its life, first under the name of Joseph Whitworth and then of Armstrong Whitworth, the Openshaw works had manufactured a wide range of steel products: small tools, machine tools, railway engines, cranes, paper-making machinery, tanks, ammunition, naval guns and gun turrets. The turrets, between 70 and 90 feet in height, were built in deep brick-lined pits and on completion were dismantled and taken, first by road to Trafford docks, then by sea to Portsmouth, where they were fitted onto warships. The gun turrets of the cruisers Achilles and Exeter, which played an important part in the battle of the River Plate, were made at Armstrong Whitworth's.

Vickers Armstrong
In 1938 when rearmament had begun, Vickers Armstrong began building three new workshops on the Whitworth Street site for the production of Bofors guns, anti-aircraft guns and guns for use on aircraft.

Ashbury's Carriage Works
Ashbury's Carriage Works closed down about 1925 and the site was sold to the London North Eastern Railway Company, who used it as a centre for the distribution of goods by road.

John Smith and Sons, Tamworth Street
The closure of the firm of John Smith and Sons shortly after 1937 may have been caused by changing fashion. Their works had specialised in the manufacture of iron fire-grates. In many homes these were being replaced by the new porcelain-finished bungalow ranges.

George Saxon and Co. Ltd
The firms of George Saxon Ltd and Saxon Brothers closed down in 1943. According to a former employee there was no apparent reason for the closure as they had plenty of work. Although there was no longer a demand from cotton mills for their engines, they had been kept busy with repair work, building grinding mills for potteries, machinery for rubber manufacturers and marine engines for the navy.

The Vaughan Crane Company, Openshaw
During the economic depression of the 1930s Vaughan's ran into financial difficulties. They were saved from going out of business by Herbert Morris of Loughborough. Although they became a subsidiary of Herbert Morris, they continued trading under their own name and with their own board of management.

James Johnstone and Co.
The firm of James Johnstone and Co., paint manufacturers, was established in Glasgow in 1890. In 1920 they moved to Gorton and set up a works at the corner of Wellington Street and Cross Lane. By 1922 Johnstone's had left Wellington Street and had taken over the old Abbey Hey School, built by John Rylands.

Long and Crawford Ltd., 200 Gorton Road, West Gorton
The firm of Long and Crawford was established in 1911. They specialise in switchgear and switchboards.

Brayshaw Tools, Belle Vue Works, Boundary Street, Gorton
Brayshaw Tools was founded in or about 1890. About 1933 the firm moved from Mulberry Street, Hulme, to Boundary Street.

The decline of manufacturing industry after 1945

By 1982 only four of the Gorton and Openshaw manufacturing firms established before 1945 were still in business. The others had either closed down completely or had moved elsewhere. The survivors were Crossleys, Holden and Brooke, Ferguson and Pailin and Lindsay and Williams.

Crossley Engines
After a series of mergers beginning in 1966, Crossley Brothers had by 1981 become CROSSLEY ENGINES functioning within the NEI APE Company. CROSSLEY ENGINES specialise in the manufacture of the Crossley-SEMT-Pielstick engines, which are used for powering both ships and generating

set installations. They have fitted them in container ships, warships, tankers, car ferries and cargo vessels for customers in New Zealand, Mexico, Norway, Russia, the U.S.A., Greece, Canada, Hong Kong and of course the U.K.

The use of these engines for the generation of electricity has almost been equally world-wide: Nigeria, Jordan, Malaysia, Guyana, Ecuador, the Sudan, Australia, the South Pacific Islands and the U.K.

Ferguson and Palin
About 1960 Ferguson and Pailin merged with the A.E.I., which is now known as the G.E.C.

Below is a list of closures:

Vickers Armstrong 1950
Vickers Armstrong was opened in anticipation of the Second World War. It ceased production in 1945, but did not officially close until 1950.

Brooks and Doxey 1956
Brooks and Doxey closed down because of the fall in demand for textile machinery and the work was transferred to Platt's of Oldham.

Crossley Motors 1956
In 1951 Crossley Motors moved to the Errwood Park Works, Crossley Road, Heaton Chapel and was absorbed into the Associated Equipment Company Ltd.

Gorton Tank 1963
Gorton Tank was a victim of the so-called "BeechingAxe", named after Richard (now Lord) Beeching. Richard Beeching was the leading member of the Special Advisory Group, which drew up a plan to restructure British Rail by closing down unprofitable lines and uneconomic workshops. When the decision was taken in 1962 to close the works,the labour force was 1700. *(Daily Telegraph 20.9.1962)*

Hampson and Wrigley Between 1960 and 1965
This closure was probably brought by a shortage of work due to a decline in the cotton trade.

Robert Williams Between 1960 and 1965
The firm of Robert Williams and Son was taken over by J. and J. Makin and the work was transferred to premises in Rochdale.

The Admiralty 1963
Gunnery Department
(A.G.E.D.)
The depot was set up in 1946, after Vickers Armstrong workers had protested against the closing of the works. It employed about 260 workers. The depot was transferred to Coventry and Glasgow as an economy measure.

Beyer Peacock 1966
The fall-off in orders, which led to the closure, was brought about indirectly by the decision of British Railways to abandon steam. Overseas railways, who were the customers of Beyer Peacock, followed suit. *(See "Beyer Peacock" by R.L. Hills and D. Patrick)*

Joseph Stubbs 1966
Falling orders and the financial squeeze were blamed for the closure. *(See the Gorton and Openshaw Reporter, 21.10.1966)*

Brayshaw Tools 1966
This firm closed down in July, 1966. The reason given in the Gorton and Openshaw Reporter of 18.11.1966 was that "it could not recruit enough workers".

Kendall and Gent 1967
The closure of Kendall and Gent was the consequence of a take-over by Staveley Indstries. The workers were offered employment at Craven Brothers of Reddish and George Richards of Altrincham. Both firms were members of Staveley Industries. *(Gorton and Openshaw Reporter, 4.10.1966)*

Hugon and Co. early 1970s
Hugon's moved to Hartlepool.

Johnstone's Paints 1974
Johnstone's moved to a new works on Edge Lane, Droylsden.

Follows and Bate 1978

The Vaughan Crane Company 1979
Shortly after the war, new offices and works were built on Vaughan Street, Ardwick, to which all the manufacturing and administration functions of the Openshaw works were transferred between 1949 and 1950. The company was at this time prosperous, employing about 600 workpeople and manufacturing a wide range of overhead electrical cranes. In the 1970s its business was gradually transferred to the parent company, Herbert Morris of Loughborough. The final closure took place in 1979.

The English Steel Corporation 1970
Edgar Allen (Steels) and Edgar Allen (Tools) took over the North Street works of English Steel about 1970. They closed down in 1980.

B. and S. Massey 1981
"Heavy losses and difficult trading conditions have led to the decision (to close) at B. and S. Massey's works in Ashton Old Road, Openshaw." "The 120 year-old business remained under family control until 1971, and is now owned by the Davy Corporation. It is to be merged with the Hydraulic Machinery division of Davy- Loewy, based at Darnall, Sheffield." *(The Manchester Evening News, 10.7.1981)* There was a loss of 150 jobs.

Laurence Scott 1982
and Electromotors
In 1981 the management decided to transfer most of their work to their Norwich factory, retaining only ten jobs in Louisa Street. The workforce was 650. A bitter struggle followed, ending in 1982 when machinery was lifted by helicopter out of the factory.

Other Gorton and Openshaw manufacturers which have closed down *(based on a list at the Greater Manchester Record Office, compiled by F. Wightman)*

Bratby and Hinchcliffe, manufacturers of bottling machinery, moved from Sandford Street, Ancoats, to the Crossley Motors Works, when the latter closed down. They ceased production in the 1970s.

Carrington Sellars, makers of Portland cement, Fairfield Road, Higher Openshaw, Closed in 1933.

T. Davies and Son , Brook Street/James Street off Pottery Lane, West Gorton, manufacturers of foundry equipment, tanks, galvanised baths, steel plate work.

Garner's Foundry, Victoria Street, Openshaw, heavy iron founders, engine and machine tool casting. Closed down 1950.

R.A. Hicks and Sons , Cornwall Street, Openshaw, makers of candied peels and cherries.

Lambourne and Co., Constructional engineers, Wheler Street, Openshaw, specialists in theatre steel work. Closed 1939.

H.O Morrison and Co., Ltd , heavy chemical manfacturers, Gorton Road, West Gorton. This firm manufactured phosgene gas, which was used in the 1914-1918 war. The firm closed in 1922.

A.S. Main and Co., Thames Street, West Gorton, manufacturers of gas stoves and ranges etc.

Robinson's Bridge Foundry, Openshaw, Closed 1924.

Robinson's Engine Works, Lees Street, Openshaw.

United Steel Wire Mills Ltd., 85 South Street, Openshaw, bead wire for cycle tyres and motor vehicles.

Walker Hannah Bearing Co., Birch Street, West Gorton, manufacturer of cheap, light, cast-iron bearings. The firm, which employed about 25 workpeople, closed in 1933.

George Wood and Son, Wesley Street, Openshaw, mineral water manufacturers and botanic beer brewers. There was a branch of the firm in Dyer Street.

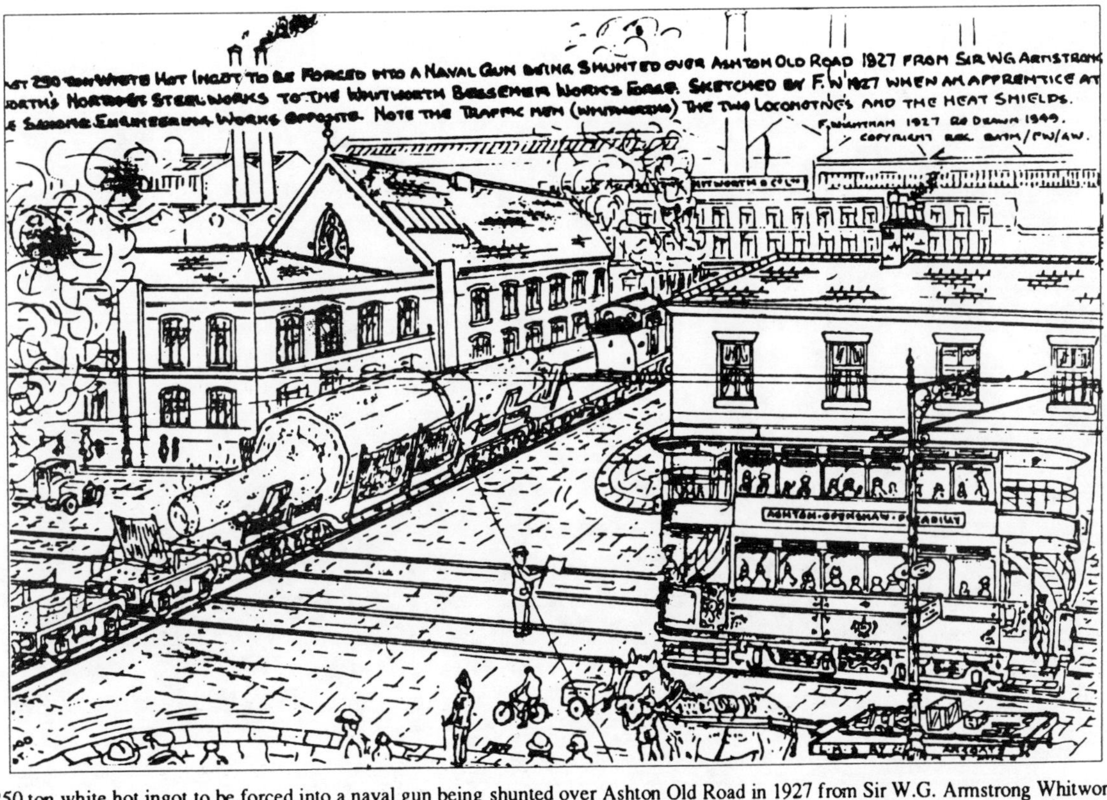

The last 250 ton white hot ingot to be forced into a naval gun being shunted over Ashton Old Road in 1927 from Sir W.G. Armstrong Whitworth's North Street steel works to the Whitworth Bessemer Works forge. Sketched by Frank Wightman when an apprentice at Saxon's engineering works opposite. Note the traffic men *(Whitworth's)*, the two locomotives and the heat shields. *(courtesy F. Wightman)*

Gorton Mills, Abbey Hey Lane, began working in 1825. Closed down in 1919.

Gorton Tank - photograph taken from the round tower *(the Smithy)*.
The building with the lancet-shaped windows in the right-hand top corner is the Press Street side of Cornwall Street Baptists Chapel.

CHAPTER VI

LOCAL GOVERNMENT

Local Government in Gorton up to 1863

Until the development of manufacturing industry brought about an increase in population, the main concern of local government in Gorton was care of the poor, maintenance of law and order and upkeep of roads.

Care of the poor
The Poor Law of 1601 made each parish responsible for its poor. This responsibility was delegated to churchwardens, assisted by overseers of the poor. The overseers were empowered to levy a rate and to buy stocks of material on which the unemployed could work. Until 1662 care of the poor of the whole of the Manchester parish was in the hands of the churchwardens and overseers of the poor of St. Mary's Church, (the old name for the cathedral). In 1662 the Poor Relief Act ordered the division of overlarge parishes for poor relief purposes and the people of Gorton became responsible for looking after their own poor.

The 1722 Workhouses Act forbade the distribution of outdoor relief and ordered each parish or township to build a workhouse. The poorhouse, as Gorton's workhouse was called, was on High Bank, at its junction with Hyde Road. It was often referred to humorously as "Chatsworth House" after the residence of the Dukes of Devonshire. In 1830 it was pulled down and a new one erected in Wellington Street.

Law and Order
Responsibility for maintaining law and order was in the hands of two village constables. Village constables were chosen every year from among able-bodied ratepayers between the ages of 25 and 55. They were not paid a salary, but they were reimbursed for their expenses, usually incurred by way of liquid refreshment. In 1623 the village constables for Gorton were James Worthington and Thomas Graver.

The Overseers of the Highways
By the 18th century Gorton had become responsible for the upkeep of its roads and overseers of the highways were appointed. In 1772 there were voluntary subscriptions towards maintenance of roads. In 1834 a highway rate was levied. After Stockport Road and Hyde Road were turnpiked, Gorton still made a contribution to their upkeep.

Town's meetings and "select vestries"
Originally the "vestry" was the ruling authority of the parish. This was a meeting of members of the parish held in the vestry. When parishes became overlarge, individual townships were allowed to hold their own "vestries". In Gorton these meetings were called "town's meetings". They were open to all householders.

From 1830 "select vestries" were held in Gorton. These were committees of well-to-do householders. Without their orders no poor relief could be given by overseers of the poor. In 1834 a Gorton select vestry of thirteen men included: John Shawcross, a dyer with a works at Gorton Brook; Aaron Lees, a director of Gorton Mill on Abbey Hey Lane; Thomas Pownall, the owner of the tannery on Tan Yard Brow; John Buckley, the owner of the Chapel House Inn and the nearby brewery and bleachworks.

Formation of the Chorlton Poor Law Union, February 1837
In 1834 Parliament passed the Poor Law Amendment Act, the purpose of which was to replace the old system of poor relief with one that would reduce the burden of the poor rate. Parishes and townships were to be grouped in Unions, each of which would maintain a workhouse. These were called Union workhouses. Popularly they were known as "Bastilles".

The Act ordered that only the aged and the infirm were to be given outdoor relief i.e. in their own homes. The able-bodied poor and their families were to be given the choice of starving at home or going to the workhouse. Conditions were to be made harsh to discourage the able-bodied from seeking relief. The Act was based on the recommendations of a Poor Law Commission, whose secretary, Edwin Chadwick, was born in Longsight.

In February, 1837, the Chorlton Poor Law Union was formed. It comprised the eleven townships of Chorlton on Medlock, Hulme, Ardwick, Gorton, Rusholme, Levenshulme, Burnage, Stretford, Moss Side, Withington and Didsbury. Chorlton Cum Hardy and Openshaw were added before the end of the year.

It was soon found impossible in the north of England to enforce that part of the Act which forbade the giving of outdoor relief to the able-bodied.

The Wellington Street, Gorton, workhouse continued to operate as a Union workhouse for a time, together with one in Stretford. By 1841 it had apparently closed down for it is not shown in the census returns for that year.

Chorlton Union Account Book
1837 Dec. 23 In maintenance in the Gorton W:House a pauper 10 days 4s 3d

Nell Lane Workhouse
In 1855 a new Union workhouse was built in Nell Lane, Withington, replacing the one in Stretford. In December, 1859, the Nell Lane workhouse was looking after 350 men and women who were either disabled or old and infirm, 40 able-bodied men and women and 195 children of all ages up to 16,

61 idiots and 7 vagrants. A workhouse school had an attendance of 133 boys and girls. Industrial training was given to 82 boys and girls.

As time went on the workhouse in Nell Lane found itself more and more dealing with the sick who could not afford the cost of medical treatment. Gradually it was transformed into a hospital and a new workhouse was built across the road. When in 1928 an Act of Parliament abolished workhouses, the "institution", as it was then called, found a new use as a home for old people.

Local Government in Openshaw up to 1863
No records of local government in Openshaw before 1863 have survived. However one can say with certainty that the township must have had the same system of local government by a vestry, supported by Overseers of the Poor and of the Highways and village constables.

The Gorton Local Board of Health and the Gorton Urban District Council

On 18.1.1864 the Manchester City News reported, "Two new local boards of health have been recently established in our neighbourhood - Gorton and Openshaw. Manchester is now almost completely surrounded by boards of health in which is placed the local government of all our surburban districts." It was the increase in the populations of the townships, a consequence of industrialisation, which had made a change in the system of local government essential.

Population	1801	1811	1821	1831	1841	1851	1861	1871
Gorton	1,127	1,183	1,604	2,623	2,422	4,476	9,897	21,616
Openshaw	339	459	497	838	2,283	3,759	8,623	11,108

Population	1881	1891
Gorton	33,096	15,215
Openshaw	16,153	

The decrease in the population of Gorton between 1881 and 1891 is due to the amalgamation of West Gorton with Manchester in 1890.

In Gorton the decision to replace the old system of local government was taken at a public meeting in 1863, convened by the surveyors themselves, who felt that ".... their powers were inadequate for carrying out useful and general improvements". Two thirds of the Gorton ratepayers present voted to adopt the general Government Act of 1848. This Act, passed after an outbreak of cholera and when the death rate was abnormally high, encouraged the setting up of local boards of health as the best way of stamping out disease.

The minutes of the Gorton Local Board of Health begin on 18,11,1863. In 1894 the Board became the Gorton Urban District Council. In 1908 Gorton amalgamated with Manchester. Openshaw had already amalgamated with Manchester in 1890.

The "ashpit question"
In 19th century Gorton the equivalent of the w.c. or lavatory was usually called the "privy" and occasionally the "closet" or "necessary". The privy was at the back of the house and was built over an ashpit. It was customary for the privies to be in pairs to serve adjoining houses, with one ashpit to each pair. In 1889 the number of ashpits in Gorton was 5,145, whilst the number of privies was 9,192. *(Collection, Treatment and Disposal of Town Refuse by C.J. Lomax, P.38)* No detailed description of a Gorton privy and ashpit has survived, if ever one existed, but it is reasonable to assume that like most others throughout the country the privy was brick built with a roof of stone slabs and that the ashpit was lined with bricks.

The ashpit was a depository for the domestic refuse such as ashes and potato peelings and for excreta from the privy. The ashpit and privy together were usually termed the "privy-midden", "midden" being a synonym for "ashpit".

The problems arising from the "privy-midden" were known collectively as the "ashpit question". The most urgent problem facing the newly formed Gorton Local Board was the problem of emptying the ashpits. This duty lay with the owners of the property but it was not satisfactorily carried out and in May, 1868, the Board decided "to purchase two carts and to hire two horses and men to remove the night soil and rubbish from the streets night or day for six months". *(Gorton Local Board Minutes)*

In 1869 the Board invited tenders for emptying the ashpits and in 1870 awarded the contract to Peter Clough, the proprietor of the Pineapple public house, Openshaw. The contract was for three years and Peter Clough was paid £500 per annum. His work however proved unsatisfactory. In November, 1870, he was reported for removing night soil at noon from Belle Vue Street. By law it should have been removed between 10 p.m. and 6 a.m. In the same month he received a writ from Mr Whyatt for dumping manure opposite the gates of Belle Vue gaol for sale to farmers. *(Gorton and Openshaw Reporter, 26.11.1870)*

Eventually the Gorton Local Board used its own labour for emptying ashpits. The night-soil men were paid 22s per week, well above the 12s which was the average pay for a labourer. From statistics given by C.J. Lomax in his "Collection, Treatment and Disposal of Town Refuse" it appears that ashpits in Gorton were emptied once a year and that 20 men and 6 carts were employed. The system was still inadequate. Emptying once a year was insufficient and in February, 1889, the ashpits were so full that "refuse was coming out of doors (of the ashpits) and running into passages". *(G.O.R. 9.2. 1889)*

Under the Gorton Urban District Council (1894-1908) there was an improvement. Ashpits were not to exceed 6 cubic feet and were emptied once a week. The pail system was also introduced. This consisted of a pail under the seat and admitted of a much more complete cleaning than the privy-midden system. It was also more expensive, because it required regular removal of the pail and its replacement by a clean pail. It was known as the "Dolly Varden" system, because of some real or imaginary similarity of the pail to the Dolly Varden hat. The carts on which the "Dolly Vardens" were carried were called "Dolly Carts".

When in 1908 Gorton amalgamated with Manchester both the pail system and the privy-midden system were in common use. Manchester had already converted to water-closet system. The City of Manchester Proceedings for 1910-11 reported a rapid conversion of pail-closets in Gorton to water-closets. The same publication for 1911-12 shows that 2,734 privy-middens in Gorton were replaced by water-closets.

Gas lighting
Rate books show that Gorton received its first supply of gas - from the Manchester Gas Committee - in or before 1858. Gas was first used for street lighting. Hyde Road and Cross Street each got two gas lamps in 1864. Gas was paid for according to the number of lamps and the length of time they were burning. The minutes of the Gorton Local Board record that in September, 1864, two lamplighters were appointed and were paid threepence per lamp per week. As regards houses the owner decided whether a house should be supplied with gas.

Water Supply
Although there were water mains in Gorton in the 1840s, the supply of water to the township as a whole was unsatisfactory until late in the century. The inadequacy of the water supply was described in graphic terms by the Gorton Medical Officer of Health in a report dated the 29th May, 1873. He wrote:
"In some cases there is no provision of drinking water. Some people depend on the goodwill of the proprietors of neighbouring pumps. One clump of cottages drew their supply for all hot cooking purposes from a foul puddle, whose only feeder was a filthy ditch, the outlet of a filthier duckpond, the receptacle of the drainage from a midden. Chemical knowledge was superfluous in deciding as to the purity of such water, the analysis by the senses being absolutely conclusive."

One of the problems was the cost of laying water pipes. In 1871 the Manchester Corporation refused to supply Upper Gorton and Reddish Lane with water because the outlay would have been £600 and the income expected was expected to be only £45. Between 1872 and 1878 a series of Public Health Acts placed upon sanitary authorities the duty of supplying clean and wholesome water for their areas. In Gorton the cost was met by a charge on owners of the property in question.

Infectious diseases
Outbreaks of typhoid, cholera and smallpox continued during the period in office of both the Local Board and the Gorton Urban District Council. From 1870 an annual donation of £10 was made to the Manchester Royal Infirmary and to the Monsall Hospital to pay for treatment of infectious cases, but only when amalgamation with Manchester brought in a hygienic system of sewage disposal did the outbreaks end.

Infant mortality was high. Of 25 deaths reported in St. James's Parish magazine for October, 1905, 13 were children 14 months and below. The common children's diseases were measles, whooping cough, croup, diphtheria and scarlet fever, the latter occurring in a severe form that sometimes resulted in death. In recent times they have been almost eradicted by improved social conditions and immunisation.

Maintenance of Roads
In 1865 the Gorton Ratepayers Association complained that "The whole township was a sea of mud". *(Gorton and Openshaw Reporter 4,3.1865)*

The Fire Brigade
Gorton did not have its own fire brigade. When, in February 1860, a fire broke out in John Rylands' mill, the blaze was put out by one fire engine from Fairfield and two from Gorton Tank. *(Ashton Reporter 4.2.1860)* In 1870 the Gorton Local Board came to an arrangement with the Manchester Fire Brigade whereby in return for an annual retainer of £100 they would come out to any fire in Gorton, but the owners of the building would have to pay for each service.

Problems of communication made the service given by the Manchester Fire Brigade less than adequate. The engines were stationed in Pollard Street, Ardwick, and for a time there was no telephone. When a fire broke out in Birch Street, Gorton, the Manchester engines took over forty minutes to get to the scene of the fire only to find that the fire brigade of the Union Iron Works was already there. *(Gorton and Openshaw Reporter 21.8.1880)* The Reporter commented on the absence of a telephone in its edition of 28.8.1880.

Education - *see Schools*

The amalgamation of West Gorton with Manchester
As early as 1867 a meeting was called in Gorton to discuss the question of amalgamation with Manchester. In 1889 the issue was still a very live one and it was discussed together with three other alternatives: the retention of the Local Board, a charter of incorporation for Gorton and amalgamation with Openshaw to form a borough.

There were strong arguments for amalgamation with Manchester. Gorton was dependent on Manchester for water and gas and both could be obtained more cheaply if Gorton became part of Manchester. The biggest problem, however, was the disposal of sewage which could only be solved by amalgamation, for Manchester was refusing to take drainage from any other extra-municipal area. An article in the Gorton and Openshaw Reporter of 22.3.1889 on the subject went on to say "Gorton had been governed for 25 years by a Local Board and at the present time has less to show for it than any other other district round Manchester. The streets are unfinished and many are badly lighted".

In February, 1890, a poll of ratepayers and property owners was held to decide the question of amalgamation. St. Clement's ward and St. Mark's ward voted for amalgamation whilst the Town Hall ward and St. James's ward voted against. The first two wards, which comprised West Gorton, became part of Manchester.

The amalgamation of the rest of Gorton with Manchester
In 1907 the question of amalgamation with Manchester was again to the fore in independent Gorton. A letter from Councillor W. Walker, published in the Gorton and Openshaw Reporter, gave the main arguments in favour:

1. There were no schools in Gorton equipped to prepare children for the salaried pupil teachers examination and therefore children who wished to sit the examination had to attend schools outside Gorton.
2. 1700 Gorton children received elementary education outside Gorton.
3. Gorton Urban District Council had an overdraft of £10,000 for which the banks were pressing.

4. There was no hospital accommodation in or near Gorton.
5. The sewage works was too small and out of date.
6. Manchester provided Gorton with gas, electric light and power, trams and a fire brigade.

In November, 1907 Gorton voted in favour of amalgamation and in November, 1908 became part of Manchester.

The Openshaw Local Board of Health

The Openshaw Local Board of Health was established towards the end of 1863. It faced the same problems as the Gorton Local Board and the main one was the disposal of sewage.

In 1865 the Openshaw Ratepayers Association was complaining that the contents of the ashpits were left on the surface of South Street and they recommended that the Local Board should undertake the work of emptying them. The association also complained that workers on their way to Beyer Peacock were up to their knees in mud in Wellington Street. One of the members added that the streets of Gorton were as bad as Openshaw's and that there was no advantage in moving house. *(Manchester City News, 25.11.1865)*

By 1875 the Local Board was undertaking the emptying of ashpits and privies. Its methods met with a good deal of criticism. It was claimed that untreated sewage was drained into Gorton Brook, which also contained refuse from dye and bleach works, paper staining and waste water from the boilers of cotton mills. Excreta was carted onto a plot of land adjoining the canal from where it was disposed of to farmers.

Openshaw, like Gorton, paid the Manchester Corporation for the use of their Fire Brigade.

The question of amalgamation with Manchester does not appear to have caused the controversy that it did in Gorton. Possibly the issues were more clear cut. Openshaw had a smaller population - in 1890 it was about 20,000 against an approximate 40,000 for Gorton - and so was too small to continue as an independent township. In 1889 the Openshaw Local Board recommended amalgamation on the grounds that it would bring about better street lighting, better policing, free use of Manchester's fire brigade and a reduction in the price of gas and water. A majority of Openshaw rate-payers voted in favour of amalgamation and in 1890 Openshaw became part of Manchester.

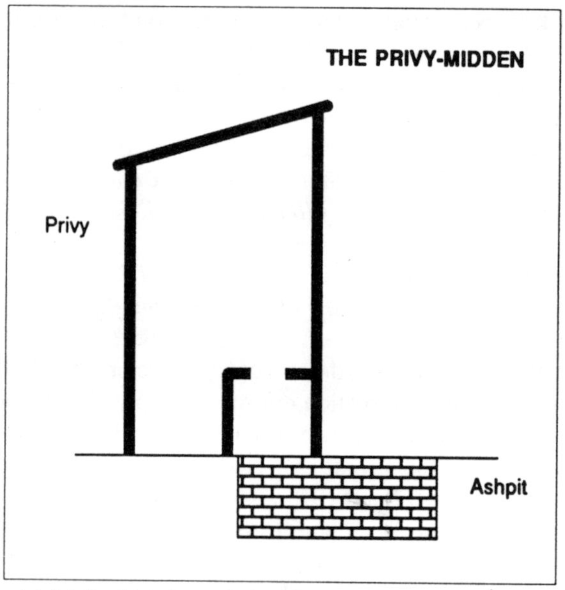

A brick-lined ashpit or midden served each pair of privies. The ashpit was also used as a repository for household rubbish.

A rear view of Ashton Fold. Wellington Street Baptists is at the back on the left and Garlick Street on the right.

CHAPTER VII

ROADS

Stockport Road is believed to have been a Roman road, linking, via Stockport, the fort in Manchester with Buxton.

THE SALTER-GATES - REDDISH LANE, TAN YARD BROW AND ABBEY HEY LANE

Before the agricultural revolution a shortage of winter fodder made it necessary for farmers to slaughter a high proportion of their stock in autumn. To preserve the meat for later consumption large quantities of salt were needed. Salt from Cheshire was brought into South Lancashire across the Mersey at the Didsbury ford and then along Saltergate, the old name for Burnage Lane and Slade Lane. There was also another salter's track, leading from the same ford over Heaton Moor, across Stockport Road at Heaton Chapel and then on into Reddish Lane. The track then ran north along Reddish Lane and via Tan Yard Brow into Abbey Hey Lane. From Abbey Hey Lane it continued into Edge Lane and on through Droylsden and Failsworth. *(History of Newton Chapelry, Vol. 55, page 440)*

Pink Bank Lane was originally Pink Pank Lane, an old pack-horse road, which ran from Stockport Road to Gorton. It is possible that its name came from the sound made by pack-horses or clog-shod passengers on the cobble-stone surface between high banks. *(History of Newton Chapelry, Vol. 55, page 432)*

The Turnpike Roads

When in the 18th century expansion of trade made an improvement in roads essential, turnpike trusts were granted parliamentary powers to erect toll-gates and exact tolls from the road users in return for making and repairing some particular stretch of highway. Up to 1773 tolls were collected by servants of the turnpike trust. In that year it became compulsory for trustees to auction the collection of tolls. Avoiding toll-bars by turning off the turnpike road into a side lane was common practice. To prevent this happening side bars were erected.

STOCKPORT ROAD AND THE MANCHESTER AND BUXTON TURNPIKE TRUST

When the Manchester and Buxton Turnpike Trust was established in 1724, Wellington Road had not been built. The route from Manchester was along Stockport Road and into Stockport via Lancashire Hill, then along Hillgate, eventually emerging on the Buxton Road.

Yates' map of 1786 shows only one toll-bar on Stockport Road, a little south of the Slade Lane junction. This was known as the Longsight Bar. A sketch by F.C. Tavare of Longsight Bar shows a side bar on Slade Lane. By 1803 there were toll-bars at Heaton Norris and Heaton Chapel.

In or shortly before 1851 a toll-bar was set up on Stockport Road at the junction with Plymouth Grove - this part of Plymouth Grove is now Plymouth Grove West, being renamed after Plymouth Grove was extended some time after 1890. There was also a side-bar on Plymouth Grove West. The bar, shown in some detail on a map of 1851 and marked as the Longsight Bar, presumably replaced the Slade Lane bar. The Manchester to Buxton Turnpike Trust expired in 1873.

ASHTON OLD ROAD AND THE MANCHESTER AND SALTER'S BROOK TURNPIKE TRUST

Ashton Old Road formed part of the turnpike road which passed through Ardwick, Openshaw, Droylsden, Ashton-under-Lyne, Stalybridge and Mottram in Longdendale and which was administered by the Manchester and Salter's Brook Turnpike Trust. The Trust was established in 1731. At the Trinity Street library, Stalybridge, there is a minute book of the Trust covering the period 1733-1771 together with other documents relating to the Trust.

On 21.7.1733 the trustees agreed to erect turnpikes at Woodhead in Cheshire, at Three Lane Ends, Mottram, and at a point "midway between the two crosses of Manchester and Ashton-under-Lyne". This midway point was in Openshaw, presumably near where the Halfway House is now. On 16.8.1733 it was decided to move the toll-bar to the junction of Manchester Road and Audenshaw Road. Toll-keepers were appointed at an annual salary of £12 per annum. To guard against dishonesty they had to find sureties which varied between £200 and £500.

A turnpike was erected at a later date on Ashton Old Road on the Manchester side of its junction with Gorton Lane. It was known variously as Gorton Lane End Gate, Openshaw toll-bar and Ardwick toll-bar. In 1851 the toll-bar was removed, with the result that Gorton farmers with their horses and carts could drive to Manchester without payment. *(John Higson, Gorton Historical Recorder)* To prevent loss of revenue new side-bars were erected on Hyde Road at Church Lane, at that time called Kirkmanshulme Lane, and at the Plough Inn, to intercept traffic going up Wellington Street. The Gorton Lane toll-bar must have been replaced at a later date for a Mr Shaw, interviewed by the Gorton and Openshaw Reporter (25.2.1955), said that when he was a boy, "Ashton Old Road was a turn-pike with toll-gates and a toll-house in the centre of the road near St. Silas's Church". Mr Shaw was born about 1865.

Auctioning of tolls

An Act of 1773 made it necessry to auction the right to collect tolls. In 1801 and 1831 the auctions brought in the following amounts:

Gorton Lane End Gate	1801	£206	1831	£2300
Audenshaw Gate		£441		£2000
Mottram Gate		£386		£880
Woodhead Gate		£184		£370

The increase in the value of the tolls at the Gorton Lane End and Audenshaw gates reflects the rising prosperity of Manchester and Ashton.

The first new surface

The first new surface, built by the Turnpike Trust in 1733, was only three and a half yards wide. It was described as a "causeway". In 1736 the road was widened to eight yards and the surveyor was asked to "take note of any person's land they take into the road". Stones were bought in Openshaw and Ardwick or brought from the River Irwell in Clifton.

The diversion of Ashton Old Road at Little Droylsden

In his Historical and Descriptive Notices of Droylsden *(p.11)* Higson writes that Little Droylsden was "once intersected by the old road from Manchester to Ashton...." In the same book *(p.142)* he refers to the diversion of the road to what must have been its present line. This was probably the work of the Turnpike Trust.

The tolls

The tolls for coal, levied at the Audenshaw toll-bar in 1733, were: a halfpenny for every horse load, sixpence for every cart load and 12d for every waggon load. The horse would be a pack-horse. A cart had two wheels and a waggon four. An important concession was made in the case of corn. Corn going to the Ashton mills was allowed through the Audenshaw toll-bar without payment of toll. In 1755 the charge for post going from Manchester to Ashton via the Audenshaw toll-bar and carried by "one horse, mare or gelding" was 6d for three months.

In 1826 tolls at the Audenshaw and Gorton Lane End Gates were: gig with 1 horse, 6d; chaise with 2 horses, 1s; cart 6 inch wheels 2 horses, 10d; cart 6 inch wheels 1 horse, 9d; waggon 6 inch wheels 4 horses, 2s; single horses, 1d

A gig was a light two-wheeled carriage. A chaise was a light, open carriage for one or more persons. A six inch wheel was one which had a tyre six inches thick. The narrower the tyre the greater the damage to the road surface and the higher the toll.

Side bars and additional main road bars

To prevent road users avoiding payment of tolls, bars, often a chain bar, were erected across side streets. The first such bar - it was a chain bar - was fixed across Gorton Lane in 1742 at its junction with Ashton Old Road. A concession was made to people who lived in Gorton and the townships beyond and "whose direct way led them into the turnpike road through Gorton Lane". They were to pay full tolls on coal only. Until Hyde Road was built in 1818 the quickest way to Manchester from Gorton was via Gorton Lane and Ashton Old Road.

As the land at the side of the turnpike road became built up, so the opportunities for avoidance of tolls increased and additional side bars were requried. About 1865 a side bar was erected across Tipping Street and in 1878 one at the end of Rider Street. There was a side bar on Abbey Hey Lane.

In 1879 the trustees recommended the erection of bars across Ashton Old Road at three points. One bar was to be immediately to the east of Grey Mare Lane and Pottery Lane, another was to be a little to the west of the two lanes and a third was to be "near to and on the east side of Fairfield Lane and Ogden Lane". The latter became know as the Half Way House Chain-bar. The second bar may have been the one which was remembered by Mr Shaw. The Half Way House Chain-bar caused a good deal of resentment locally and a petition, dated 26.1.1882, was drawn up for its removal:

"We are engaged in the locality as milk sellers etc. many of us passing only a short distance along the road and we feel this toll to be a serious burden on our trade. We do not go forward to Manchester and therefore are not evaders of tolls for which this bar was fixed".

The petition bore the signatures of F. Ilderton M.D. and a number of milkmen, farmers and fishmongers. Dr Ilderton's residence was near St. Ann's and his surgery was on the far side of the canal bridge. There is no record of the outcome of the petition.

Criticisms of the surface of Ashton Old Road

In reply to a complaint that Ashton Old Road was dusty, the Trust said that all macadamised roads were dusty. *(G.O.R. 12.8.1871)* The system of road building devised by John Macadam entailed a ten inch layer of stones, each about the size of a golf ball, on the natural subsoil. The top stones would be crushed by the vehicles using the road to give a smoother surface.

In 1871 a patent crushing machine was used on Ashton Old Road. It weighed 17 tons and included "a wide crusher and two narrow ones behind used to consolidate the road. *(G.O.R. 3.8.1872)*

The macadamised surface was later replaced by one made of stone setts. This in turn with the coming of the motor car was replaced by an asphalt surface.

The end of the Manchester and Salter's Brook Turnpike Trust

The Trust expired on the 1st November, 1884.

The Manchester, Hyde and Mottram Turnpike Trust

Unlike Stockport Road and Ashton Old Road, which were in existence centuries before they were turnpiked, Hyde Road, or Sheffield New Road as it was at first called, was a completely new road, built by the Manchester, Hyde and Mottram Turnpike Trust through the fields that lay between Ardwick and Hyde. The Trust was established in 1818 by an Act of Parliament. Before Hyde Road was built, the way from Manchester to Hyde was along Ashton Old Road, Gorton Lane, Far Lane, Thornele Lane and Windmill lane.

Johnson's 1819 map shows only one toll-bar on the Gorton and Denton section of Hyde Road: the Canal Bridge Toll Bar at the Reddish Lane junction. The Ordnance Survey map of 1848 shows the Canal Bridge Toll Bar and one at Devonshire Street, then called Summer Place. Presumably traffic turned right here to follow the Chancery Lane, Great Ancoats and Piccadilly route to Market Street.

In 1851 side bars were erected at Church Lane, then known as Kirkmanshulme Lane, and at the Plough Inn. In his reminiscences of Gorton in the 1870s Sam Kirkman wrote of a toll-bar on Hyde Road at Grey Street, a little to the east of the railway viaduct, and of a side-bar in Belle Vue Street.

Expiry of the Manchester, Hyde and Mottram Turnpike Trust

The Manchester, Hyde and Mottram Turnpike Trust was due to expire on November 1st, 1878. However, the trustees applied to Parliament for an extension. A number of Gorton ratepayers opposed the extension. The Local Board were divided on the matter. The argument against the extension was that abolition would increase the rateable value of property on Hyde Road as it had done on Stockport Road and that if toll bars were not removed side streets would be more used and more money would have to be spent on repair.

The argument for extension was that abolition of tolls would result in traffic being diverted onto Hyde Road from Ashton Old Road - the Salter's Brook Trust did not expire until 1884 - and the expense of repair would fall heavily on Gorton ratepayers. *(Gorton and Openshaw Reporter, 16.2.1878)*

Eventually it was agreed that the life of the Trust should be extended until November 1st, 1879.

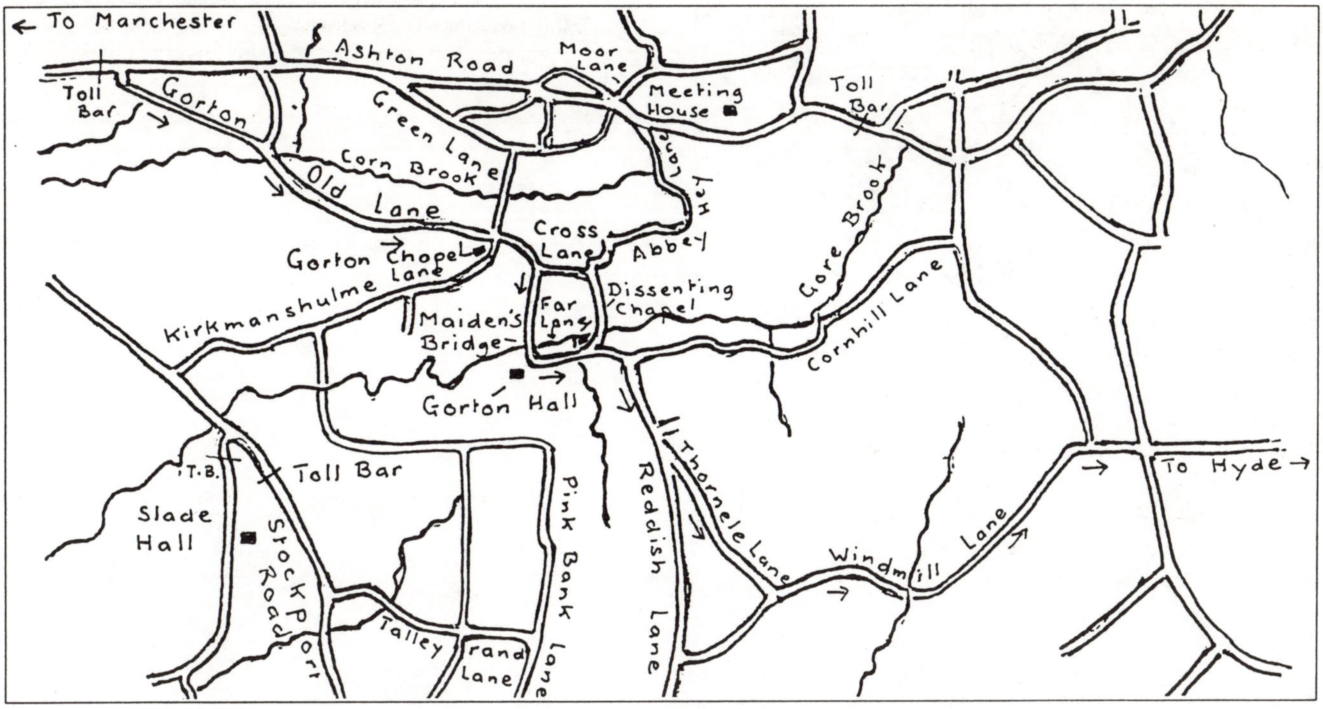

The arrows show the route from Manchester to Hyde before Hyde Road was built.

The Stockport Road toll-bar and the Slade Lane side bar.

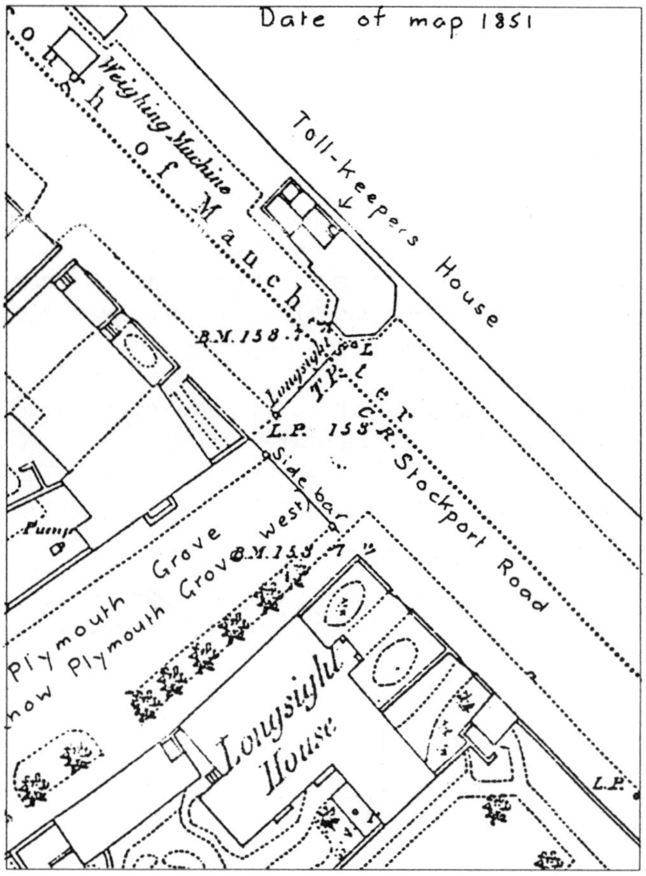

The Longsight Bar or Toll Point.

Toll-Bar on Ashton Old Road at the junction with Gorton Lane.

Audenshaw Side Bar. At the junction of Manchester Road and Audenshaw Road.

CHAPTER VIII

COACHES, BUSES AND TRAMS

Coaches

There was a coach service through both Gorton and Openshaw in the early 19th century. At least two coaches called at the New Inn, which stood on the site of the Half Way House. There was the "Fair Trader", which plied between Manchester and Stalybridge and the "Tantivy", which ran between Manchester and Sheffield. Coaches between Manchester and Newton and Hyde passed through Denton and Gorton every weekday.

Horse buses

Horses buses were the idea of John Greenwood, a Pendleton toll-keeper. In 1824 he opened a service between Pendleton and Market Street, carrying thirteen passengers. In 1852 a Mr McEwen introduced a new style of omnibus, which accommodated seventeen passengers inside and twenty five on top, sitting back to back. It was drawn by three horses abreast. He sold his entire property to a Mr Alderman Mackie, who with others established the Manchester Carriage Company in 1865. The Company enlarged its operations until a service of three-horse buses ran along most of the main roads.

There were two local omnibus companies. In April, 1863, George Kirkpatrick started the Denton Omnibus Company with only one bus, working Hyde Road as far as Denton. His vehicle was drawn by three horses. *(Gorton and Openshaw Reporter, 16.9.1871 and 2.11.1872)* On the 10th February, 1872, a new bus company, the Gorton Omnibus Company, began a service along Hyde Road to Manchester from the Plough Inn. *(G.O.R. 10.2.1872)* By 1876 it was operating services to Openshaw and to Ashton via Openshaw.

Competition between bus companies using the same route often took the form of "nursing", when a bus-driver would keep immediately in front of his rival to prevent him picking up fares. *(G.O.R.,10.9.1870).*

Some local services

1858

To Belle Vue gardens and Longsight to and from the corner of New Brown Street, every quarter of an hour. *(Source - street directory. Name of company not recorded, but probably McEwen's which had premises in Grey Street, Longsight.)*

1865

To Denton and Hyde via Gorton from the Angel Inn, Market Street, at 10 a.m. 1 p.m. 2.15 p.m. 4.15 p.m. 7 p.m. *(Source - street directory. Name of company not recorded).*

1866

The Manchester Carriage Company ran buses to Ashton via Openshaw and Fairfield and to Stockport via Stockport Road. The fare was 6d inside and 4d ouside. *(See "The Manchester Carriage and Tramways Company" by Edward Gray)*

1876

The Gorton Omnibus Company had a service to Manchester from the Plough Inn. An 1876 street directory advertises a service from Market Street to Gorton every 15 minutes from 8.30 a.m. to 8.15 p.m., but does not give the name of the company.

To Openshaw from Market Street every half hour from 8.30 a.m. to 9.30 p.m. To Ashton via Fairfield and Openshaw from Market Street at 9 a.m. and then every hour from 9.30 a.m. until 8.30 p.m. On Saturday every half hour from 1 p.m. until 7 p.m. *(Source - street directory)*

Horse-trams

The first horse-tram service in the Manchester area was instituted in 1877 between the Grove Inn, Bury New Road and Pendleton via Deansgate. In 1880 the Manchester Carriage and Tramways Company was formed. The new company opened the following routes from Piccadilly:

Levenshulme and Stockport	7.5.1880
Gorton	7.5.1880
Openshaw	28.3.1881
Ancoats, Ashton and Stalybridge via Ashton Old Road	4.6.1881
Gorton to Denton	17.8.1883

(See "Manchester Carriage and Tramways Company" by Edward Gray,p.75)

The earlier trams had a long knife-board seat on the top, open to the weather, similar to that of the horse-buses. The speed was 6-7 m.p.h. and the horses had to be rested at the termini. Most cars were reversible i.e. they were made to pivot on their "truck" or bogie, thus not requiring a turntable at the terminus. The Openshaw depot was on Louisa Street at the corner of Ashton Old Road. It was taken over by Lindsay and Williams in the 1920s. There were no fixed stops on the horse-tram routes. A car would stop wherever a passenger wished to alight.

Electric tramways

In 1897 the Manchester City Council decided to take over the tramways from the Manchester Carriage and Tramways Company and to adopt the system of overhead electric traction. The Company continued to operate individual routes until electrification was completed. Local routes began to operate electric trams on the dates given below:

Service	Date of Commencement
Belle Vue and Victoria Street	1.6.1902
Denton to Manchester via Hyde	1.6.1902
Audenshaw and Piccadilly via Openshaw	1.4.1903
Fairfield and Piccadilly	31.10.1904

Trolley boys were introduced in 1902 on the workmens cars. Their duty was to assist the guards by giving the driver the bell signals at the stops and helping the passengers to board and alight, as well as lending a hand with the reversal of the trolley. In 1933 as part of an economy drive the post was abolished.

Fares were much cheaper than those of the horse-trams. On the horse-trams there were no half-penny fares. On the electric trams one could travel three quarters of a mile for a halfpenny. For a penny the distance was a little over two miles, almost twice as far as on a horse-tram. As time went on fares were reduced, reaching their lowest in 1913, when the average length of the penny stage became nearly three miles. The electric trams were so profitable that for years they made a contribution to the rates.

The effect of the introduction of the electric tram

As fares were reduced, the electric tram became increasingly popular. It was used for visiting and for shopping trips to town. It enabled the shop assistant, the office clerk and the warehouseman to live in the outer suburbs and work in the city. Yet the artisan, who began work at 6 a.m. before the Great War and at 7.45 a.m. after, still preferred to live within easy walking distance of his place of employment.

The decline of the electric tram and its replacement by the motor bus

In the 1920s private bus companies began to operate services which competed with the tramways. To prevent an increase in competition, the Manchester Corporation began to run single-deck motor buses along the principle tramway routes. Charges were made higher to discourage short-distance traffic leaving the tramcar, but limited stops increased the speed for the journey. In 1929, when renewal of some lengths of the tramway track became due, it was decided to convert the route to buses. From then on it was the policy to replace trams by buses. There were two reasons for the change in policy: the high cost of track renewals and the lack of flexibility of the tram. The tramways closed down completely in 1949.

Trolley buses

In 1938 the Corporation substituted trolley buses for trams on the Ashton Old Road route. The experiment was continued on other routes. The great advantage of the trolley bus over the tram was the low capital cost as no track was required, but like the tram they lacked flexibility. On the 30th December, 1966, all trolley bus services were ended and replaced by the motor bus.

Horse tram on Ashton Old Road at the corner of Fairfield Road. The shafts of a second horse are visible. *(Courtesy Chris Makepeace)*

Clowes Street in 1906 looking towards the library.

Left: The smallest house in Gorton. It stood on Cross Lane at the corner with Kirk Street. The front door 5'6" high opened into a room barely 8' square.

Below: Old cottages on Abbey Hey Lane, Little Droylsden. Now demolished.

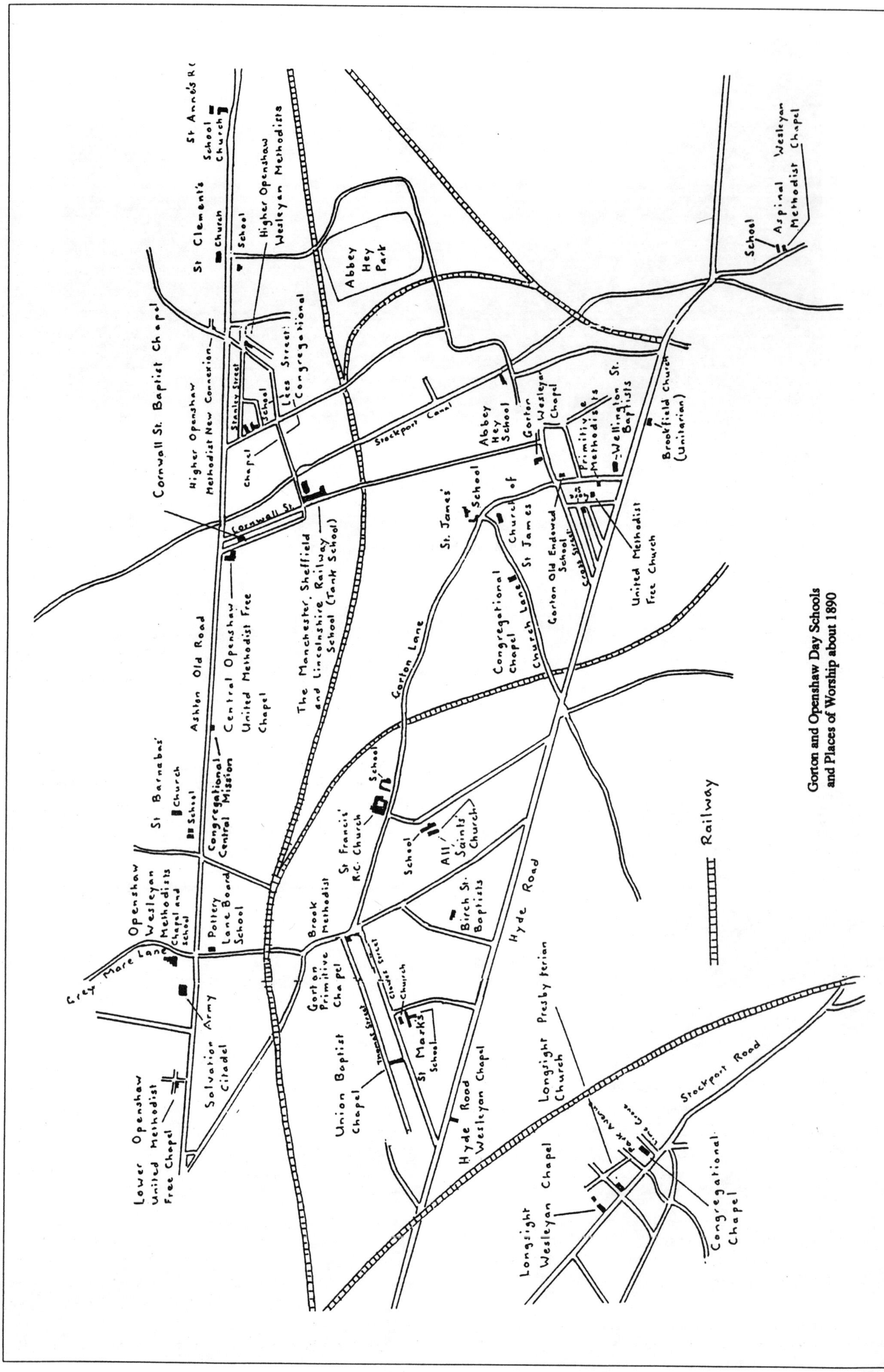

Gorton and Openshaw Day Schools and Places of Worship about 1890

CHAPTER IX

PLACES OF WORSHIP

GORTON

Gorton Parish Church, St. James

An entry in the Gorton Historical Recorder states that "Denton (St. Lawrence) Chapel was erected 1531-2; the inhabitants previously worshipping at Gorton".The first Gorton chapel is believed to have been a "chapel of ease" i.e. a chapel built for the convenience of the people of Gorton and districts nearby, who previously had to walk to St. Mary's - the old name for the Cathedral.

This chapel was replaced in 1755. The new chapel was often referred to as St. Thomas's chapel, although it had not been dedicated to the saint in question. In 1839 a new parish of St. James was formed and Gorton chapel became the parish church, but it was still known as St. Thomas's.

In 1870 it was decided that a new church should be built, because the existing church was unsafe. The old church with its burial ground lay on the west side of Church Lane (now Cambert Lane). The new church was built on the east side of Church Lane and so, to link it to the burial ground, Church Lane was diverted at its Wellington Street end around the burial ground.

The Dissenting Chapel

After the Reformation Protestantism spread throughout England and Gorton, too, was affected. At the bishop's visitation in 1592 it was found that the Puritan minister of Gorton chapel and the people were Puritans. The Victoria County History states that in 1662 the Puritan minister in charge of Gorton Chapel, William Leigh, "appears to have been ejected, but the chapel was used indifferently by both Episcopalians (members of the Church of England) and Presbyterians (Puritans) for some time afterwards".

By the end of the 17th century the dissenters were assembling for worship in the upper chamber of a house near the junction of Abbey Hey Lane and Cross Lane. A ladder was used to gain access. In 1703 a chapel was built behind Far Lane, at an angle of the Gore Brook, for the scattered dissenters of Gorton, Openshaw, Droylsden, Denton and Levenshulme. It was known as the Dissenting chapel or Independent Chapel. *(see the Manchester Guardian cuttings, 1901, Manchester Local History Library)*

According to the Victoria County History the congregation became Unitarian a century later. In 1871 the Dissenting Chapel was replaced by Brookfield Church

Brookfield Church, Unitarian

In 1871, Richard Peacock, a partner in the firm of Beyer Peacock, commissioned the erection of Brookfield Church, the successor to the Dissenting Chapel. At the same time, his partner, Charles Frederick Beyer, had assumed responsibility for the building of St. James's Church. The partners vied with each other as to which church should be completed first, as the winner would have the privilege of installing in its tower a peal of eight bells. Brookfield won and the tower was equipped with eight bells, each of which was inscribed with the name of a member of the Peacock family. *(Gorton and Openshaw Reporter, 28,12,1962)*

St. George's Church, Abbey Hey Lane

An 1871 street directory shows a Gorton Parish Church Mission Room on Abbey Hey Lane between Green Fold and Lake Street. The first St. George's Church, begun in April, 1902, now forms part of the Parish hall. In 1903 the parish of St. George was formed. The present church was built in 1912.

St. Philip's Church, Brookhurst Road

The parish of St. Philip was formed in 1904 out of the parish of St. James. Services (Evensong) were first held in a workshop in the back garden of a house in Levenshulme Road and there was a Sunday School in the upstairs room of a house in South Road. Later in the same year a temporary church, now the Church hall, was built and services were held there until the dedication of the present church in 1909. The temporary church was also used as a day school until the opening of Old Hall Drive School in 1914. *(See the "History of the Parish of St. Philip, Gorton, 1904-1969" by C.J. Coulson)*

The Church of our Lady of Mercy and St. Thomas of Canterbury, Mount Road

Shortly after the first world war housing development in the Mount Road area led to an increase in the number of residents. To meet their spiritual needs Church of England services were held, first in an army hut and then in a wooden hut.

In 1925 or 1926 a decision was taken by the Manchester ecclesiastical authorities to accept a bequest under the will of Mrs Angelina Frances Clarke. Mrs Clarke had left £10,000 with which to build a church in a poor area, but, so exacting were the conditions of the bequest and so at odds with the prevailing mood of the Church of England, the money had lain dormant for a number of years. Mrs Clarke made the following stipulations:

The church was to be called the Church of Our Lady of Mercy and St. Thomas of Canterbury. It was to be in the Renaissance style with three domes and was to carry the inscription "Out of your charity, Pray for the repose of Edward Clarke and Lena, his wife".

There was to be an annual requiem mass for the husband and

wife.
The altar was to be of marble with a baldachin or canopy.

The money left by Mrs Clarke proved insufficient to build the church exactly as she desired. Only two domes were built. The church was opened in 1927.

The Church and Monastery of St. Francis of Assisi, Gorton Lane
In 1861 Father Cardinal of St. Anne's, Higher Openshaw, built a school on Gorton Lane, which also served as a chapel. In the same year a group of Belgian friars of the Order of St. Francis of Assisi were sent to Openshaw on a teaching mission, at the same time accepting responsibility for between 400 and 500 Catholics in West Gorton. They began teaching in the school chapel built by Father Cardinal and later moved to Bankfield Cottage on Gorton Lane. The need for more permanent premises led to the building of the friary, which was begun in 1863 and completed in 1864. The church was opened in 1872.

The Sacred Heart Roman Catholic Church, Levenshulme Road
On the 25th January, 1902, the Gorton and Openshaw Reporter reported the opening of a "new Roman Catholic Church" in Levenshulme Road, Gorton. This new church was known as the "tin hut". It was replaced in 1926 by a new building, which in turn was replaced by the present church.

Aspinal Wesleyan Methodist Chapel, Reddish Lane
The history of Aspinal Wesleyan Chapel begins in 1795, when a class of thirteen members first met for instruction in Methodism in Brook Green. In 1808 a school-chapel was opened over a cottage on the site of the old school. It was known as "Aspinal Smithy". A chapel was built on an adjoining site in 1877, followed by new schools in 1887. A third chapel, opened in 1909, proved too large for modern needs and was replaced by a smaller building to accommodate both church and Sunday school. The opening ceremony of this new building was the 21st October, 1972.

Gorton United Methodist Free Chapel, Hyde Road, corner with Crosfield Grove
This chapel was opened in 1903. The money for the building was provided by a prominent local Free Methodist, J.H. Crosfield. The chapel replaced a school-room in Short Street, off Gore Street. With the closure of the Cross Lane and Wellington Street chapels in 1958, it became the central Gorton Chapel.

Abbey Hey Wesleyan Methodist Chapel
In 1897 the Methodists decided to start a mission in Abbey Hey. Two cottages were bought from a Mr Bousfield and used as a Sunday school. Two years later a plot of land at the corner of Jackson (Jetson) Street and Harrop Street was bought from Mr Harrop and a mission school-chapel was built on it. In 1953 a small chapel was built at right angles to the school.

St. Paul's Presbyterian Church, Abbey Hey Lane
This church was built in 1905 at the Openshaw end of Abbey Hey Lane. In 1965 a brick shell was built round the existing walls and the interior was modernised.

The Congregational Chapel, Cambert Lane
The Congregational Chapel on Cambert Lane was opened in 1883 and extended in 1905. It is now known as the Gorton United Reformed Church.

The Trinity Baptist Church, formerly known as Wellington Street Baptists
In 1828 two Baptists, Mr and Mrs Brooks, started meetings in their house in Ashton Fold and later used a larger room in a neighbouring cottage. In 1829 they opened a Sunday school. In 1832 a site was bought on the other side of Wellington Street and on it a school room was built. *(See John Higson's Historical Recorder).* The present chapel was opened in 1873. Some time in the 1970s Birch Street Chapel and Clowes Street Union Chapel closed and their congregations joined the Wellington Street Baptist Chapel. The union was recognised by changing the name of the latter to the "Trinity Baptist Church".

PLACES OF WORSHIP IN GORTON WHICH HAVE CLOSED

St. Mark's, Clowes Street Opened in 1865. Closed in 1978 and replaced by Emmanuel Church.

All Saints, Queen's Road Opened in 1869. Burned down in 1964.

St. Clement's, Ducie Street Opened in 1876. Closed in 1970s when area was cleared. Replaced by St. Luke's Church at corner of Stockport Road and Devonshire Street South.

The Crescent Chapel Built by John Gomm Baker, a Manchester merchant, about 1800. Situated in Longsight Crescent. Used in turn by Longsight Sabbath School, Congregationalists and Methodists.

Gorton Wesleyan Chapel, Cross Lane School room opened in 1866, chapel in 1873. Closed in 1958.

Gorton Brook Primitive Methodist Chapel, Gorton Lane First chapel built about 1852, replaced in 1893. Society dissolved in 1964. Chapel demolished in 1965.

Longsight Wesleyan Chapel, Stockport Road Chapel and school opened in 1860 at corner of Richmond Grove East. New chapel built in 1868. In 1966 chapel demolished.

West Gorton Wesleyan Chapel, Hyde Road In 1859 Methodists from Longsight began using a hayloft behind the Justice Birch Inn as a Sunday school. In 1864 school built at corner of Chapel Street. New chapel built in 1873. Chapel closed in 1969.

Wellington Street Primitive Methodist Chapel Building bought from Baptists in 1874. Closed in 1958.

Crossley Street Primitive Methodist Chapel A school-chapel was built in 1903/4.

Longsight Presbyterian Church, Stockport Road In 1868 the Presbyterians bought the Longsight Wesleyan Chapel. Church closed in 1960.

Ivy Congregational Chapel, Stockport Road, between Park Avenue and Lime Grove
In 1830 William Holt commenced Sunday services in his own kitchen. In 1834 a cottage was used. Chapel opened in 1842. New and larger church built in 1852, known as Ivy Congregational Chapel on account of ivy on walls. Closed 1933. *(There is a detailed account of this chapel by Rev. H.C. Long in Manchester Central Library.)*

Union Baptist Chapel, Clowes Street Built in 1868. About 1970 joined with the Birch Street Baptists to form the West Gorton Baptist Fellowship. Services were held at each chapel on alternative weeks. About five years later the chapel closed and the Fellowship joined the Wellington Street Baptists.

Birch Street Baptist Chapel In 1878 a Baptist chapel and school were opened on Ainsworth Street. In 1880 a larger building was opened on Birch Street. *(See Union Baptist Chapel above)*

Gore Street Mission Free Evangelical Church Began life in 1875 as Gore Street Ragged School. Continued to function as a chapel. When Gore Street was pulled down as part of redevelopment of Gorton, a new hall was built on Turner Street. It was opened on Sunday, 23rd May, 1976. Closed because of falling attendances. Final service held on Sunday, 29th November, 1987.

OPENSHAW

The Church of St. Barnabas, Ashton Old Road

In 1824 the church authorities opened a Sunday school on a site later occupied by Ashton Old Road Council School. It was known as the "Bunghole" school. In 1828, George Cornwall Legh of High Legh in Cheshire, the owner of almost the whole of the land in Openshaw, gave a plot of land for use as a site for a church. On June 5th, 1837, the foundation stone was laid.

"Openshaw went on holiday for this event with feasting and a procession, in which those taking part included the clergy and the committee responsible for the erection of the church; the Sunday school children and their teachers and superintendent; the Openshaw band; the township and parochial officers of Openshaw, Droylsden and Gorton; the deputy constable of Openshaw and Droylsden; and workmen, walking three abreast, from the dyeworks, bleachworks and Clayton coal pits." Refreshments were provided for all concerned.

The church was opened on Easter Day, 1839. In 1959, after the building was found to be so affected by both dry rot and wet rot as to be unsafe, services were held in the Parochial Hall. The old church was demolished and replaced by the present church. This was dedicated on the 3rd March, 1962, by the Lord Bishop of Manchester.

(See St. Barnabas rebuilt by the Rev. K.P. Bullock, M.A.)

St. Clement's Ashton Old Road

In 1870 the Rector of St. Barnabas opened a Sunday school in the basement of four cottages in Fairfield Road - the ground and upper floors were in use as a warehouse. In the same year the Sunday school was transferred to a disused workshop at the end of Vine Street. In 1872 a Church of England school was built on the south side of Ashton Old Road. It opened on 16th January as St. Luke's school. Sunday evening services were also held there.

In 1876 Mr Legh gave land on the opposite side of the road for a church. There was, however, difficulty in raising money for the building. Towards the end of 1877 the difficulty was overcome by an offer of assistance by St. Clement's Charity Fund of Manchester. This fund had been formed from the proceeds of the sale of St. Clement's Church, built in 1793 at the corner of Stevenson Square and Lever Street. Its purpose was to make grants to new churches in the Manchester parish. One of the conditions for a grant was that any church receiving help should be called "St. Clement's".

In 1879 whilst negotiations were in process, an "iron church" was built in front of the day school. It continued in use as a church until early 1881, when the present church was completed. From then on it served as a parish hall until it was demolished in 1976.

(See the "Parish Church of St. Clement, Higher Openshaw, Centenary 1881:1981")

St. Anne's Roman Catholic Church, Ashton Old Road

In 1846 the first Roman Catholic Sunday school in Openshaw was opened in a house adjoining the Bridge Inn on Abbey Hey Lane, Little Droylsden. In 1849 a building, previously used as a warehouse, was acquired on the south side of Ashton Old Road, opposite to the present St. Anne's Church. It consisted of three storeys, the lower one being used as a boys Sunday school, the upper one for the girls and the intermediate storey as a temporary chapel.

The area was then known as Seven Thorns. The parishioners were mainly Irish peasants, who had left Ireland because of the potato famine. Employment was found for them in the cotton mills and engineering works.

In 1882 the building on the south side of Ashton Old Road was sold and the present St. Anne's church and a day school were built.

(See History of Droylsden, p.138, by John Higson and Centenary Memoirs of St. Anne's Fairfield, 1849-1949 by W.J. Timms)

St. Vincent of Paul, George Street

This Roman Catholic Church was built in 1899.

Higher Openshaw Methodist New Connexion, Gransmoor Road

In 1839 a small school-chapel was opened in Moor Lane (Fairfield Road) near to Ashton Old Road. In 1902-3 a new chapel and school were erected in Gransmoor Road.

Higher Openshaw Wesleyan Methodist Chapel, Stanley Street

In 1872 a small joiners shop in Harley Street was opened as a place of worship and as a Sunday school. A school-chapel was opened in 1877 at the corner of Ogden Lane and Stanley Street and the present chapel built on the adjoining site in 1890.

Lees Street Congregational Church

In 1865 Congregational services began in Higher Openshaw at the Co-operative Hall on Ashton Old Road. In 1871 the Congregational chapel on Lees Street was opened.

The Mersey Street Tabernacle

In 1921 the Reverend James Lawson became the pastor of the Cornwall Street Baptist Chapel. A dispute amongst the congregation led to Mr Lawson and a number of members leaving in 1922. For sixteen months they used a room in the Whitehall Cinema and then moved to Holland's bakehouse in Stanley Street. The bake-house was eventually registered for weddings. In 1926 the break-away group acquired a plot of land on Mersey Street, where they built the new Baptist Tabernacle, a wood and asbestos structure. In 1954 a brick shell was erected around the existing walls. In 1963 the Tabernacle was extended.

The Fairfield Road Citadel
The Salvation Army Citadel on Fairfield Road was opened in the early years of this century.

PLACES OF WORSHIP IN OPENSHAW WHICH HAVE CLOSED

Openshaw Wesleyan Methodists, Grey Mare Lane Opened in 1864. Demolished in 1956.

Central Openshaw United Methodist Free Chapel Built on south side of Ashton Old Road opposite Wood Street in 1860. In 1889 a new Methodist chapel was opened on Press Street. Known as "Saxon's chapel" because of support from Saxon family. Old building sold to Congregationalists. Press Street Chapel closed 1966.

Lower Openshaw United Methodist Free Chapel, Barmouth Street Built in 1909. Demolished in 1959.

Higher Openshaw Primitive Methodist Chapel, Ashton Old Road. School chapel built in 1872 corner of Margaret Street. New chapel fronting road built in 1894. Closed 1966.

The Congregational Chapel, Ashton Old Road. Purchased from Methodists in 1864. Stood near Pottery Lane. Closed in 1890 and replaced by a new chapel in Gresham Street.

The Congregational Central Mission, Ashton Old Road, Opposite Wood Street.
Building bought from Methodists in 1889. Closed about 1912.

Cornwall Street Baptist Chapel. School-room built on Cornwall Street at corner of Whitworth Street East in 1878. Chapel built in 1906. Both closed in 1970. In 1971 the Cornwall Street Baptists united with Mersey Street Baptists.

The Dyer Street Citadel The Salvation Army Citadel on Dyer Street near Grey Mare Lane opened in 1880. It closed in 1970.

(The notes in this chapter on Methodist chapels are based on "Methodism in East Manchester" by E.A. Rose B.A. in the Journal of the Lancashire and Cheshire Branch of the Wesleyan Historical Society, August 1966)

Central Openshaw United Methodist Free Chapel.
Whitweek walk, 1908 (?). Ashton Old Road, probably corner of Press Street.

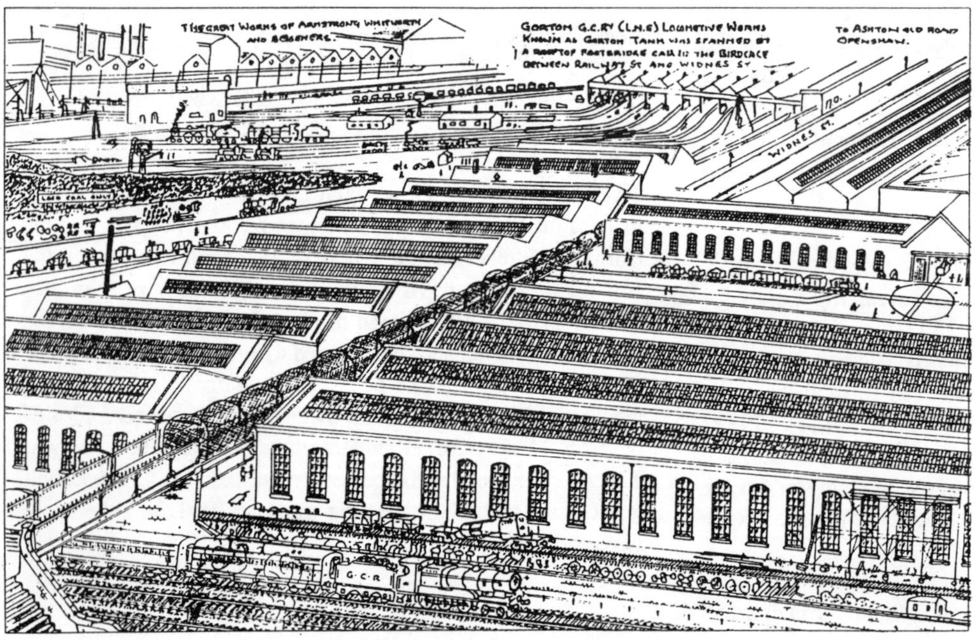

The "Birdcage".

CHAPTER X

SCHOOLS

GORTON

Gorton's first day school

When the Bishop of Chester visited Gorton Chapel in 1592, he found that "the curate taught a school". *(Transactions of the Lancs. and Chesh. Antiquarian Society, 1895, p.63)* This does not necessarily mean that there was a separate school building. It was not unusual for children to be taught in the church. By 1717, however, the Gorton school had its own building for Bishop Castrell of Chester wrote in his Notitia Cestriensis: "A school, built by contributions and the Master nominated by the township but no endowment, only a penny a week paid by the children". This school stood in the chapel yard of St. Thomas's on Church Lane.

By 1783 the school had become too small to accommodate the increased number of children and a new one was built at the corner of Cross Lane and Wellington Street. Money was raised by public subscription. It became known as Gorton Old Endowed School.

Gorton Old Endowed School

A Schools Enquiry Report, published in 1869, said that there were between 120 and 130 boys on roll, but no girls. There was no income apart from school fees which ranged from 4d to 10d. The subjects taught included French, Euclid (Geometry), Algebra, Book-keeping. The headmaster, William Rose, was neither a graduate nor a certificated teacher and the school was not under government inspection. In 1882 the school, now under James Green, a qualified teacher, was brought under government inspection and qualified for a government grant. The school closed in 1905.

The National School, also known as St. James C. of E. and Gorton C. of E., The Bishop Greer School and the Trinity High School

In 1786 a Sunday school was opened in the Gorton Old Endowed School. In 1834 a new Sunday school was erected at the corner of Green Lane and Wellington Street. Control of this school was firmly in the hands of the church. In 1838 a grant from the National Society, a Church of England organisation, was used to enlarge the school room and it appears that in the same year a day school was begun. The school building was 86 feet by 25 feet and 12 feet in height. The school room was divided by a movable partition into two compartments, one for girls and one for boys. It was built of brick and blue slate and heated by two stoves. The ventilation was imperfect. There were two proper conveniences. It was enclosed by wooden rails. *(Council of Education report of 1845)*

In 1872 new buildings were opened adjoining the old school, which continued in use as an infants school. In 1968 the senior children were transferred to the new Bishop Greer School on Taylor Street. This school, a comprehensive school planned for 600 pupils, proved to be too small to offer a sufficiently wide range of subjects and in 1984 it amalgamated with the Fallowfield Church of England High School. A new school, the Trinity High School, was built in Cambridge Street. In September, 1985, all the pupils were transferred to this new school.

In the meantime the Junior School took over the premises vacated by the seniors in 1968. In 1972 the Junior and Infants amalgamated and became "controlled". This means that the fabric of the buildings became the responsibility of the Manchester Education Committee but in return religious education became non-denominational.

In 1976 the St. James C. of E. Primary School moved into new buildings on Stelling Street.

The School in Gorton Mill

The Factory Act of 1833 laid down that all children between nine and thirteen employed in textile factories were to receive two hours schooling daily. To implement this provision a school was opened in Gorton Mill in 1837. 38 boys and 16 girls, divided into three sets, were taught Reading, Writing, Arithmetic and Geography. *(Gorton Historical Recorder by John Higson)* The Gorton Mill closed down in 1840 and was re-opened in 1844 by Messrs John Rylands, who sent their child workers to the National School at the corner of Green Lane.

Sunday schools and ragged schools

Before elementary education became compulsory Sunday schools and ragged schools were opened to give children a few hours schooling each week: on Sundays in the case of Sunday schools, on Sundays and weekday evenings in the case of ragged schools. Reading was the principle subject, sometimes the only one, taught.

In addition to the Sunday School in the Gorton Old Endowed School, which moved to a new building in 1834 at the corner of Green Lane, there was a Methodist Sunday school built in 1826 on William Street by Mr W.H. Lees of Gorton Mills. When he attempted to introduce Arithmetic, the Methodists would not agree and were ejected.

A minute book, dated 1854, of the Longsight Wesleyans Sunday school, Richmond Grove, has survived. School began at 9 a.m. and continued at 2 p.m. Spelling and Reading, based on the Bible, were taught.

A ragged school was opened in Josiah Street, Gorton Brook, in 1870. Within four months the attendance had increased to 184 and the cottage was too small. *(Gorton and Openshaw Reporter, 15.4.1871)* The best known local ragged school was the one in Gore Street. It opened in September, 1875, with accommodation for 300 children. Classes were held every Sunday, one night per week, Christmas Day and Good Friday. *(G.O.R., 11.8.1875)*

The introduction of compulsory education in 1876 reduced the role of the ragged schools. However, they survived well into the 20th century, providing recreation for youngsters during the week and religious teaching on Sunday.

GORTON SCHOOLS TODAY

St. James C.E. Primary *See Previous pages*

St. Francis R.C. Primary is on Ellenbrook Street.

St. Alban's R.C. High School was formed by amalgamation of the senior schools of St. Francis with St. Alban's. The site is on Holmcroft Road, Gorton.

All Saints County Primary School, Windicott Close off Gorton Lane.

St. Luke's C.E. Primary School, Langport Avenue, built 1969, was originally St. Clement's C.E. Primary School. As the church is now dedicated to St. Luke the name was changed.

Aspinal Primary, Broadacre Road, was opened on 20th March, 1930, as an all age school. In 1952 the senior pupils were transferred to neighbouring schools.

Sacred Heart Roman Catholic School, Knutsford Road The first school was opened in 1902 with 68 children. Today there is a junior school on Knutsford Road and an infants school on Glencastle Road.

Abbey Hey Primary School, Abbey Hey Lane. The first school, an all age school, was built in 1911. The school was replaced in 1937 by a new junior and infants school. In 1959 the school was extended and the infants department became a separate school.

Old Hall Drive Primary School was opened in 1914, the children having previously been accommodated at the temporary church of St. Philip and the parish hall of Brookfield Church. It was an all age school. In 1932 the school became a junior mixed school, the senior scholars transferring to Spurley Hey Secondary School. It is believed that during the First World War it served as a hospital.

Peacock Street School was opened in 1928 as Peacock Street Primary School. It closed as a primary school in 1983. The building is now used for special education.

Gorton Mount Primary School, Mount Road. This school opened in 1928 as the Gorton Mount Municipal School taking children up to the age of 14. In 1932 it closed as an all-age school and became a junior and infants school. The older children transferred to Spurley Hey Secondary School.

Spurley Hey High School This comprehensive school was created in 1967 by using the buildings of Spurley Hey Secondary School and Ryder Brow Secondary School as upper and lower schools respectively. The former school, named after a Director of Education, was opened in 1932. The latter was opened in 1952.

Wright Robinson High School, Abbey Hey. This purpose built comprehensive was opened in 1967. It was named after a former chairman of the Manchester Education Committee.

GORTON SCHOOLS WHICH HAVE CLOSED

The School in Gorton Mill, 1837 - 1840
Gorton Old Endowed School, 1783 - 1905
The Wesleyan School, corner of Richmond Grove East and Stockport Road. Opened in 1865. After the area amalgamated with Manchester the school changed its name to Longsight Municipal. It closed in 1936.
St. Mark's, Clowes Street, opened in 1866 and closed in 1983.
St. Francis's, Gorton Lane. The first school, known as the Monastery Boys School, was opened in 1870. The Girls School was opened in 1877. Closed in the 1970's.
The Wesleyan School, Hyde Road, corner of Chapel Street. Chapel Street was between Redgate Lane and Grey Street.
All Saints School, Queens Road, was opened in 1875.
St. Clement's School stood in a triangle formed by Grey Street, Ducie Street (Dillon Street) and New Bank Street. School closed in 1960s.
John Rylands School The correct name of this school was "Abbey Hey School". It was built by John Rylands and Sons in 1876 on the opposite side of Abbey Hey Lane from the present Abbey Hey Primary School and near to the west bank of the canal. It closed in 1894, because there were 222 more school places in Gorton schools than were required.
Aspinal Gorton Wesleyan Day School This mixed school opened in 1888, using the building of the newly built Aspinal Wesleyan Sunday school. It closed in 1930.
Thomas Street Board School Opened in 1894. When Thomas Street was renamed Wenlock Way, Thomas Street Primary School changed its name to Wenlock Way Primary School. This school closed in 1978.
St. George's Temporary Council School opened in 1914 in the parish hall of St. George's Church on Abbey Hey Lane. It closed in 1911, when the children moved to the newly built Abbey Hey Municipal School.
Hyde Road Temporary Council School opened in 1905. It stood between Sunny Brow Road and Chatsworth Road. It closed in 1938.

OPENSHAW

Openshaw's first day school

The first day school in Openshaw was St. Barnabas's, a Church of England school. It opened in 1833, twelve months before the church from which it took its name. Both church and school were in South Street. The average attendance was 150, there being twice as many boys as girls. School fees were 4d, 6d and 8d, according to age. They were reduced to 2d, 3d and 4d in 1847 or, where there was more than one child from the same family attending, to ½d, 2d and 3d. The school received a Treasury Grant from the National Society. A local benefactor,

Mr Neden gave £500 to the school. The money was used to buy five houses in South Street, the rents being used to pay the fees of poor children.
For some years there were only two teachers: a master for the boys and a mistress for the girls. Usually they were husband and wife. The syllabus consisted of Reading, Writing and Arithmetic - popularly known as the "3 R's" - together with Spelling, Geography and Scripture. It is probable that the boys and girls were taught in separate rooms. The master and mistress were assisted by paid monitors, usually aged between thirteen and fifteen. These monitors would frequently take charge of a class. In 1855 a new school mistress was guaranteed a wage of 14s a week whilst the headmaster received £2 14s a week.

In 1877, Mrs W.Brundet, a patron of the school and church, built a new infants department. In 1973 a new school was built on Parkhouse Street. Its official title is "the Openshaw Church of England Primary School".
(See St. Barnabas Rebuilt by the Rev. K.P. Bullock)

St. Clement's Day School
The school that eventually became known as St. Clement's opened on 6th January, 1873. It stood on the south side of Ashton Old Road. It was at first called St. Luke's because it was intended to build a church nearby and dedicate it to St. Luke. However the church when built was dedicated to St. Clement and so the school changed its name. In 1899 the mixed department moved into a new building on Gransmoor Road. The infants occupied the old school building. In 1967 the introduction of comprehensive education resulted in the school losing all pupils over eleven. In November, 1978, the school moved into new premises on Ackroyd Street.
(See "The Parish Church of St. Clement Higher Openshaw Centenary 1881:1981)

St. Anne's Day School and St. Gregory's R.C. High School
The first St. Anne's Day School used the church building which was acquired in 1849. The earliest record of a school there is in a street directory of 1858. By 1876 the school had moved, for a street directory of that year shows that it was next door but one to the church. In 1882 a new school was built on the opposite side of Ashton Old Road, immediately behind the site of the present church.

In 1964 two new secondary modern schools, dedicated to St. John the Evangelist, were opened on Stopford Street for the senior boys and girls. In 1977 the two schools amalgamated with St. Gregory's, Ardwick, to form a mixed comprehensive school. In 1985 there was a further amalgamation with Sir Thomas More School, Palmerston Street. At present the Stopford Street schools are the lower school, but it is intended to phase out the Palmerston Street site and build an upper school on Stopford Street. The schools are now dedicated to St. Gregory.

The St. Anne's Primary and Nursery School is now in Clarendon Road, Audenshaw. The junior department was built in three phases, which were completed in 1966, 1970 and 1974. The infants school was opened in 1974 and the nursery unit was added in 1979.

Varna Street School
Varna Street School was opened in 1897, replacing the Tank School. Between 1924 and 1934 part of the building was used to accommodate the Varna Street Central School. It resumed in 1934 as a senior and junior mixed school. In 1967 with the introduction of comprehensive education it lost its older pupils and continued as Varna Street Primary.

Openshaw Technical College
The Openshaw Technical College was opened on Whitworth Street in 1955 and extended in 1968. It is now the Openshaw Centre of the Manchester Central College.

SCHOOLS WHICH HAVE CLOSED

The Manchester, Sheffield and Lincolnshire Railway School, or "Tank School" as it was popularly known, was opened in 1856 on Cornwall Street for the children of railway employees. Other children were admitted at a higher fee. In 1892 all fees were abolished. In 1894 it was taken over by the Manchester School Board. In 1897 it closed and the children moved to Varna Street.

The boys had the reputation of being very unruly until Arthur Moxon was appointed headmaster in 1888. He was a tall, broad man of powerful physique. When he walked into the interview room, so the story goes, the committee took one look at him and said, "He'll do". The committee had done their work well for within six months he had transformed the school. He took over the headship of Varna Street in 1897. Long after his retirement in 1920 Gorton and Openshaw children used to chant, when Shrove Tuesday arrived, their version of the old rhyme:

Pancake Tuesday is a very happy day
If you don't give us a holiday,
We'll all run away.
Where shall we run to?
Down Edge Lane,
To see Paddy Moxon with his big fat cane.

The Mechanics Institute, Pottery Lane, was opened in 1872. The cost of building was met from money left by George Whyatt, the Openshaw dyer. Classes were held in the evening. Girls were admitted in 1875. In1881 a day school was opened in the building. After Openshaw amalgamated with Manchester in 1890, the school changed its name to the Pottery Lane Board School. It appears to have closed in 1923.
Ashton Old Road Council School was opened in 1898. The building was demolished in1969.
Wheler Street Council School was opened in 1902. It closed in 1967. The building is now used as a community centre.
Elysian Street Council School was opened in temporary buildings in 1904. It moved into new buildings in 1911. The school was demolished in 1983.
Lees Street Congregational School was opened in 1872. In 1902 the senior department was transferred to Wheler Street school. In 1915 the Junior school closed.
The Wesleyan Day School, Wesley Street, off Grey Mare Lane, was opened in 1865 and closed in 1914.
The Openshaw School of Technology, a branch of the Municipal Technical School on Princess Street, was opened between 1895 and 1900 in the Whitworth Hall, Ashton Old

Road. It appears to have closed in 1917 or 1918.

The Openshaw Junior Technical School was founded in 1914, when it was realised that the war was going to be a long one and there would be a serious shortage of foremen and what we now call technicians. Entry was by examination from the top classes of elementary schools. At first the school was housed in part of Crossley Lads Club and the basement of Whitworth Library. In 1931 it moved to a new building on Gorton Road. About 1960 it changed its name to the Openshaw Technical High School. It closed in 1967.

EXTRACTS FROM SCHOOL LOG BOOKS

Until late in the 19th century the master or mistress was usually the only adult teacher in the school. He or she was assisted by monitors or monitresses, aged between thirteen and fifteen, in return for a small wage. This assistance included taking charge of a class. When the pupil teacher system was introduced, monitors and monitresses could become pupil teachers.

Monitors, monitresses and pupil teachers were given tuition after school by the master. At the age of about nineteen, the pupil teacher could sit the Queen's Scholarship examination and, if successful, gain admission to a teacher training college. Successful students at the college became qualified teachers. Teachers who failed the Queen's Scholarship examination or who failed at college could stay on as teachers, but were unqualified and were paid less.

Gorton C. of E. Boys School

Nov. 14th 1865

Mill boys generally untidy. *(Mill boys were "half-timers", who worked two and a half days each week at a local cotton mill.)*

Nov. 15th

Very few *(of the boys)* learnt their "Home Lessons" properly.

Dec. 11th

Boys left school to work at Gorton factory.

Jan. 31st 1866

Two mill boys viz Chapel & Stewart inclined to be rebellious.

May. 3rd

1 boy Half Timer admitted. Age, 12 years, knows letters only. 1 girl admitted. Age 14 years. Letters only. One left to work "full time".

May. 17th

Several boys principally "Half timers" without either slates or books.

July 17th

Boys very noisy in coming in after "Recreation". Clogs made a great noise on boards.

Jan. 23rd 1867

Several of Mr Grimshaw's half timers without either copy books or slates. *(Mr Grimshaw was the owner of High Bank Mill, Ogden Lane.)*

March 13th

Some children bring very short pieces of pencil. *(i.e. slate pencils)*

July 26th

Had to flog a "Half Timer", Bardsley, for disobedience.

August 29th

Girls attendance small owing to the wakes. *(Mr Canner was the master in charge of the boys school, but he had also responsibility for the girls school. The mistress in charge of the latter was Mrs Tatton.)*

March 10th 1868

The boy who taught the 3rd class received Bribes.

Nov. 23rd

Some boys allowed to come free this week, the father being without work.

Dec. 16th

Punished Eastwood for spending his school fee.

Feb. 2nd 1869

The Paid Monitor late this morning.

July 14th

Several in the hay-fields this week.

April 7th 1870

Several away picking stones off the fields.

Jan. 7th 1871

The Monitor spells very indifferently & works his sums incorrectly.

July 14th 1873

Admitted 2 boys one a half-timer in Brickfield.

St. Barnabas' Infant School

Oct. 11th 1877

Sarah Stelfox absented herself from school without leave. There being so many scholars this week, a girl required from the Girls School to teach in the place of the above mentioned. Weekly av. 180

Dec. 17th

Maud Robertson aged 14 of 486 Ashton Old Road appointed monitress of this school. Duties to commence on Jan. 7th, 1878. M.R. came to take lessons with the other monitresses to prepare for the Pupil Teachers examination.

Feb. 6th 1878

The teachers had a written examination in Grammar after school hours. The papers were done very fairly with the exception of Sarah Stelfox's which was done somewhat carelessly.

Apr. 28th 1879

S.Stelfox's name has been removed from the Register of P.T.s serving in this school.

July 23rd 1880

School closed on Thursday of this week until Monday July 26th. The children were taken by boats to Stockport Park. A pleasant day was spent and all seemed to enjoy themselves.

Nov. 4th 1881
Notices came from Cheltenham Training College respecting the result of the Scholarship examination last July: Maude Robertson has obtained a place in the first class and purposes entering the college named, January 25th, 1882.

Lessons 1883
Reading, Spelling, Arithmetic, Object Lessons, Recitation, Singing, Needlework, Marching Exercises and Drill. Object lessons for five year olds: ostrich, whale, duck, rabbit, table, clock face, school, school slate, umbrella. *(In an object lesson the teacher would draw from the children as much information about the object as possible.)*

St. Barnabas' Mixed School
Master William Bamford

April 9th 1887
Found out today that a bag containing about 18s school fees etc. was missing from a drawer in the table.

April 10th
On April 10th Mrs Edgar brought her boy John Taylor to school and said he had been spending money. He was eventually taken to the police station, where he confessed to the theft. The sum of 9/4 was recovered. The boy was brought before the magistrates and ordered to receive twelve strokes with the birch rod.

Sept. 1st 1890
Thomas Perfect appointed headmaster.

October 17th 1893
This morning the Rector and other managers gave a free breakfast to needy children attending this school. There were present this morning 57 children. It is intended to continue the free breakfast as long as necessary.

November 13th
Free breakfasts still going on as the great coal strike still drags on. There is great distress in the neighbourhood.

July 10th 1895
School cricket club organised. With 5 neighbouring schools organised a cricket league.

April 27th 1897
D. Farnworth has obtained a First Class in Queen's Scholarship
(Dora Farnworth eventually became headmistress of Lilley Lane Infants School, Moston.)

November 30th 1904
This morning we commenced giving free breakfasts (consisting of bread, butter or jam and cocoa) to poor scholars. There are 60 fathers of families out of work.

December 23rd
Free breakfasts are being continued throughout the holiday. I am raising the funds by private efforts having been unsuccessful in attempts to get assistance from the Lord Mayor's fund. *(Note - the breakfasts were prepared by the teachers.)*

Aspinal Gorton Wesleyan Day School (Mixed School)
1890 Week ending October 17th For the last few weeks I have been taking the first year teachers from 5.00 p.m. to 5.30 p.m. on the Geography of Mountains and Rivers.

1891 Week ending January 9th Eleven scholars were admitted. These are mostly in a very backward state being supposed to have attended a cottage school in the neighbourhood kept by a young lady who combines the work of school teaching with the making of womens garments at one and the same time.

1900 29th October In the Infant Department, he (Mr Jalland HMI) found the certificated Mistress with the aid of a very young Monitress, attempting to manage 110 children. The pupil teacher, who generally assists the Mistress, was absent, attending the Pupil Teachers Centre.

THE EVACUATION OF SCHOOL CHILDREN

As there was a widespread belief that the outbreak of war would be accompanied by heavy bombing of cities, plans were drawn up in the early months of 1939 for the evacuation of school children. Below are extracts from Evacuation Handbook No 2, a copy of which was sent by the Manchester Education Committee to the heads of all local authority schools.

"The imminence of evacuation, if ever it became necessary, would be notified by the radio, in the press and by other means. It is to be hoped it would be possible to send two messages to all Manchester Head Teachers, either at school, if it were in session, or at the home or holiday address.

First message: get ready for evacuation
Second message: evacuation on - day

On receipt of the second message the Head Teacher will tell all Assistant Teachers and helpers to come to school at a specified time. 8.15 a.m. is suggested.

Hand luggage only - own gas-mask, a change of underclothing, night clothes, house shoes or plimsolls, spare stockings or socks, a tooth brush, comb, towel, handkerchiefs.

Supply of food for one day. Trains will not be corridor trains."

The evacuation began on Friday, September 1st. Higher Openshaw children were evacuated to Glossop, Hadfield and district and Lower Openshaw children to Blackpool. Gorton children were evacuated to Hazel Grove and Poynton. Mothers with children under school age were evacuated the following day.

When the expected air-raids did not take place, mothers and children began to return home. Some children came home on Friday or Saturday for the week-end only, returning on Sunday or Monday morning. Of the 50,000 Manchester children who were evacuated in early September only 20,000 remained by the end of December. Twelve months later the number had fallen to 5,000.

The Manchester Blitz of December 22nd and 23rd, 1940, brought about a second evacuation, but on a much smaller scale than that of September, 1939. Of the 80,000 children eligible, only 11,600 registered.

THE EVACUATION OF GORTON C. OF E. (ST. JAMES) SCHOOL

On Friday, September 1st 1939, Gorton C. of E. (St. James) School was evacuated to Hazel Grove. The children were taught part-time in the Norbury C. of E. School until December, when the St. James Infant Department moved to Napier Street Methodist School. This made it possible for the Boys and Girls Departments to work full-time.
The Department log books record the preparation for evacuation, some aspects of school life in Hazel Grove, and the return to Gorton.
Here are some extracts:

Boys
July 20th, 1939. All labels for evacuation purposes have been completed and stored away in the cupboard in the Head Teacher's room.

August 25th, 1939. This week has been one of intense activity in preparation for evacuation: everything has been done in accordance with the orders issued from the Education Office.

August 26th, 1939 (Saturday). Teachers assembled in school this morning to give advice to parents and children for the evacuation rehearsal which is to take place on Monday, August 28th.

August 27th, 1939. A skeleton staff was present at school this morning to answer questions and give advice to parents and children. The same procedure was adopted this afternoon from 2.00 to 4.30.

Girls
August 28th, 1939. The children whose parents wished them to be evacuated attended school this a.m. for a rehearsal of evacuation arrangements. Labels were issued and checked. Kit bags were inspected and reported on. Girls were accompanied by other members of their families of school age, grouped together in tens under one helper and marched into queues in the yard with full kit. Members of the staff of Rackhouse School, Wythenshawe, along with four mothers, Mrs Thorpe and Mr Artingstall completed the number of helpers.

September 1st, 1939. Train from London Road to Hazel Grove. 118 children evacuated. After medical examination and receiving a package of food the school was divided off for billets.

10 children Woodford, 12 Bramhall, remainder Norbury Hazel Grove.

September 2nd, 1939. Evacuation of mothers and children. 12 more girls evacuated.

September 11th, 1939. Girls commenced school 1.30 - 5 p.m.

Boys
September 11th, 1939. We opened school this afternoon at Norbury C. of E. School, Hazel Grove, after 1 week from the date of evacuation from Manchester, 1 September. The week intervening has been spent in collecting the children from their billets, verifying addresses, making enquiries as to children who had returned home and compiling registers. Time had also been spent in outdoor pursuits - organised games, walks and nature rambles.

Girls and Boys Departments were formed from Std. 111 children upwards, Std. 11 (Boys and Girls) being with the Infants Department.

Owing to an error by the Billeting Authorities a number of Gorton C. of E. children were sent to Bramhall and a number of St. Mark's, Holland Street, Miles Platting, were sent to Hazel Grove. St. Mark's, Holland Street, at Bramhall would incorporate Gorton C. of E. Gorton C. of E. at Norbury would incorporate St. Mark's children billeted at Hazel Grove.

October 27th, 1939. No on roll 50

November 13th, 1939. No on roll 34. I propose to visiti the homes in Gorton this week and ascertain reason for all the returns.
November 24th, 1939. I attended Gorton each morning for the tutorial system and was present here each afternoon for full session 12.45 to 4 p.m. No on roll 31.

April 1st, 1940. School re-opened for full time instruction. 150 boys presented themselves for instruction. *(The school in question was the school in Gorton.)*

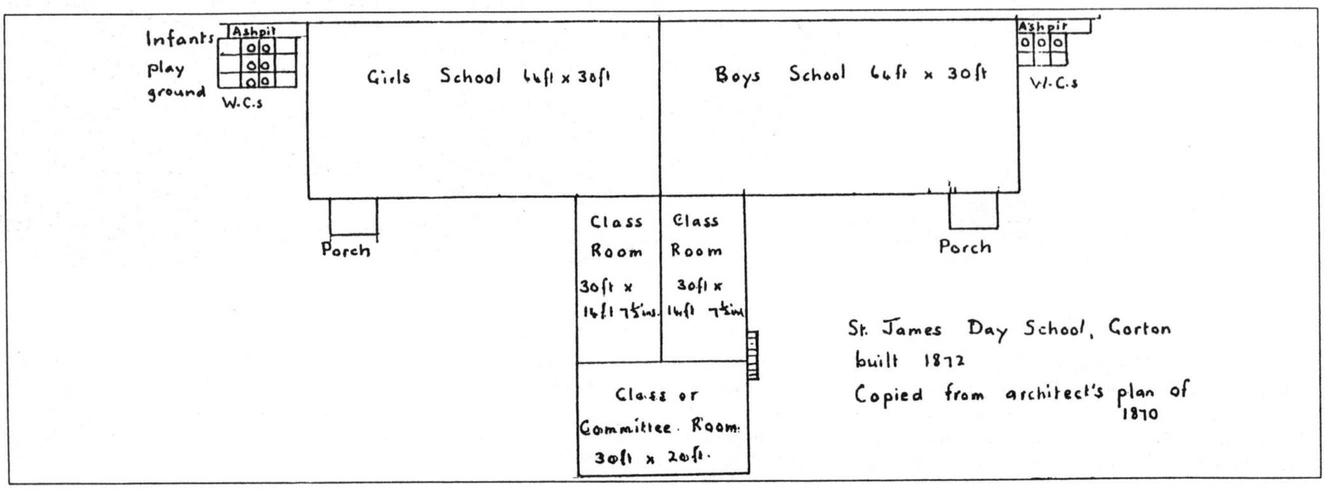

Two Evacuees from Varna Street Elementary School

Probably taken September 1st, 1939. Note the sweets: chocolate tea-cakes, owls' eggs, Swizzel fruits - 2 for 1d, "Swizzade makes 2 drinks", and on the top shelf a box of Cadbury's Milk Tray - the ladies have always loved Milk Tray - at 6d a 1/4lb. "Surely", some of you will say, "surely somewhere in the shop there must have been: Palm Toffee, everlasting strips, coconut chips, sherbet in a paper bag with a tube to suck it through, lucky horse shoes, Spanish sticks, tiger nuts, locust seeds and Packer's chocolate dragees, which tasted as though sand had been added at some stage in the manufacture!" The shop was at the corner of Varna Street and Electro Street. *(Courtesy Chris Makepeace)*

Gorton House, Debdale Park
Built in the 18th century. Between 1848 and 1850 it was the home of two hat manufacturers.

The "favourite walk",
Gorton Reservoirs, shortly before the First World War.

A Beyer Peacock locomotive,
built in 1921 for the 3'6" gauge of the South African State Railway.

CHAPTER XI

HOUSES

Cottages and Villas

It is reasonable to assume that the first houses in Gorton and Openshaw were timber framed with walls made of wattle (interwoven branches) and daub (clay) and that their roofs were thatched, as that was the customary method of building houses when the two townships were first established.

By the mid-eighteenth century, according to John Higson in his Antiquities and Fragments of Lancashire, farm buildings in Gorton were generally slate-roofed and only a few were thatched. Walls, he said, were wattle and daub or brick.

No houses built in Openshaw before the middle of the 19th century have survived and only five in Gorton: a row of three houses on Far Lane, one of which bears the inscription "ESA 1782", Gorton House, which was in existence in the 18th century, and Spring Bank Farm, which is said to be the oldest house in Gorton.

Mill Cottages

It was common practice in the 19th century for mill owners to build or buy cottages for their workers. The company of John Lees and Sons, who built the cotton mill on Abbey Hey Lane, owned 34 cottages in John Street, 7 in Bridge Street, 6 on Goose Green, 15 in William Street, 2 in Gas Street, 10 in King Street, 8 in Lees Street, 10 in Peel Street and 10 in Wilson Street. When the company closed down in 1840, John Chapman of Glossop bought all the property and in 1843 leased it to John Rylands. The conveyance contains a description of the property, including the fixtures.

All the cottages were built on the same plan and the differences, where they occurred, were trivial. For example, the cottages in Wilson Street were the only ones to have a deal partition at the door and only those in Peel Street had a stone chimney piece. The full description of the Wilson Street cottages was:

"10 cottages Wilson Street have each - Deal Partition at door - oven, grate and boiler - Flag in scullery - flag and shelves in pantry - slopstone - grate and chimney in chamber."

The grate was between the boiler and the oven, so that the heat from the fire could be used for baking or boiling water - a damper directed the heat in the required direction. The "flags" in the scullery and pantry were slabs of stone on brick pillars. They were used in the preparation of food and in the case of the one in the scullery for resting dishes after washing. The slop stone was a shallow sink, made of stone, earthenware or wood. The chamber was a bed-room. The impression given is that the cottage had only one bed-room. It is probable that there were two, but that only one was itemised because there was no grate and chimney in the other. A kitchen/living room and scullery would comprise the ground floor and a large and small bed-room the floor above.

The annual rents of some of these houses are given in the 1848 Gorton Rate Book:

John Street - £6 5s, William Street - £5 7s, King Street - £8 4s
Lees Street - £5 10s, Peel Street - £6 1s, Wilson Street - £6 3s

The house occupied by Joseph Mottram in Lees Street
This house, itemised and described separately on the conveyance, was too luxurious to be a mill-workers cottage.

"Grate - stone chimney piece in parlour. Oven, grate and boiler, cupboard with 4 drawers in kitchen. 2 shelves in scullery. 2 grates with stone chimney pieces in chambers. Large water tub in yard.

Iron boiler with door, bars and brickwork, grate, slop stone and flag in washhouse. Flag 6 feet 2 inches by 2 feet 1 inch and 23 feet shelves in larder. Stone shelves in hen coop."

None of the above dwellings had water on tap. All would be illuminated by candle or oil-lamp. What today we call a lavatory was then the "privy" in the backyard, cleared out once or twice a year.

Gorton Villa

Gorton Villa was built in 1829 by John Harrison Lees, one of the owners of Gorton Mill, and leased by John Chapman to John Rylands. The conveyance of 1843 contained a detailed description of its fittings and fixtures.

Ground Floor
Hall with suspending double bronze gas chandelier
Conservatories - one left and one to right of the hall, one with a bracket gas light
Ante Room with grate, marble chimney piece and gas light
Dining Room with 66 feet of gilt picture rods, grate, black marble chimney piece, bronze gas chandeliers
Breakfast Room 34 feet 4 inches of gilt picture rods, grate, white marble chimney piece
Drawing Room with grate and marble chimney piece
China Closet
Servants Hall with 10 bells and fixings, grate with boiler and hot hearth, stone chimney piece, painted cupboard with shelf and clothes pegs, dresser, slop bench with lead tops, decanter rack, 2 bracket gas lights
(A "hot hearth" was the space below an oven and enclosed by a door. It was used for grilling.)
Scullery with 7 painted shelves, pump, slop stone

Kitchen with 2 bells and fixings, cupboard, smoke jack, kitchen range with 2 ovens, boiler and hot hearth, stone chimney piece, jack bracket, shelf, 2 bacon rails each 10 feet long with 20 hooks, 35 ceiling hooks, dresser 13 feet long by 2 feet 8 inches wide, suspending gas light, 1 inch brass tap
(A smoke jack was a device which used the draught in a chimney to turn a spit)
Larder Meat rail with pullies, fixings and 22 hooks, shelving, 2 salting flags, slop stone, suspending gas light, 1 inch brass water tap

Basement
Washhouse with slop stone and flag 10 feet by 2 feet 3 inches, salting flag, grate with hot hearth, stone chimney piece
Boot house with two shelves
Laundry with 2 large water tubs, slop stone on brick pillars, 3 iron boilers, ironing stove, stillage, 2 gas lights
(A stillage is a frame or stand for keeping things off the floor)

Wine cellar, spirit cellar, beer cellar and a second larder

Rooms upstairs
(The conveyance does not say whether there was one or two floors above the ground floor.)

No 1 bedroom with register grate, 2 bronze bracket gas lights and 1 bronze bracket gas light in dressing room
(A register grate was a grate with a moveable iron plate in the chimney which could adjust the size of the chimney opening)
No 2 bedroom with register grate, marble chimney piece, 3 bronze bracket gas lights
No 3 bedroom with register grate, marble chimney piece, 3 bronze bracket gas lights
Water closet with bracket gas lights
Housemaids closet
Backstairs and chambermaids closet with wood slop, cistern with lead top (i.e. lined with lead), clothes rack and pegs
Servants bed room No 4 with wardrobe, fireplace, bell *(but apparently no gas light)*
No 5 bedroom with bell, register grate, stone chimney piece, double bracket gas light
No 6 bedroom with register grate, black marble chimney piece, gas light, small bell, alarm bell outside the room

In the grounds of Gorton Villa there were three stables, a hay loft, a cottage, a granary and a wooden shippon with four cow chains. Gas in the house was presumably supplied by the mill from its own retort and water from its reservoir.

The apparent absence of gas light in the breakfast room, drawing room and scullery is surprising. The absence of a bathroom is not. Baths were usually taken in a portable bath, water being carried up from the kitchen.

Gorton's smallest house

This unusual house stood on Cross Lane at its junction with Kirk Street. The front door, which was only 5 feet 6 inches high, opened into a room barely 8 feet square.

Gorton Hall

Gorton Hall was demolished in 1906. The lodge at the entrance to the Hall grounds still stands on Brookhurst Road at its junction with Old Hall Drive. The earliest reference to a "Gorton Hall" is in a feoffment made in 1681. *(See Victoria History, Vol. V p.83)*

In 1715 it was bought by John Gorton of Preston and until 1805 it was the home of the Gorton family. It then came into the possession of the Barker family and in 1834 it became the home of Robert Bennett, a solicitor and his wife Ann, the daughter of Samuel Barker. The Bennett family left in 1846 and the Hall was leased to a Mr Braham, whose insane son set it on fire in 1847. In 1865 it was taken over by Richard Peacock and afterwards was often referred to as "Peacock Hall".

The collection of Dutch 17th century paintings and English Silver in the City Art Gallery is almost entirely from the generous bequest of Mr and Mrs Edgar Assheton Bennett. The collection was finally made over in 1979. Mr Assheton Bennett was the grandson of Mr Robert Bennett.

Gorton House

Gorton House is on the north side of Hyde Road in Debdale Park. The earliest reference to it is that in 1790 it was owned by Robert Grimshaw *(G.H.R)*

In 1825 the Gorton House estate, which included Gorton House, a farm house, farm buildings, cottages and fifty-nine acres of meadow and pasture was put up for sale. By 1844 Joseph Stanfield Grimshaw had become the owner of all or the greater part of the estate. There is no evidence that he was related to Robert Grimshaw. He was the son of John Grimshaw of Audenshaw Lodge. It is not even certain that he ever occupied Gorton House. He built Stanfield Lodge where he was living in 1848 *(Gorton rate book)* and in 1861 *(census returns).*

In 1841 Gorton House was occupied by Nathanial Denton and Joseph Gillham, hat manufacturers, together with their families and servants. They had a hat works in the grounds. In 1850 it was the home of Edward Pinder, a steel manufacturer, and his family. Today it is owned by Manchester Corporation.

High Bank House

The house, known as High Bank, was situated on High Bank, the continuation of Tan Yard Brow. In 1780 it was the home of a Mr Grimshaw. In 1841 it was the home of John and Elizabeth Grimshaw, presumably man and wife, and a George Grimshaw. *(Census returns 1841)*

By a 1861 a new family of Grimshaws were in residence: John and Mary Grimshaw and their three sons. The eldest son, John, was a solicitor, Joseph S. (Stanfield?) was a barrister and their youngest son George was a cotton spinner. The father was the twin brother of Joseph Grimshaw of Stanfield Lodge. George was the Grimshaw who built High Bank Mill on Ogden Lane.

The Grimshaws of 1861 were still in residence in 1881 with the exception of Joseph and the father, John Grimshaw. By 1891 they had left. A recreation ground, opened in October 1909, occupies the site of High Bank House.

High Bank Farm

High Bank Farm was a little to the north of High Bank House and on the same side of the lane. In 1844 it was owned by James Grimshaw, who farmed 15 acres. In 1881 it was occupied by

James Brocklehurst and his wife, who with the help of one boy farmed 40 acres.

Kenyon House

Kenyon House, named after Lord Kenyon the owner of the land, was built between 1871 and 1881 for John Buckley (1834-1916), the son of the John Buckley who built Gorton New Mill, better known as Buckley's Mill. John Buckley, senior, was the owner of the Chapel House Inn, the Cornwall Inn, the Plough Inn and a brewery near the Chapel House Inn. He also had a bleach works in Prestwich Clough. By 1861 he had left Gorton and was living in Prestwich Clough.

The younger John Buckley took over the New Gorton Mill, describing himself in the 1881 census returns as "a cotton manufacturer employing 260 workpeople". He was known locally as "the Gorton millionaire". The Gorton Free Library, opened in 1900, was a gift from him to the people of Gorton.

Improvements in the home in the 19th and 20th centuries

W.C.s, hot water and baths

The acquisition of Longdendale in 1862 and Thirlmere in 1894 brought important benefits to the areas served by the Manchester Corporation Water Works. The supply of water was now sufficient for the replacement of the "privy-midden" and "pail" systems of sewage disposal by the water-closet and for the installation of a back-boiler to provide hot water on tap. The conversion to water-closets was carried out by Manchester City Council and therefore came more quickly to Openshaw, which had amalgamated with Manchester in 1890, than to Gorton which had to wait until after 1908.

The provision of a hot water tap and its corollary, the fixed bath, was however a matter for the landlord and the owner-occupier. Of the latter there were few and of the former many were not anxious to make expensive alterations. No separate figures are available for Gorton and Openshaw, but as late as 1951 31% of households in Manchester were without their own bath.

Gas light

Before William Murdock demonstrated in 1793 that coal gas could be used for illumination, buildings were lit by oil lamp, candle and taper and sometimes dwelling houses simply by the light of the fire in the hearth.

Gas was first used in Manchester in 1807, when the Manchester and Salford Police Commissioners, dissatisfied with the existing sperm oil lamps, decided to experiment with gas lighting and started with a single jet outside their headquarters in Police Street at the lower end of King Street. The commissioners, who were responsible for street lighting, then built a gas works in Water Street, which supplied street lamps and a few private houses.

The first gas mains in Gorton were laid by the Manchester Gas Committee between 1856 and 1858. By 1861 there were nearly five miles of pipe along the main roads. *(See rate books for 1856, 1858 and 1861)* Lamp lighters were paid 3d per lamp per week.

In 1855 Openshaw had 22 miles of gas mains, owned by the Manchester Gas Committee, along Pottery Lane, Clayton Lane, Wellington Street and Lees Street, Ogden Lane, Moor Lane (Fairfield Road) and Ashton (Old) Road. There was a further 4 mile of mains in Moor Lane supplying gas from the Droylsden Gas Company.

In both townships gas was first used for street lighting. Probably public buildings, industrial premises and the houses of the well-to-do were the next to have it installed. Large works such as Gorton Tank and Gorton Mill were already manufacturing their own gas. The Stockport Advertiser of 2.3.1874 reported that two sermons had been preached in St. Barnabas's Church, Openshaw, in aid of the funds for beautifying their church and for providing additional gas lights.

It is likely that the widespread use of gas came after 1886. It was in that year that Dr. Welsbach invented the incandescent mantle, which gave a light far superior to that provided by the naked flame of the old gas burners.

Electric Light

In 1879 Edison in the U.S.A produced carbon filament incandescent lamps, invented by Swan in England in 1860. This made electric light possible for domestic use. The two inventors joined forces and put the Ediswan lamp on the market in 1887.

In 1890 Paulden's of All Saints, Manchester, were lighting their retail stores with electricity generated on the premises. In 1893 Manchester Corporation opened their first power station in Dickinson Street, followed by one in Bloom Street. Preparations for an electric tramway system led to the opening in 1902 of a third power station in Stuart Street with an extension shortly afterwards. The flywheels, manufactured in Germany, came in four sections, each weighing 30 tons. Each section was hauled from the railway station on a truck drawn by 16 dray horses. The Stuart Street power station had sufficient power to supply Gorton and Openshaw.

In 1905 the Gorton Urban District Council decided to have forty electric lamps installed on Hyde Road, Wellington Street and Cross Street. The comparative cost of lighting these roads with gas and electricity was as follows:

Electricity	16,400 candle power	£325 p.a.
Existing gas lamps	3,500 candle power	£264 p.a.

As far as can be ascertained, schools and public buildings were lit by electricity before 1914. To dwelling houses electricity came slowly. Not until the 1930s was there a marked increase in the domestic use of this new power. This was brought about by increased prosperity and the success of the Central Electricity Board, established in 1926, in providing a cheap and reliable supply of electricity.

The weekly routine of a typical Openshaw or Gorton housewife in the 1920s and 1930s

Sunday: preparation for washing-day
Towels and bed-linen were put into two tubs of hot and water and left to soak overnight.

Monday: washing-day

Early in the morning the solid fuel boiler was lit. The boiler, known as a "set pot", was in the kitchen, cellar or shed in the backyard. All washing that had to be boiled was put into the set pot.

Other washing went into a zinc "dolly tub", which had ribbed sides, where it was agitated with a "dolly" or a "posser". A dolly resembled a three or four-legged stool with a long wooden handle. A posser was a perforated brass hood also with a long handle. A scrubbing board was used for particular difficult items of washing. This was a corrugated and perforated sheet of zinc mounted on a wooden board.

Each washing was followed by a wringing to press out the dirty water. Then came a rinse and another wringing. Whites were rinsed twice and then "dolly-blued". Items that needed starching were starched. Wringing was done on a "wringer", a machine which was fitted with two rollers, turned by a handle on a large wheel. The same machine was used for "mangling" or smoothing linen. It was often called a "mangle". In the late 19th century, house-wives who did not possess a mangle could take their washing to a "mangle house". By the 1920s there were few houses without one.

Drying took place outdoors or indoors in front of the fire on a large clothes maiden or on a rack suspended from the ceiling.

Cold meat, left over from Sunday, was the usual fare on washing day.

Tuesday: ironing-day
The flat iron was heated on a trivet in front of the fire. Getting the right temperature was difficult, for frequently it was too hot or not hot enough, and maintaining it at the right temperature was impossible as it cooled quickly.

It was customary to put the flat iron into a chrome "slipper" or to rub soap on it to ensure that it ran smoothly.

Wednesday: baking-day
On Wednesday most of the baking for the week was done. In the early 1920s this included bread, but by the end of the decade most housewives preferred to buy shop bread.

Baking was done in an oven, which with the fire-grate and the back-boiler formed the kitchen range. The kitchen range was for the most part made of cast iron, which had to be blackleaded. But there was also some steel, for example the oven hinges, and this had to be emery-papered. At the side of the grate was a hinged iron frame called a "crow", which could be lowered onto the fire to serve as a platform for a kettle or a pan.

On the hearth was the fender, usually of steel and therefore requiring cleaning with emery-paper. Inside the fender were the fire-irons: a poker, a scraper and sometimes a small brush and shovel.

In the 1930s the old-fashioned kitchen ranges were being replaced by "bungalow ranges", which were tiled or stove-enamelled for easy cleaning.

Thursday: bed-rooms
Thursday was the day for thoroughly cleaning the bed-rooms.

Friday: Stair-rods
On Friday the brass stair-rods were polished.

All the foregoing was of course in addition to the many household chores which were done everyday or frequently, including one which typified the era: donkey-stoning the front step and the window-sills.

Hyde Road, Gorton (between 1902 and 1925) showing the Lake Hotel and The Empire Grocers. The latter was at the corner of Church Lane.

Belle Vue, Hyde Road entrance. Photograph probably taken Easter 1944, when 120,000 paid for admission.

The Black Horse, Far Lane, at the turn of the century.

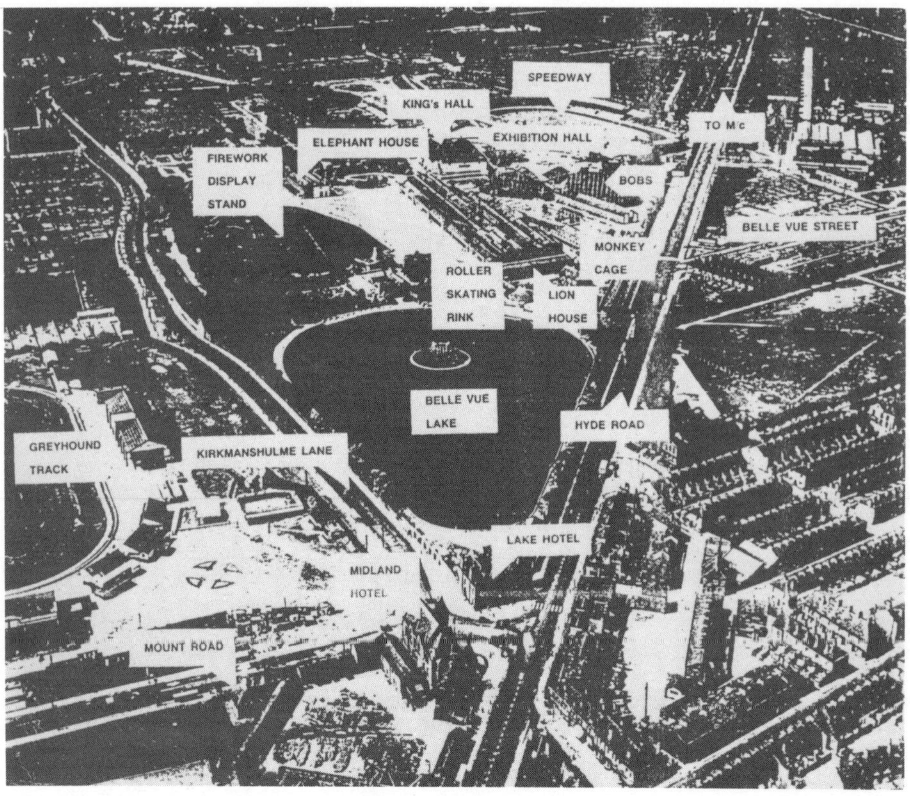

Aerial view of Belle Vue, 1957.

Gorton Town Hall, Hyde Road, at the junction with Kirkmanshulme Lane. Taken from a picture postcard sent by Fusilier John Hickson, stationed at Dover, to his mother at 11, Cross Lane, Gorton. 11.9.1916.

Belle Vue, main entrance, Belle Vue.

Gorton Lane and St. Francis's in the early years of the century.

Ashton Old Road in the early years of the 20th century.

It is the late afternoon or early evening of a summer's day and the sun is shining. Two open-top trams clank and sway as they move in the direction of Fairfield. In the distance two ladies are taking a walk. A man crosses the road and another pauses on the edge of the pavement. Two horses are pulling a waggon. Three men stride out towards the Half Way House. Will they call in or walk past? We shall never know.

The Alhambra Cinema, Ashton Old Road, advertising Gary Cooper in "Man of the West". Taken in the 1950s.

CHAPTER XII

LEISURE

May Day

Between the two wars almost every street in Gorton and Openshaw had its May Queen, usually a girl of school age. She wore a long dress, borrowed from her own or a friend's mother. An old lace curtain, fastened round the head and held up by one of the maids, served as a train. A wooden hoop, decorated with coloured paper, was held in front by two attendants in such a way that it formed a frame for her head and shoulders. Her retinue varied in number, but it was rarely more than six and all were girls. Doors were knocked on and, if fortune smiled, pennies were collected. One song which was sung by her attendants went as follows:

May Day, May Day, bright and shady,
Through the midst of April showers,
The Queen of May is here today,
To give us all a holiday.
Around this merry May-pole
And through the live-long day,
Gentle little *(here followed the name of the Queen)*
Is crowned the Queen of May.
Don't you see, she's the Queen,
Coming from the meadow green?
If you wait a little while,
We will dance the May-pole style.
Dance around the May-pole,
Merrily we go.
Hurrah for the Queen!
Hurrah for the Queen!

Another May Day custom was that of decorating horses and carts with flowers, ribbons and bells. It survived until the 1930s, disappearing when the horse was replaced by the internal combustion engine.

Welcoming the New Year

It was a wide-spread custom in Gorton and Openshaw before the Second World War for the man of the house to go into the street a few minutes before midnight on New Year's Eve, sometimes taking with him a piece of coal for good luck. On the stroke of twelve he would knock at the door and when this was opened, he would enter, bringing good luck for the next twelve months.

Guy Fawkes Night

Bonfires were common but there were no rhymes, apart from the odd couplet of doggerel, to celebrate the end of Guy Fawkes. In Denton, however, children used to chant the following jingle when collecting pennies for fireworks.

We come a cob-coaling for a bon-fire plot,
There's nowt in yon corner but an old pepper pot,
Fol-de-de, Fol-de-di, Fol-de-diddle-i-dum-day,
Up a ladder, down a hole,
Please do give us a cob of coal
Or else a box of matches.
Guy! Guy! Guy! Hit him in the eye!
Hang him on a lamp post and let him die.
Christmas is coming and the geese are getting fat,
Please put a penny in the old man's hat.
If you haven't got a penny, a aipenny will do,
If you haven't got a aipenny, God bless you.
Tramp, tramp, tramp, the boys are marching,
Who's that knocking at the door?
Oh, it's little Mary Ann with a candle in her hand
And she's going down the cellar for some coal,
For some coal, for some coal,
Yes, she's going down the cellar for some coal.

Gorton Wakes

The word "wakes" is derived from 'wake', originally a watch or vigil held in a church to celebrate the festival of the patron saint. With the passage of time the wake or wakes lost much of its religious significance and became an occasion for jollifications, which usually included a rush-bearing ceremony when rushes, fashioned in the shape of a pyramid, were taken on a cart to the church to be used as a floor-covering. There were rush-bearing ceremonies in both Gorton and Openshaw before 1775 according to John Higson:

"Until 1775 there were two rush carts, one from Gorton and one from Openshaw, with a good deal of rivalry as to who could produce the finest rush-bearings and the best dances. By that year Gorton chapel was flagged and more of less carpeted and so, the need for rushes being no longer there, the men of Openshaw discontinued their contributions. The men of Gorton, on the other hand, kept up the custom for many years afterwards." *(Gorton Historical Recorder p.164)*

Morris dancing was a feature of the Gorton and Openshaw rush-bearings before 1775, for the 'best dances' can only have been Morris dances. There is no record of rush-bearing in Gorton after 1874. Morris dancing, which died out at the same time, was revived in 1974, when the Gorton Morris Men were formed.

Amongst the entertainments of the 1804 Gorton Wakes were bull baiting and bear baiting. By 1858 an annual fair had become the main attraction of Gorton Wakes. Indeed, the fair was known as Gorton Wakes. Upto 1870 the Plough Inn was the focal point of the festivities. In that year, however, ground near the Plough Inn was closed by stumps and railings, leaving only limited space for a fair. There were in fact two fairs: a small one near the Plough and a large one on the Town Croft, a piece of land, bounded by Croft Street, Chapman Street, Cross Lane and Wellington Street.

In the early part of the 20th century the Town Croft became built up and the Gorton Fair was held on an open piece of ground between Peacock Street and Casson Street. When Peacock Street school was built in 1928, a site for the fair was found in the vicinity of Broughton Street and Waddington Street. One Gorton resident remembers the fair being behind Taylor Street.

Until the Second World War, Wakes Week, the week beginning with the first Sunday in September, was the principal holiday period in Gorton and Openshaw. All factories were closed down. It was the favourite week for weddings, as for most people it was their only full week's holiday. On 4.9.1942 the Gorton and Openshaw Reporter said that Gorton Wakes had commenced but most people had taken their holiday. On 7.8.1953 the same newspaper reported that for some years Gorton Wakes had been from July 18th to August 1st.

Whitweek
Before the 1939-1945 war the Whitsuntide holiday in Gorton and Openshaw was second only in importance to Wakes week. On the first Sunday the churches held their Whitweek walk, when the minister led the members of his congregation in a procession around the parish, usually accompanied by a brass band. On Thursday, Friday and Saturday all works closed down. The holiday appears to have been discontinued during the war.

The tradition of celebrating Whitsuntide with a few days holiday is an old one. In 1888 most Gorton Sunday schools had celebrations which lasted a good part of the week. A programme of the week's events was published in the Reporter of 26.5.1888.

Wellington Street Baptist Sunday School
Thursday a.m. procession in neighbourhood. Afternoon to field in Gorton and free tea in school.
Friday Teachers and senior scholars to Llandudno.
Saturday Lurry trip to Romiley.

Brookfield Church Sunday School
Peacock's Gorton Brass Band engaged.
Thursday Procession round township, tea at schools and afterwards to field kindly lent by R.Peacock, Esq. M.P.
Friday to Knowsley (Rowsley?) for Chatsworth.

Gorton Parish Church Schools
Gorton Parish Church band engaged
Thursday Procession round parish
Friday Games in field

Whitsuntide finery and Fairfield Wells *(from the G.O.R. 11.6.1932)*
Fairfield Wells are spoken of as St. Anne's Wells by some residents, or S'enthorn Wells by others. Some aver there was a connection between the Wells and St. Anne's church, Fairfield, but there seems to be stronger support for the belief that the name of the Wells derived from 'Seven Thorns'. The wells were situate at the corner of Station Road on the Audenshaw side, now occupied by Auburn House, which was built nearly fifty years ago. Years ago the Wells formed one of the water supplies of the district and the water was sold by young girls. An old resident says the girls used to cry, 'Who will buy my St. Anne's water, a boodle a burn'. A boodle was a fraction of a farthing, a burn was about two gallons. The girls carried the water in wooden pails, two of which they attached to a wooden hoop with the pails on either side of them. The idea of the hoop was to keep the pails clear of the legs and prevent spilling. All the money which the girls received was saved in order to buy their Whitsuntide finery. The wells were semi-circular orifices built into a low bank. The water was always clear and the wells had a constant supply of water.
(Station Road is now Manshaw Road)

Cricket
Gorton Cricket Club was founded in 1848. Its first ground, between Lees Street and the present Constable Street, is marked on the 1890 map as a rectangle to the north of Gorton Mills. Until it joined the Lancashire and Cheshire League in 1919 it played only friendly matches.

In the summer of 1890 property development near the ground with the prospect of development of the ground itself prompted the club to lease from Mr Chapman, the landowner, a ground on Chapman Street near the railway. It played there until the end of the 1933 season, when building development again compelled it to leave. In 1934 it was without a ground and played only away games. In the following year it amalgamated with the Reddish club.

West Gorton had its own cricket club with a ground near Belle Vue station. There appears to be no record of it after 1888.

Football
In the 19th century Gorton had its own football team, Gorton Villa F.C. On 20.10.1888 the Gorton Reporter said, "The Gorton Villa F.C. continues on its victorious way", and added that it had only been beaten once and that was by Bolton Wanderers.

In May, 1888, the club acquired a new ground on Church Lane (now Cambert Lane) opposite the Congregational Church, using the Chapel House Hotel as the club house and one of the rooms in the hotel as a dressing room. The ground is marked on the 1890 map.

By 1893 Gorton Villa had joined the Pottery League and was playing on a ground on Chapman Street, possibly that of the Gorton Cricket Club. In September of the same year the club was dissolved. The reason was financial - the club owed £200. A reader complained to the Gorton and Openshaw Reporter that he and many other supporters had subscribed £1 each towards the cost of a new ground.

Parks, Recreation Grounds and Playing Fields - Dates of Opening
The difference between parks, recreation grounds and playing fields is a question of amenities. Parks have the most amenities and playing fields the least.

1891 - Greenside Street (originally George Street) Recreation Ground, Openshaw.

1893 Gorton Park
1897 Whyatt Street Recreation Ground, Openshaw
1899 Delamere Park, previously known as "Burkitt's Meadow".
1909 Sunny Brow Park. Named after one of the fields which formed the park.
1909 High Bank Recreation Ground. Developed on the site of High Bank House.
1909 Abbey Hey Park. It lay between High Bank and Green Fold and was later converted to an allotment. It is again a playing field.
1912 Debdale Park. One of its great attractions before the Second World War was the brass band that played in summer on Sunday afternoons and evenings.
1915 Casson Street (off Gorton Lane) Recreation Ground
1950 King George's Playing Field, Chapman Street. During the war it was used by the R.A.F. as a site for barrage balloons

All the above are owned by the Manchester Corporation. The two important playing fields that follow are the property of the Manchester and Salford Playing Fields Society:

The Melland Playing Field opened in 1907, Mount Road, Gorton, was bought with funds raised after a public appeal. The name "Melland" was chosen in appreciation of the work of Alderman William Melland, a chairman of the Playing Fields Society. During the war it was the site of a P.O.W. camp.

The Godfrey Ermen Playing Field was opened in 1931. Godfrey Ermen was born in Holland about 1812. About 1835 he joined his older brothers, who had a cotton mill in Blackfriars, eventually taking charge of the business. He died in 1899, leaving a vast fortune of which £200,000 was in trust for the support of any object deemed worthy of assistance. In 1928, A.G. Roby, one of the trustees, gave £5,000 out of the fund to the Manchester and Salford Playing Fields Society for the purchase of land in Abbey Hey and for the land to be laid out as a playing field. In 1907 money from the fund was used towards the building of Gartside Street Children's hospital. In Eccles there are the Godfrey Ermen Memorial Schools.
(See Godfrey Ermen Memorial C of E Schools by K. Joyce)

William Barker, Stunt Athlete
William Barker of Woodhouse Street, High Bank, died in February, 1965, aged 84. As a music hall entertainer he had cleared two cart horses in a standing jump and snuffed out two five feet high candles with his feet. He won local fame for jumping over the nine feet wide canal at Higher Openshaw in two leap-frog hops. So light was he on his feet that he could touch the water with his feet without sinking. He carried two 25lb. weights, one in each hand, to gain momentum. *(Gorton and Openshaw Reporter, 5.8.1960)* A claim that he could jump in and out of a crate of eggs without breaking any has been disputed.

Gorton Public Houses
John Higson, in his Gorton Historical Recorder, writes that there were four inns in Gorton in the 18th century: the Red Lion, the Packhorse, the George and Dragon and the Horse and Farrier. The Red Lion was in the Gorton portion of Longsight. The Packhorse, which later changed its name to the Midway, was on Stockport Road at the corner of what is now Matthews Lane. The George and Dragon was near Gorton chapel and later became the Chapel House. It was rebuilt at the corner of Croft Street *(Stelling Street).*

The Horse and Farrier, better known by its later name, the Black Horse, was on Far Lane. Before Hyde Road was built in 1818, Far Lane was on the main road to Hyde and it was to this that the Black Horse owed its prosperity. After 1818 it lost much of its trade and in 1833 it was adversely affected by the opening of the Waggon and Horses at the corner of Far Lane and Hyde Road. In 1912 Sarah Peacock surrendered its licence and it then became a dwelling house. It was demolished in the 1950s.

The Lord Nelson in Foxfold is one of many public houses that began as a cottage. It opened about 1860. The first public house in Abbey Hey was the Old House at Home, which in 1861 was owned by John Williamson. There is some evidence that it is the same public house as the Hamlet. The Hamlet was named after a successful whippet dog, probably one that ran at the Abbey Hey Grounds. *(See the Gorton and Openshaw Reporter, 4.7.1931)*

An old handbill, discovered some years ago, advertised the delights of the Pomona Hotel. In addition to attractive gardens, it had a "Grotto, Vinery, Fernery and Hot Houses, Bowling Green, Billiards, Pleasure Boats on hire". The boats were for use on the canal.

The Waggon and Horses on Hyde Road at the corner of Far Lane was a recognised halt for traffic to and from Manchester in the 19th and early 20th centuries. Travellers could purchase food and drink. Drivers, taking taking loads into Manchester, made a habit of putting their dinners into a huge oven so that they would be piping hot on their return. For the horses there were drinking troughs and tubs full of corn. In the days of the charabanc, the Waggon and Horses was a popular stopping place. In 1936 the old Waggon and Horses was pulled down and replaced by the present building. At the same time a car park was laid down to accommodate the new motor coaches. *(G.O.R. 14.1.1949)*

The Plough Inn, licensed in 1823, was for many years the focal point of the Gorton Wakes festivities. The Abbey Hey Hotel was opened in 1863 by Henry Ackroyd, who was also the proprietor of the adjacent Abbey Hey Gardens.

Openshaw Public Houses
One of the earliest Openshaw public houses was the Red Lion, which in the early 18th century stood in little Droylsden on the main road from Manchester to Ashton. Shortly after it was turnpiked in 1733, the road was diverted to its present line i.e. to the north of little Droylsden. The owner and occupant of the Red Lion, John Thelwell, nick-named "old Maccaroni", then built a new Red Lion on Ashton Old Road between what is now Ogden Lane and Vine Street. The Red Lion changed its name to the Halfway House. *(History of Droylsden by John Higson, p.142)*

Some years later the New Inn was built at the corner of Ogden Lane next to the Halfway House. When the licence of the Halfway House lapsed, the New Inn took its name and became known as the Halfway House. About the same time the New Inn was rebuilt. There is no certain date for the rebuilding but from conveyances it appears to have been about 1872.

Three other public houses were in existence in the 18th century: the Drover's, the Grey Mare and the Pack Horse. The Drover's was known locally as "the Sheepshouters" and the Grey Mare's official name was "the Plough". From 1831 the Pack Horse was the headquarters of the Lancasterian Friendly Burial Society, popularly known as the "Neck or nowt".

The Gransmoor Hotel was completed in 1876, but, according to the licensing register, it held a licence prior to 1854. The present building must have replaced an earlier one.

The Abbey Hey Gardens

The Abbey Hey Gardens occupied a piece of land which was bounded on its south east and sides by Abbey Hey Lane, on its north side by the Manchester-Sheffield Railway and on its west side by Hodson Street, the old name for the Gorton portion of Vine Street. They were opened in 1869 by Henry Ackroyd, the proprietor of the Abbey Hey Hotel. They were also known as Abbey Hey Park and and Abbey Hey Grounds.

The Gardens offered a variety of entertainments. According to the Stockport Advertiser of 22.8.1873, the Denton Original Brass Band played for dancing every Saturday and Monday and there was accommodation for 2,000 visitors. The price of admission was 4d. It was however for their sporting attractions that the Gardens were famous. There was a bowling green and a trotting track with a perimeter of half a mile. There was quoits, curling, wrestling, football, May Day horse shows and in 1878 a "run pudding" match between W.Worrall and J.Greenwood, both of Droylsden, for £10 a side. Greenwood won. *(Gorton and Openshaw Reporter, 15.5.1878)*

Blood sports in the form of pigeon shooting, sparrow shooting and rabbit coursing were particularly popular. In the first two sports shot-guns were used. These threw out a string of lead pellets. It is customary to use one when shooting at birds on the wing. There was sparrow shooting at the Sportsman Inn, Hall Street and at the Old House at Home, Abbey Hey.

The gardens closed in 1893 and houses were built on the site. The Lodge Garage, Butman Street, is a reminder of the lodge that stood at one of the entrances to the gardens.

The Belle Vue Zoological Gardens

The Belle Vue Zoological Gardens took their name from a tavern, called Belle Vue, built by John Walker, the son of a local farmer, on Sheffield New Road, as Hyde Road was then called. Sheffield New Road was formed and turnpiked by the Manchester, Hyde and Mottram Turnpike Trust in 1818 and it is likely that Belle Vue tavern was erected about the same year.

Johnson's map, 1820, shows a small open space in front of the tavern to serve as a parking space for waggons whose drivers sought refreshment there. Adjoining the tavern were thirty six acres of ground, to which John Walker gave the name of Belle Vue Gardens. The only attraction in the Gardens was the bowling green.

John Walker sold the estate to William Crisp, who in 1836 sold the tavern and half an acre of land to John Jennison, a Stockport handloom weaver. In 1829 John Jennison had started a small pleasure garden in Stockport, which had attained considerable popularity and encouraged him to embark on his Belle Vue enterprise.

As the popularity of Belle Vue grew, John Jennison bought more land and added to the attractions of the gardens. In 1842 he bought a number of animals from the Vauxhall Gardens in Collyhurst and these formed the nucleus of his collection. The Vauxhall Gardens lay between Rochdale Road and Collyhurst Road near the River Irk. The site of the Gardens is commemorated in the name Vauxhall Street. They were established by Robert Tinker and were also known as Tinker's Gardens.

From an early date Belle Vue was famous for its displays of fireworks, for John Higson recorded:

"Splendid fireworks exhibited at Belle Vue by Signor Pietro (Mr Richardson) of Chapel Houses. 1842, May 2nd."

Ten years later John Jennison introduced a spectacle, which for nearly one hundred years thrilled tens of thousands of children and their parents. This was the pictorial drama, usually some historic battle, re-enacted by a stage army of soldiers, who ran about wildly, firing blank cartridges, and from time to time throwing themselves on the ground in make-believe that they were dead or wounded. The entertainment culminated with a display of fireworks, the magnificence of which was enhanced by their beauty being reflected in the water of the lake which separated spectators from actors. The theme for 1852 was the Bombardment of Algiers.

As the population in and around Gorton increased in numbers and wealth so did the demand for entertainment. Although only a small proportion of the wealth generated by the Industrial Revolution had found its way into the pockets of the working class, the latter were far better off than earlier generations of workers had been. Moreover, communications had improved: the horse bus and the train made Belle Vue more accessible. To meet this demand there was a corresponding increase in the variety of entertainments offered by Belle Vue. Two newspaper accounts illustrate the rise in Belle Vue's prosperity:

Zoological Gardens at Belle Vue

To the Zoological collection many additions have been made, the more noteworthy being a full-grown African lion, imported only a few weeks ago. Two new lakes have been constructed, in order that the waterfowl may revel more unrestrainedly in the element they love so well.

The maze has been retrimmed......... During the forthcoming holidays, two bands will each day delight the ear and give occupation to the feet of thousands of town and country visitors: while the vast music hall, capable of sheltering 20,000 persons, stands ready offering a welcome and gorgeous place of refuge, should the weather prove unpropitious. Opposite the music-hall and above the large lake arises a magnificent scene picture of the siege of Charleston and bombardment of the world-famous Fort Sumter. *(Two episodes of the American Civil War.)*

The whole concludes with a grand display of fireworks, representing the American eagle and the stars of the several state.

(Manchester City News, 28.5.1864)

Belle Vue Gardens
There is, perhaps, no place of public resort in Great Britain, which attracts a larger concourse of visitors than these popular gardens during the Whitsuntide holidays. Mammoth excursion trains from all the surrounding towns and villages pour in their thousands, in addition to the proportion of Manchester folk who would not believe in Whitsuntide if they were not permitted to visit Belle Vue during the holidays. It is therefore not unusual for 50,000 to 60,000 persons to crowd the gardens daily during Whitsun week.

The great pictorial attraction provided this year for the patrons of Belle Vue is a magnificent al fresco painting of the City of Lisbon previous to the earthquake of 1755. At dusk the fearful earthquake, which destroyed the City of Lisbon, will be exhibited and this will form the subject for the usual grand pyrotechnic display, arranged by Mr Danson with the assistance of his two sons.

The music hall has been enlarged and now measures 72 yards by 35 yards.
(Manchester City News, 3.6.1865)

In 1889 the price of admission was 6d each, but on firework days patrons were charged 1s each if they entered after 4 p.m. *(Gorton and Openshaw Reporter 29.6.1889)*

The Belle Vue management encouraged their customers to arrive early, in the belief that the longer they were in the grounds, the more money they would spend. Eventually the surcharge for late admission was dropped. Forty two years later, inspite of inflation and the doubling of wages the admission charge was 6d for adults and 3d for children. The spectacle was the Battle of Waterloo followed by a display of fireworks.

A change of ownership
On January 1st, 1925, Belle Vue was floated as a public company, named Belle Vue (Manchester) Ltd. and the Jennison family were now no longer in control. A series of enterprises followed. In July, 1926, greyhound racing was introduced. In August, 1928, the Manchester Central Football Club with headquarters at Belle Vue made their debut in the Lancashire Combination and beat Lancaster before 10,000 spectators. Dirt-track racing began in April, 1929. At the second meeting there was a crowd of 12,000. The fun-fair side of the business was also developed.
By 1956 all caterings outlets had been taken over by a company belonging to Mr Charles Forte. Gradually this company took over the whole of Belle Vue and the gardens became part of a group called ENTAM.

The end of Belle Vue Zoological Gardens
Belle Vue continued to prosper. During the war, when stay-at-home holidays were encouraged, the Gardens attracted huge crowds. Their prosperity continued for years after the war and in 1962 they were reported as having a bumper Easter Bank Holiday.

In the 1970s they ran into financial difficulties, brought about by falling attendances. There was now competition from other centres of entertainment, such as Blackpool, Alton Towers and Chester Zoo, which, with the increase of motor-car ownership, were becoming increasingly accessible for the day tripper.

On the 12th September, 1977, the Manchester Evening News told the sad story of the departure of the animals:

"It was Noah's Ark in reverse today as, on a wave of nostalgia, the animals continued to leave two-by-two. After 141 years, financial problems forced the Zoo to close yesterday - and the sad exodus began."

In 1981 Belle Vue closed down completely.

Music
The Gorton Singing Club met between 1809 and 1812 at the Horse and Farrier on Far Lane. Its orchestral section included violins, violincellos, bassoons, oboes and clarionettes. The club formed the choir at Gorton Chapel and the Dissenting Chapel. After the service they would adjourn to the Horse and Farrier. In 1812 anxious not to jeopardize its licence, they began to meet at the Old Endowed School at the corner of Cross Lane and Wellington Street. After the change of headquarters the membership dwindled and the club went out of existence, possibly because the school lacked the attractions of the Horse and Farrier. *(Gorton and Openshaw Reporter, 14.9.1872 and a letter signed J.R., dated 1854, in the Manchester Public Library)*

The Gorton (Aspinall Smithy) Old Band In 1838 this band took part in a grand procession in Manchester to celebrate the coronation of Queen Victoria. They were the only equestrians in the procession. *(John Higson, Gorton Historical Recorder)*

The Gorton Tank Prize Band was formed in 1851. It changed its name to the Gorton Silver Prize Band and then to the Gorton and Openshaw Old Silver Prize Band. *(Gorton and Openshaw Reporter, 4.1.1957.)*

The Gorton Philharmonic Society was founded in 1854 by a number of local musicians at a meeting at the home of R.B. Blackshaw of Brook Green Lane, Gorton. Having played together only at the Aspinal Nonconformist Chapel, they wanted to have more frequent opportunities for musical collaboration.

The orchestra met on alternate Sunday mornings, for a time at a private house on Hyde Road and then at the Aspinal Smithy. Later they moved to the old Pomona Hotel. Three more moves took place until in 1891 the Gorton Urban District Council provided accommodation at the Gorton Town Hall, where they stayed until the 1960s. In 1965 a room was provided at the Central High School for Boys on Kirkmanshulme Lane. In 1982 they moved to the East Manchester Music Centre on Ryder Brow Road.

The Society did not find any place where they could regularly give public performances until May, 1887, when the orchestra gave its first "Open Rehearsal" at Belle Vue. "Open Rehearsals" were in fact concerts, but the term was used because the concerts, held on Sunday afternoons, were open to members and patrons of the Society and to members of the public visiting Belle Vue Gardens, free of admission charge. In 1973 a charge of 20p was introduced for members of the public. During this period the Jennisons, the founders of Belle Vue Gardens, had been generous patrons of the Society and the advantageous terms they gave were continued under their successors.

However, when Charles Forte acquired Belle Vue, the terms were changed and the Society had to look elsewhere. From 1977 concerts were held at Stockport Town Hall, with occasional ones at the Manchester Town Hall and the Free Trade Hall. It now holds five concerts per year, four at Stockport Town Hall and one at Manchester Town Hall.

The officers of the Society include Sir William Downward, J.P.,L.L.D., formerly Lord Lieutenant of Greater Manchester, who is the President; Godfrey Somech. the vice-president; Colin Touchin, the conductor and John Boydell, the secretary.

The Gorton Male Voice Choir

In 1906 Tom Beveridge formed a quartet, which met at a house in Wellington Street. By the following year the quartet had grown into the Gorton Male Voice Choir and a room at the Co-operative Hall on Wellington Street was hired for rehearsals. Apart from a short period during the Second World War, the Co-operative Hall continued as the Choir's headquarters for more than fifty years. After leaving the Hall it moved to the Labour Club. Since 1970 the school room of Brookfield Church has been used.

In its hey-day the Gorton Male Voice Choir was essentially a festival choir. On eleven occasions they won the Burbage Shield, awarded at the Buxton Festival. Between the two wars they found outstanding conductors in Tom Corlett and William Mitchell. When in 1936 they were awarded the highest number of points, the composer, Sir Granville Bantock, paid a tribute to the Choir by setting to music Robert Browning's A Grammarian's Funeral, a poem chosen by Mr Mitchell. Another of their successes was in 1967 at the Bromborough Festival, when after winning the trophy for the 3rd successive year they were awarded 99 points out of 100 in the Bebington Corporation Trophy.

In recent years recruitment to the choir has fallen off and today their efforts are devoted to charity and church concerts and participation in mass male voice choirs.

Today's officers are: William J. Hanson, chairman and treasurer (over 35 years service), Derek Edwards, conductor (over 30 years service), Mrs Dorothy Fisher, pianist (over 30 years service)

Lark singing contests were sufficiently popular in the late 19th and early 20th centuries for the Gorton owners of the birds to form the Gorton Lark Singers Association. The contests took place in public houses. The winning lark was the one that could sing for the longest time. The following account of a contest was published in the Gorton and Openshaw Reporter of 25.1.1902. "The first contest of the season took place on Saturday last at the house of Mr John Warburton, Sportsman Inn, Hall Street (Now Hengist Street), Gorton. There were 22 birds entered for the prizes offered by the landlord, which consisted of some very useful articles. There was some good singing considering the weather we have had of late."

The larks were timed over 13 minutes. The winner was I.J. Warburton's bird. It sang for 12 minutes 29 seconds.

John Beswick of Gorton, singer, fiddler, flautist was known to everyone as Parish Jack. His services were often in demand at 'stirs' and merry makings. He was author or compiler of the words of the song 'Gorton Town' and composer of the tune. 'Gorton Town' was sung in February, 1865, by Samuel Beswick, at the naming of a dog 'Ringwood' at the Hare and Hounds Inn, Abbey Hey. *(Songs and Ballads of Lancashire by John Harland)*. The writer of the song tells of his return to Gorton Town and the changes he found. In days gone by there were honest men in Parliament, the mills worked full time, there were no strikes and wages were never reduced. But, now, he says, things are different. Poor folk go hungry. They live on soup and bad beer, provided by the Poor Law. He is in fact describing the devastating effects that the American Civil War (1861-65) had upon the lives of Gorton men and women. *(See Chapter 1, 1862-63)*

Theatres

The Metropole Theatre was opened in 1898 as a member of the Broadhead Circuit. It stood on the site of the old Whyatt's dyeworks. Its stage productions were in the early years music hall and melodrama, two-well known examples of the latter being The Face At The Window and Maria Marten And The Red Barn. The first play was a Woman's Victory, a story of the South African War. The record audience was 4,725, possibly when the seating consisted mainly of forms, for in 1938 the accommodation was given as 3.700 seats.

In October, 1905, the King's Theatre, Stockport Road, Longsight, was opened and on February 6th, 1909, the Alhambra Theatre, Higher Openshaw, gave its first stage production. The entertainment at the Alhambra appears to have been mainly of the music hall kind. Harry Tate, a famous comedian in his day, and his No1 company gave a performance in October of the same year. Adjoining the theatre were the Assembly Rooms, which held between 1,400 and 1,500 people.

The Change to cinema

In 1889 Friese-Green patented the first kinematograph device, but the performance that showed the possibilities of the new invention was given by the brothers Lumiere of France in 1896. The first British showing on the Lumiere machine took place in the same year.

Only twelve months after its opening the Alhambra Theatre was experimenting with moving pictures. In the Gorton and Openshaw Reporter of 26.2.1910, a review of variety turns ended with, "The bioscope pictures are up-to-date and interesting and the orchestra as usual play well under Mr J. Harvey, musical director".

By August, 1910, a separate hall for the showing of moving pictures had been built at the rear of the Alhambra Theatre. Entrance to the Alhambra Pavilion, as the picture hall was called, was by way of Buckley Street. A review of a performance appeared in the Gorton and Openshaw Reporter of 13.8.1910:

"Alhambra Pavilion, Openshaw

There is a fine array of pictures at the pavilion this week, including 'Crippen', 'The Girl and The Fugitive', 'Winning of Father', 'The Converts', 'Old Sleuth', 'On the Border Line', 'The Gipsies', 'Hand', 'The Love Of Lady Irma', etc, an admirable medley of pathos, tragedy, comedy and scenery to please all tastes and fancies."

In 1909 an Act of Parliament was passed requiring cinemas to be registered. The Act became operative in March 1910. In that year five Gorton and Openshaw cinemas, including the Alhambra, were registered. The others were: Belle Vue Gardens which closed in 1914; the King George Picturedrome, Gorton Lane, which changed its name to the Plaza in 1916; the Labour Hall Picturedrome, Knutsford Road, which closed in 1916 and the Imperial, 690 Ashton Old Road, which closed in 1916 or shortly after. Note that 1910 was the year of registration and that any one of the four cinemas may have been open before 1910. After 1910 it can be assumed that the year of registration and the year of opening were the same.

The Labour Hall claimed to be "the original picture house of the district". It had twice nightly performances at 7 p.m. and 9 p.m. with matinees four afternoons each week.

In 1913, a billiard hall near the canal bridge on Ashton Old Road was converted into the Openshaw Picture Hall and later given the name "Rex".

On 3.1.1914, the Gorton and Openshaw Reporter gave its readers a description of a "New Electric Theatre", which had just opened in Old Lane, Openshaw. It was called the Whitehall Cinema. "The tip-up chairs are practically the only ones in the neighbourhood for the humble 'tuppence' and their equipment is quite sanitary." Charges for admission were 2d, 3d, 4d. The films for the week were: "A message from Mars" and "The Peril of the Law".

The question of hygiene was important. The upholstery of some cinema seats was flea-ridden and in consequence the cinemas in question were often referred to as "bug-huts".

In 1916 the Alhambra Theatre went over to cinema and the Alhambra Pavilion became a dance hall.

"The Talkies"

On November 14th, 1928, the New Oxford Cinema, Manchester, presented the first complete "talkie" programme shown outside America. It was a 12-reel film of "Uncle Tom's Cabin" with an "all-recorded background". But the astounding success of "The Singing Fool", starring Al Jolson, had already demonstrated that for the silent screen the writing was on the wall and within a year or so all the Manchester cinemas were equipped for sound.

The coming of the "talkie" brought to an end the career of thousands of cinema pianists, whose job it was to accompany the action on the screen with appropriate music, which could range from Suppe's "Light Calvary", as the hero galloped to the rescue, to Lizt's "Liebestraum" for a romantic love scene. It also brought to an end, much to everyone's relief, the irritating habit of cinema-goers of reading in a loud voice, for the benefit of their illiterate companions, the captions, which appeared at frequent intervals on the screen.

The 1930s were the hey-day of the cinema. Everywhere theatres were closing down or going over to films. The King's Theatre, Longsight, was converted to cinema in 1933 and the Metropole in 1938. Theatrical producers inveighed against the "celluloid monster", but in vain. Luxury cinemas were built to satisfy new demand. On Mount Road, Gorton, there was the Rivoli opened in 1935. It changed its name to "the Essoldo" after the war. Not very far away for patrons who lived in north Gorton or in Openshaw, there was the Carlton cinema in Clayton, a name, which successfully conjured up a vision of opulence and comfort.

Programmes were changed twice a week and there were so many local cinemas, that it was possible to spend every night at the cinema without having to use bus or tram and without seeing any film twice. Price of admission varied between 3d and 1s.

At the outbreak of war, places of public entertainment, including cinemas, were closed for a time, as it was considered unwise to permit large gatherings when there was a danger of air-raids. When the expected air-raids did not materialise, the regulations were relaxed. In the late summer of 1940 Germany's long expected air offensive began, but by this time the authorities were taking the view that entertainment was essential in war-time and cinemas and other places of entertainment were allowed to stay open. Nevertheless, enjoyment was considerably reduced by the frequent "alerts" which were flashed on to the screen to warn of the approaching enemy. In March, 1941, cinemas were allowed to open on Sunday.

The end of the cinema era

It was the invention of television that bought to an end the dominance of the cinema world of entertainment, but its effect was not immediate. A physicist, Campbell Swinton, envisaged the invention of the cathode-ray tube as far back as 1908, but it was not until the 1930s that the first cathode-ray tube was built at the Electrical and Musical Industries Ltd. laboratory. In 1936 the B.B.C. opened the world's first full scale television service, operating from the Alexandra Palace Transmitter. By the outbreak of war, however, there were only a few thousand viewers in the country and they were all in the London area.

When the war ended, production of television sets began again and transmissions could be received throughout the country. Screens were small, pictures lacked clarity and the cost of renting was by modern standards exorbitant. Fifteen shillings, the modern equivalent of about £10, was the usual charge for a week's viewing. Yet demand went on increasing and the cinema were powerless in face of the competition. One by one they closed down, many of them catering for the new craze - Bingo.

Gorton and Openshaw Cinemas - a summary

1910

The Alhambra Pavilion, Buckley Street, Openshaw. This cinema closed 1916, when the Alhambra theatre was converted to cinema.

The King George picturedrome, Gorton Lane, Gorton. In 1916 it changed its name to "the Plaza". The Plaza closed in 1957.

The following cinemas were licensed in 1910 but they may have opened before that year.

Belle Vue Gardens. Closed in 1914

The Labour Hall Picturedrome, Knutsford Road, Gorton. Closed in 1916.

The Manchester Picture Palace, also known as "the Imperial",

690, Ashton Old Road, Openshaw. Closed 1915.

1911
Olympia, Hyde Road, Gorton. The building, which lies between Knutsford Road and Parkdale Avenue, has been taken over by Safeways. The cinema closed in 1959.

1912
New Central Picture Palace, Clowes Street, West Gorton. This cinema changed its name to "Conway" in 1915. It closed in 1961.

The Prince's, Grey Mare Lane, Openshaw. Closed 1961.

1913
The Cosmo, Wellington Street, Gorton. Closed 1960.
The Openshaw Picture Hall stood on the north side of Ashton Old Road, a little to the west of the canal and to the east of Elysian Street, which then joined the main road. It changed its name to the Rex. It closed before 1951.

1914
The Whitehall, Old Lane, Openshaw. It changed its name to "the Regal" in 1958 and closed in 1964.

1915
The Corona, Birch Street, West Gorton. It closed in 1958.

1916
The Alhambra Theatre, Ashton Old Road, Openshaw, near the corner of Old Lane. Closed 1960.

1935
The Rivoli, Mount Road, Gorton. It changed its name to "Essoldo". It closed in 1968.

Other local cinemas

1912
The Queen's Ashton Old Road, Ardwick. The cinema closed in 1961

1913
The Roy, Ashton Old Road, Ardwick. Closed 1951

1930
The Carlton, Ashton Old Road, Clayton. Closed 1964.

1933
The King's Theatre, Stockport Road, Longsight. The King's Theatre opened in 1905. It was converted to cinema in 1933. Closed 1964.

Children's activities in the inter-war years

(B) denotes a boys activity, (G) a girls and (B and G) one that was pursued by both boys and girls.

Marbles (B) Marbles often known as "allies", vied with "flirty on" for being the most popular of games played by boys. To win your opponent's marble you had to hit it with your own. There was a variety of marbles, ranging upwards from the clay ones, which could be bought for as little as twenty for a penny, to the large coloured glass marbles which might cost a penny each.

Meccano (B) Of all indoor toys none could have given more enjoyment to boys than the Meccano. Meccano was sold in graded sets, each of which contained a variety of pieces of this steel, drilled with holes and suitably shaped for building engineering models. The popularity of Meccano lay in the scope it gave for imagination.

Photographs (B and G) For a penny one could buy a kit, consisting of a negative, a piece of what was called "sentisized" paper and a cardboard frame to hold them firmly in position. The frame and its contents were propped up on a window sill in the sun to allow the picture to develop on the "sentisized" paper.

Rally-vo (B) The name "Rally-vo" is a corruption of "Relievo". The game was derived from a game played in the 19th century by adults and known as "Prisoner's base" or "Prisoner's Bars". The object of the game was to capture a member of the opposing team. This was done by chasing and touching. Every person touched was sent to prison and could only be released by one from his own side touching him.

Piggy (B) The "piggy", a short piece of broom handle, tapered so that it resembled a pig's snout, was placed on a brick or stone with the tapered end protruding. One of the contestants would give the piggy a sharp blow with a stick causing it to jump up into the air.While it was still in the air, he would hit it as far as he could. He would then estimate the number of leaps - each one from a standstill - that his opponent would have to make to reach the "piggy" and then mentally subtract one or two from that number and challenge him to reach the "piggy" at the lower figure. If the boy thus challenged succeeded, he scored that number of points. If he failed, the points went to the challenger. The skill lay in hitting the "piggy" a good distance and making a challenge which was just beyond the powers of your opponent.

Bicycles, tricycles and scooters (B and G)

Bobbers and Kibs (G) Nowadays this game is called "jacks".

Toys, guns and bomb firing explosive caps (B) A roll of caps was inserted into the gun and fired individually by pulling the trigger. The bomb, spherical in shape and made of metal, was in two sections. A cap was placed between the sections and exploded by throwing or dropping the bomb.

A key and nail bomb (B) This was not as fearsome as it sounds. It was made by ramming charcoal, saltpetre and sulphur into a hollow key into which a nail was then pushed. Nail and key, tied together by a piece of string, were swung against a wall with sufficient force to explode the mixture.

Collecting cigarette cards (B and G) This was a universal hobby amongst boys. Its great attraction was that the cards were free and could be found in discarded cigarette packets. Cigarette cards were also used for playing a very popular game called "flirty on". This was a boys game. Two contestants would kneel on the kerbstone and in turn "flirt" (=flick) a card in the direction of the wall. The cards would of course drop onto the pavement. The game would continue until one of the boys succeeded in "flirting" a card so that it fell on another card. He had then won all the cards on the pavement.

Corkwork (G) Corkwork was a form of tubular knitting. The term is, however, a misnomer, as no cork was used. At least four nails were tapped in around one of the holes in a wooden bobbin. These nails acted as knitting needles. Using woollen thread, stitches were put onto the nails by hand and looped onto the ones above with a darning needle. Eventually, a wooden tube emerged from the hole at the other end of the bobbin. When this was of sufficient length it was sewn into a spiral-shaped mat.

Fighting (B) If a boy wanted to challenge another boy to a fight, he would tap him on the chest with his clenched fist and say "here are your cagings." The phase was, no doubt, derived from the gage thrown down by knights of old.

Hoops (G) Metal hoops were popular. Sometimes they had a metal rod attached, which was used for driving and guiding.

Hopscotch (G)

Fretwork (B) Although advertised as a hobby for boys, it was suitable only for those endowed by nature with a high degree of manual dexterity and patience.

Jack, Jack, show your light (B and G) This game, one of a variety of hide and seek games, probably had an ancient ancestry. Most likely Jack was Jack o' Lantern, the elusive Will-o'-the-Wisp. Autumn was the best time for "Jack,Jack, show your light", when the dark had set in early and the air was still mild.

The boy or girl chosen to be Jack was equipped with a lantern improvised out of a jam jar, to which a string handle had been attached, and a piece of candle. Carrying the lantern in such a way that its light could not be seen, Jack would run away and hide. At the shout of "Jack, Jack, show your light", he would give the seekers a brief glimpse of the light and then hurry away to find a new hiding place.

Mrs Sadie Currie in her reminiscences of Gorton gives an interesting account of other children's games.

The amusement park, Belle Vue. The photograph was probably taken Easter, 1944, when 120,000 people paid for admission.

Gorton Hall and lodge in the late 19th century. The letters RP above the lodge window are the initials of Richard Peacock. The hall was demolished in 1906 but the lodge in the picture is still in existence. It stands on Brookhurst Road.

Fairfield Wells once supplied the district with water. They were at the corner of Station Road. (Manshaw Road). They were filled in when Auburn House was built.

CHAPTER XIII

MEMORIES OF OLD GORTON AND OPENSHAW

"Gorton in the 1870's" by Sam Kirkham.

Published in the Gorton and Openshaw Reporter on 26.12.1931. Samuel Kirkham was born in 1860 in the turret of Belle Vue goal, where his father was a warder.

Old Toll-Bars Older people will remember two of the well-known toll-bars at this end of Gorton: the one at Hyde Road near the railway arch and the other in Belle Vue Street. In summer time when traffic was heavy with visitors to Belle Vue, the drivers of conveyances, buses, wagonettes, cabs etc would come together in groups. While the toll-collector was collecting the money off the first two or three, and, of course, they all wanted change, the others would slip round a side street into Grey Street and then on again to Hague Road, thus avoiding payment. All along Hyde Road could be seen barefooted lads turning cart-wheels and standing on their heads for coppers.

Diddling visitors What diddling and cheating there was with the small omnibus proprictors! The regular Manchester Carriage Company's buses were run under proper conditions with always a fixed fare, but the "pirates!" What twisting, especially after the fireworks. Many a time a "pirate" would get as far as Ardwick Green and pretend the bus had broken down. They charged as much as the regular service and, on getting rid of their passengers, they would turn round again to get a last load and charge as much as a shilling into town.

Scuttling gangs The scuttling gangs were going about this time. A gang would cross over Donkey Common from Miles Platting or Bradford way to meet an Openshaw or Gorton gang. They would be drawn up, not in echelon but in mass formation. They would approach nearer and nearer. Then the leader would shout their battle cries. The weapons were belts, slings, sticks and stones. Both sides would give a yell as the police came on the scene, then the two armies would scatter in all directions to meet some other day.

Mr Alfred Pemberton's memories (Gorton and Openshaw Reporter, 10.6.1960 and 24.6.1960) Mr Pemberton was born about 1884.

The first house I remember being in was at the top of Vine Street, the Abbey Hey end. There was only one row of houses, on the right, perhaps seven in all. We used to go upstairs and watch the trotting, rabbit chasing and other sports connected with the Abbey Hey Hotel. I remember that people used to gather outside the boards, waiting for the rabbits which sometimes got away from the dogs. We did not stay long for the houses were demolished to make way for the railway. Half way along Vine Street was a bridge known as the "double bridge", which has since been rebuilt. Vine Street was then a muddy lane. *(The Abbey Hey stretch of Vine Street was then called Hodson Street)*

Local butchers killed their own beasts and put the cattle in the meadow to graze until they were wanted for killing. The cattle came on the hoof from Manchester market.

Women do not do the housework now as they did years ago. Nearly all the washing was done at home and a wash-boiler was a common sight. Better off people sent their washing out or paid a washer-woman to come in and do it. A fore-runner of the laundrette was the communal mangle. There was one in Mary Street. It was a kind of big press, worked by a wheel, four and a half feet in diameter which was turned by hand. The price paid for turning the handle was 2d or 3d a basket. The mangle occupied half a house and the man who turned it was quite a character. He used to attend the sports grounds in the district with a small push-cart, selling hot potatoes and green peas.

There were some unusual sights in the streets in those days, one of which was a dancing bear. It was also common to see German bands and hurdy-gurdy organs. A few of the ladies used to dance to them and, needless to say, so did the children. I remember a touring theatre that used to park behind the Half Way House Hotel and entertain the locals with blood and drama. I wonder how many of Openshaw's residents remember Crossley's penny concerts on Saturday night in the Whitworth Street Hall.

(The communal mangle in Mary Street appears to have been a box mangle. There is one in the museum at Ordsall Hall. See sketch on p.95)

Mrs Sadie Currie's Memories *(Manchester Evening News, 15.9.1973)*

I was born in 1905 and lived there until I was 23 years old. Our days were punctuated by the siren - everybody called it "the buzzer" - which blew for the start and finish at the works. It blew at 7.45 a.m. as a warning and we could hear the clatter of hundreds of feet walking past. The buzzer went again at 8 a.m., after which the gates were closed and anyone late lost half a day's pay. Again at 12 noon and 1 p.m. and 6 p.m. sounded the buzzer - and then the feet walked back again.

We lived in Gorton, because my father and my mother were in business there. We had no garden and I remember playing out in the streets with the local children. Many games seemed seasonal, but I have no idea how we knew when each was in season. One day all the children would bring out whips and tops and we would all play with them for weeks. We used to decorate our tops with coloured chalks to make pretty patterns as they were spinning. Then suddenly everybody was skipping and the tops disappeared until next year. We chanted various rhymes while we skipped and we had different rhymes and counting rhythms for ball games. Sometimes we tied clothes-lines to the lamp-posts to make swings and then for a change, we would jump higher and higher over these ropes. Hop scotch was very popular, for which we chalked out the pavement flags into numbered squares.

In its season all the little girls played Bobber and Kibs. We all squatted in the gutter to play this game on the kerb. The boys played marbles a great deal and a game called Piggy and Stick. The lamp-posts were also used for wickets in games of soft-ball cricket. We all joined up for Hide and Seek, London Bridge is falling down, but the most popular game was "There came three labourers out of work". In this game three would dance up to the rest, singing

"There came three labourers out of work,
Please can you oblige them?"

The rest would ask, "What can you do?", the reply being, "Anything". Then they were told, "Get agate". That must have been a colloquial expression. It meant, "Start working". This was the signal to mime some employment which had to be guessed.

There was no radio when I was young. We made our own amusements. People played cards, chess and draughts. Many people learned to play the piano and some had singing lessons. It was the custom for families and friends to gather round the piano and sing the popular songs of the day. Sheet music sold as freely as records today. On Sundays I always went to church service, both morning and evening. I also attended Sunday school until I was 18. When I was 15 we had a vicar with modern ideas, who allowed us to hold a dance each Saturday night in the church hall. On Sunday night, after church, it was the custom for all young people to take a walk up Hyde Road to Denton and back. Older folk called it, jokingly, the Monkey Parade. Two, three or four girls would walk together and the boys did the same. We would eye each other and maybe stop to chat with groups of acquaintances.

Elections were quite exciting for the children. All wore the colour of the party supported by their fathers. Liberals sported red rosettes and Conservatives, blue. Groups of children went round singing in competition with rival supporters

*"Vote, vote, vote for Mr 'Brown'
He is going to win the day.
We are voting very fast
And we'll have him in last.
And we'll throw old 'Robinson' away."*

At Whitsun each Sunday school walked round the parish. On the Friday everybody turned out to watch the Roman Catholics, who made a wonderful display. They had a long procession with at least four brass bands and a score of banners.

Children used to make their own fun and played some old games in the streets when I was a boy: "Ring-a-ring-a-roses", "Jack, show your light", "Kick stone", "Rally O" and the "Button and cotton game" were the most popular. In the latter we used to stick a pin in a window frame with a button and cotton attached. When the cotton was pulled from the other side of the street, the people in the house (our victims) would find no-one there.

One thing we do not see nowadays in Openshaw is the queue, generally down an entry or side street, for the pawnshop. The queue generally formed on a Monday, when there was very little money about. Most of us had what were called "Sunday best" clothes, which were worn only on special occasions. They were pawned on Monday morning in order to raise enough money to get food and coal to last the week. When pay day came round, we went to the pawnshop and redeemed our clothes.

Mrs Tipping's memories *(Gorton and Openshaw Reporter, 3.11.1939)*

Mrs Tipping, of the School House, South Street, Openshaw, was born in 1853.

I can remember water pipes being laid on in Openshaw. As a girl I played on the big water pipes placed at the side of Ashton Old Road. Until water was laid on, we got our washing water from Whyatt's Dyeworks and our drinking water from a tap near the Travellers' Call on Ashton Old Road. We had to carry water in buckets to our houses.

Mr McEwen's memories *(Gorton and Openshaw Reporter, 1.1.1937)*

Mr McEwen, of Grey Street, Abbey Hey, Gorton, was born in 1858.

When I was a child, I used to get up at four in the morning and go with my mother to the market. I would wheel back an old perambulator, full of garden produce and Eccles cakes. I made up small bundles of watercress and radishes, packed them in a basket and about eight o'clock I would sell them to regular customers at the gates of Whyatt's Dyeworks on Ashton Old Road. Later I crossed over to Ashbury's Works to sell more produce to the workmen. I started work as a boy and I worked until I was nearly seventy. One of my first jobs - for a mere handful of coppers - was in a rope-walk on Ashton Old Road near the Clock Face.

I can remember the old "five-in-hand", which went along Ashton Old Road. Children used to wait for it and as the bugler sounded his tune, they would sing out, "Will you buy, will you buy hot potatoes?"

Mrs Amelia Cooke's memories *(Gorton and Openshaw Reporter, 29.1.1943)*

Mrs Cooke, of 97 Old Lane, Openshaw, was born in 1853. The following brief account of her working life was published shortly after her death.

Mrs Cooke was 90 years of age. She began working at the age of seven at a linoleum factory, which stood near the canal bridge on Ashton Old Road. From six in the morning until six at night, Mrs Cooke picked up bobbins for the women workers. Later she became a back tenter. After the mill had been damaged by fire, she went to work at Rylands' mill on Abbey Hey Lane and then at Grimshaw's mill on Ogden Lane.
(The linoleum factory was owned by the Imperial Oil Cloth Co. Ltd.)

Mr Hyde's memories of employment and unemployment before the Second World War.

My first job

I was born in 1902 and lived the early part of my life near the Bradford Gas Works. When I was thirteen I got a job with Sutton's, the carriers, in German Street off Oldham Road. The name was late changed to Radium Street. My work entailed collecting mail from the post office in Newton Street and delivering outgoing mail to the post office in Spring Gardens. As I did the round six times a day, I must have walked at least seven miles. I had to be out in all weathers and, as I was not provided with water-proof clothing, I was often soaked through. One day, when I arrived at Spring Gardens dripping wet, a clerk offered to solve the problem. He made a poncho out of a double sheet of brown paper and slipped it over my head!

At the cinema

I left Sutton's to work at a warehouse and about the same time got part-time evening employment at the King George's cinema, Gorton Lane. King George's cinema shared films with the Prince's cinema on Grey Mare Lane and I was kept busy all evening, carrying films from one to the other, so that they could be shown at both cinemas on the same evening.

My work must have been satisfactory because I was given a full time job, working with the assistant operator. Everything went well until, one night, I handed her the reels in the wrong order, with the embarrassing result that one character was shown on the screen, alive and well, some minutes after he had been murdered. However, the operator was a good sort and soon got over her annoyance. There were no complaints from the audience. People were more patient then than they are today.

Cleaning out the animal cages at Belle Vue

Although I enjoyed my work at the King George cinema, I found the heat in the projection room oppressive, so I left and got a job at Belle Vue, helping Mr and Mrs Lambert to clean out the animal cages. Animals such as the lion and the tiger had two cages, a big cage and a bedding cage. We would secure them in one of the cages by fastening a gate and then clean out the empty cage. This done, we would manoeuvre them into the other cage and complete the work. Cleaning out the bear pit involved driving the animals, with the aid of a long pole, into a cage at the side and, after closing the gate, getting into the pit with our cleaning tackle.

Tea was provided by Belle Vue and Mr and Mrs Lambert always made sure that all who worked for them got plenty to eat. Tragically, Mrs Lambert was killed by a tiger, but that was after I left. She took too many risks.

Thirty minutes notice

After working at Belle Vue I got on the night shift at Beyer Peacock's. The shift terminated at 7.30 am. One morning at seven o'clock a number of us were told that we were to finish at the end of the shift - that was just 30 minutes notice.

Potato picking

One day at the labour exchange, I saw a notice asking for potato pickers at a farm in Northenden. The pay was 9d an hour, which was the going rate for unskilled labour. The clerk advised me against applying, but as work was not easy to find I thought it worth a try. I walked from Mount Road to Northenden, where I was told by the farmer to report the next morning at 8 a.m.

At 8 o'clock the following morning there were sixteen of us ready to start work, but the farmer said that the ground was too frosty and that we must report again at nine. Nine o'clock came, but the ground was still too frosty and we must come back at ten. Eventually at eleven the farmer suggested that we should have dinner - we had all brought sandwiches - and start immediately afterwards and work through. He took us to a barn and brought us tea in jam jars. We didn't mind that; we weren't expecting the Ritz.

On the way to the field I asked the farmer whether we would get any money for the time we had been waiting for the ground to thaw. "Certainly not,", he replied. Then he went on to make it clear that in no circumstances would we be paid if the weather held up. That was enough for me and a dozen other men and we went home.

The upshot was that six men lost their unemployment pay for six weeks, because, after being instructed to take a job, they had turned it down. Seven of us, including myself, were more fortunate. Because we were, so to speak, volunteers, our pay was deferred for one week and a fortnight later we received two weeks money together.

The means test

About 1930 the government introduced the means test. That meant the incomes of the working members of a family were taken into account before the unemployment pay - we called it the "dole" - of the out-of-work member was assessed. At one time, because my sister was a highly paid shirt machinist, my money was reduced to threepence a week.

Danger money

In the middle thirties I worked on the demolition of Armstrong Whitworth's. I got the basic pay of 9d an hour plus an extra 1d, danger money for working at heights. My work involved walking along girders forty feet above the ground. I think I earned the extra money. One of my fellow workers was killed. He was thrown off a wall.

At last, a permanent job

My last job- and I am happy to say that it lasted thirty five years until I retired - was driving a crane at Gorton Tank and at Longsight. But I nearly missed it. It happened like this. One afternoon about half past two, a note was delivered to my home, asking me to report at one o'clock at the Tank for a medical examination. The note was signed by the manager's secretary.

Of course by the time I arrived at the Tank, it was late afternoon and the foreman of the erecting shop, where I was to work, was for sending me home. When I gave him the full story, He exclaimed, "Ah, that's Mr - 's game is it. I'm the foreman here. You're in." Mr - was the manager's secretary.

It was said of Mr -, that if you were a Catholic, you were half in and that if you were from Ashton, you were half in and that if you were a Catholic from Ashton, you were in. That day I wondered if it was true.

Gore Street Mission and the Gorton Carnival between the two world wars by Mrs Edna Haughton

Many of my happiest childhood memories are associated with the Gore Street Mission. In particular I remember the Whit walks, in which most Gorton churches participated, taking it in turns to lead the procession. The men who played on the Mission cricket team wore their white flannels and it was they who carried our banners. The girls, also dressed in white, carried shepherds crooks and baskets of flowers.

Another of the highlights of the year was the Christmas pantomime, which we always played to a crowded hall.

Then there was the Whit Friday outing. In my early years at the Mission we were taken to Reddish Vale in horse-drawn carts, belonging to Mr Clancy, the local coal merchant. The carts were first scrubbed clean and forms were put in for us to sit on. Refreshments consisted of milk and currant buns. In later years we were taken by train to Marple, Middlewood or Hayfield.

We all had star cards, which were marked at the Mission each Sunday to show that we had attended, and at Christmas we were given books as prizes. Then we had what we called a foot of pennies. This was a length of card with twelve slots, each of which would hold a penny. The money was used to buy Whitweek dresses for poor children.

Carol singing is another of my memories. On Christmas Eve we would be dancing at Brookfield Church hall until eleven, when we would dash across to the Mission to change into our winter clothes. In the early hours we would return to the Mission for breakfast, prepared by the ladies of the Mission, and then off we would go again, finishing our singing at about six in the morning.

The Gorton Carnival, on the other hand, was a day-school affair, involving children from my own school, Old Hall Drive, and from Hyde Road Council School, St. James's and Peacock Street. It took place on Alexandra Rose day and the object was to raise money for the hospitals.
Every year a Rose Queen was chosen in turn from the schools taking part. Tableaux were arranged on floats. One that I took part in was a hospital scene, complete with a bed and a patient in it. We assembled in Gorton Park and, after being given prizes for fancy dress, we paraded along Hyde Road, collecting from the bystanders as we moved along. We finished in Miss Hatton's field near Debdale Park.

Life at the Ashbury Rail, Carriage and Wagon Works.

An article in the Manchester Evening News 4.6.1972

My tale about the quaintly named street in Openshaw, Dining Room Street, brought back a flood of memories to 86-year-old John Forsyth. Mr Forsyth, of Bristowe Street, Clayton, Manchester, confirms that the street took its name from the mess room where the workers at the Ashbury Rail, Carriage and Wagon Works used to eat.

He was an apprentice in the coach-body shop where they built railway carriages to send all over the world.

"My wage was 4s a week minus one penny for the provision of hot water in Dining Room Street," says Mr Forsyth. "The timber used in carriage construction was 'pickled' to eliminate fire risk. An inspector would occasionally gather up some of the wood shavings to see if they would ignite. The works was locally called 'Starvation', the Dyer Street Citadel (a Salvation Army barracks), 'Salvation', the school opposite (Ashton Old Road School), 'Education', and the Metropole Theatre, 'Damnation'.

Memories of Lower Openshaw in the early years of the century, by Mr P Manley

Mr Manley was born in 1910.

The Crossley Lads Club house on Ashton Old Road was built as a hospital by the Crossley Brothers. Its correct title was House of Peace for Persons in Consumption. Consumption or tuberculosis as we call it today was very common at that time.

On the opposite side of the road from the Club was a police station and next to the station was a cinema, owned by an Englishman and a North American Indian. Before each performance, the Indian, dressed in full regalia and mounted on a white horse, would ride round the cinema, followed by his eight year old son on a pinto pony. I used to get in for a penny and a pass from the chip-shop. During the First World War the Englishman joined the army and the Indian was left in charge. Eventually he disappeared, taking with him, so it was said, all the takings.

I remember a character called Isaac the Jew. He was a glazier. He used to walk round the streets, touting for custom, with sheets of glass in a frame on his back and carrying a bag of tools.

There was little or no hire purchase when I was a boy. There were knick-knack clubs for women who wanted to buy clothing, and pawnshops, which usually had a queue outside every Monday morning. Pubs and shops gave credit, but bad payers soon had their credit exhausted. A woman who lived in a side street opposite the Drovers had a profitable business lending money. She charged one penny per week on each shilling borrowed. She had an ingenious way of making an additional profit out of women who were short of money to buy meat. She would take their orders to the Co-op butchers on Vincent Street, where I worked, and keep the divi for herself - it was two shillings in the pound then. I remember, that, when she got home she would put the parcels on the grand piano in the front room. Eventually she went to live in Droylsden.
(The cinema was the Manchester Picture Palace)

Mr J. Green's Memories,

published in the Gorton and Openshaw Reporter, 5.3.1932

Link with horse cars

Mr J. Green, who has just retired from the Manchester Corporation Transport, joined the Manchester Carriage and Tramways Company in 1887 as a driver of the old horse cars. The usual run between Manchester and Stalybridge took two hours, but on Sundays they were allowed three hours for the journey. The trams were open and the fare from Manchester to

Ashton was 4d for those who travelled on the upper deck and 6d for those inside. In the early days there were no penny fares. The lowest were 2d on the upper deck and 3d below. The guard called at all the hotels on the way to let people know that the tram had arrived.

Mr F. Craven's memories of Openshaw

I was born in Gate Street, Openshaw, in 1912. I lived there with my parents, my brother and my sister until 1932, when we moved to Wythenshawe.

One of my earliest memories is of a Zeppelin dropping a bomb on the Belsize factory during the First World War. Belsize was on war work then, not making motor-cars. In a panic a shell was knocked over and it fell on a man's foot. It was so badly crushed that he had to have it amputated. My mother worked there and became very ill with T.N.T. poisoning.

My father worked at Saxon's controlling the "pear-drop" and starting up the donkey-engine. The "pear-drop" was a heavy weight suspended on a cable. It was used for breaking pig-iron. The donkey-engine drove the shafting.

We were poor as so many people were then. My father's wage was £2 8s per week and my mother brought in another 7s by cleaning at a school on Friday evening and Saturday morning. That was after she had finished working at Belsize.

Breakfast was often bread and beef dripping. Lunch was a few sandwiches. Sometimes we would have a stew for our evening meal. This was cheap, because it was made out of 9d worth of meat from the butcher and a 2d "pot-herb" from the greengrocer. A "pot-herb" was an assortment of vegetables such as potatoes, carrots and onions.

On Friday when my father arrived home, he would tip up all his wages to my mother apart from 2s, which he kept for woodbines - 5 for2d. Then my mother would give me a half-crown and send me off to Bill's, the confectioner, for a quarter of boiled ham and seven fancy cakes. The ham was 9d and the cakes, 6d.

I sold newspapers on the street for Mr Berry, the newsagent. The Manchester Evening News was a penny and I got 3d for every baker's dozen (13) I sold. On Saturday I took out the football papers. They were 2d. Mr Berry gave me a half penny for every one sold.

I made Mr Berry's first wireless set. He bought a Melody Maker kit and gave me 10s for assembling it.

Some people talk about the good old days. For me in many ways they were the bad old days.

Mrs Jessica Martin's war-time memories

I was born Jessica Goodwin. There were ten children in the family, but when war broke out there were only three of us still at home. We lived at 3 Gorton Road, Lower Openshaw. My most lasting memories of the war are the Blitz and my wedding day.

On the Sunday night of the Blitz the Germans dropped a landmine on Royal Street, which was on the opposite side of Ashton Old Road from Gorton Road. They were aiming for the railway goods depot at the side of Gorton Road. When we heard the explosion, we all rushed down into the cellar, which we used only in an emergency because it was damp. Some of the house windows were broken, but we were protected from flying glass by thick rubber blackout curtains.
The next morning we went to Royal Street. Most of the houses were in ruins and many people were killed or badly injured. One family - I think their name was Mycroft - was almost wiped out. I heard that one son survived. It broke my heart to see the rescue teams bring out the bodies, so badly burnt that they were unrecognisable.

There was a young soldier, Harry Hardy, helping in the rescue. He called on everybody to be quiet and then with his bare hands he dug his way into the heap of bricks and rubble that had once been a house. Then his efforts brought their reward - a mother and her small child were still alive. The father was dead.

I married Frank - he was in the R.E.M.E. - on Saturday, May 3rd, 1941, at St. Barnabas's. I wore a grey dress with burgundy trimmings and a trilby hat to match. The reception was at the Old Farm House at the corner of Tipping Street and Gorton Road. I prepared the meal myself. We had roast beef - the butcher was very helpful - and salad, trifle, tinned fruit, biscuits and a fruit cake. Afterwards there was a sing-song. It was a family affair because there was so many of us.

When we got home the siren sounded and we all went down into the cellar, where we spent most of the night. As Frank was only on a week-end leave, he went back the following day, so it was not much of a honeymoon. Frank came home again a few months later on embarkation leave and after that I did not see him until 1946 when he came out of the army. During that time he was in Iraq, North Africa, Sicily and Italy.

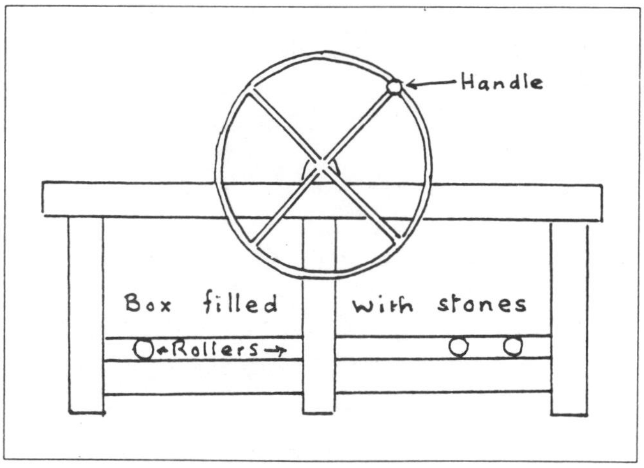

A BOX MANGLE
When the wheel is turned, the box travels backwards and forwards over the rollers around which the washing is wrapped.